TOOLKIT FOR INTERMEDIATE ACCOUNTING

FIFTH CANADIAN EDITION

Accounting for a Capital Lease

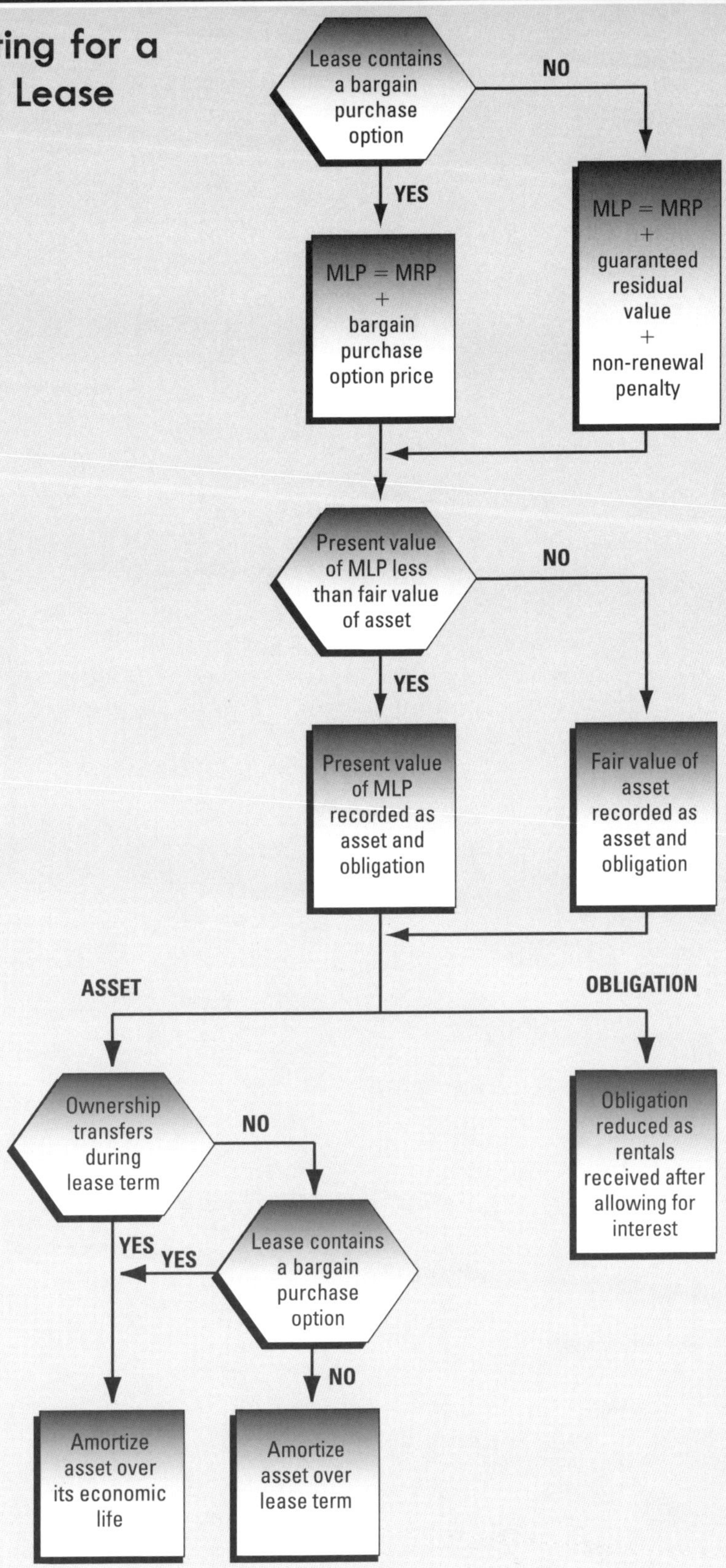

MLP = Net minimum lease payments
MRP = Net minimum rental payments called for over the lease term

TOOLKIT FOR INTERMEDIATE ACCOUNTING
FIFTH CANADIAN EDITION

Accounting for a Sales–Type Lease

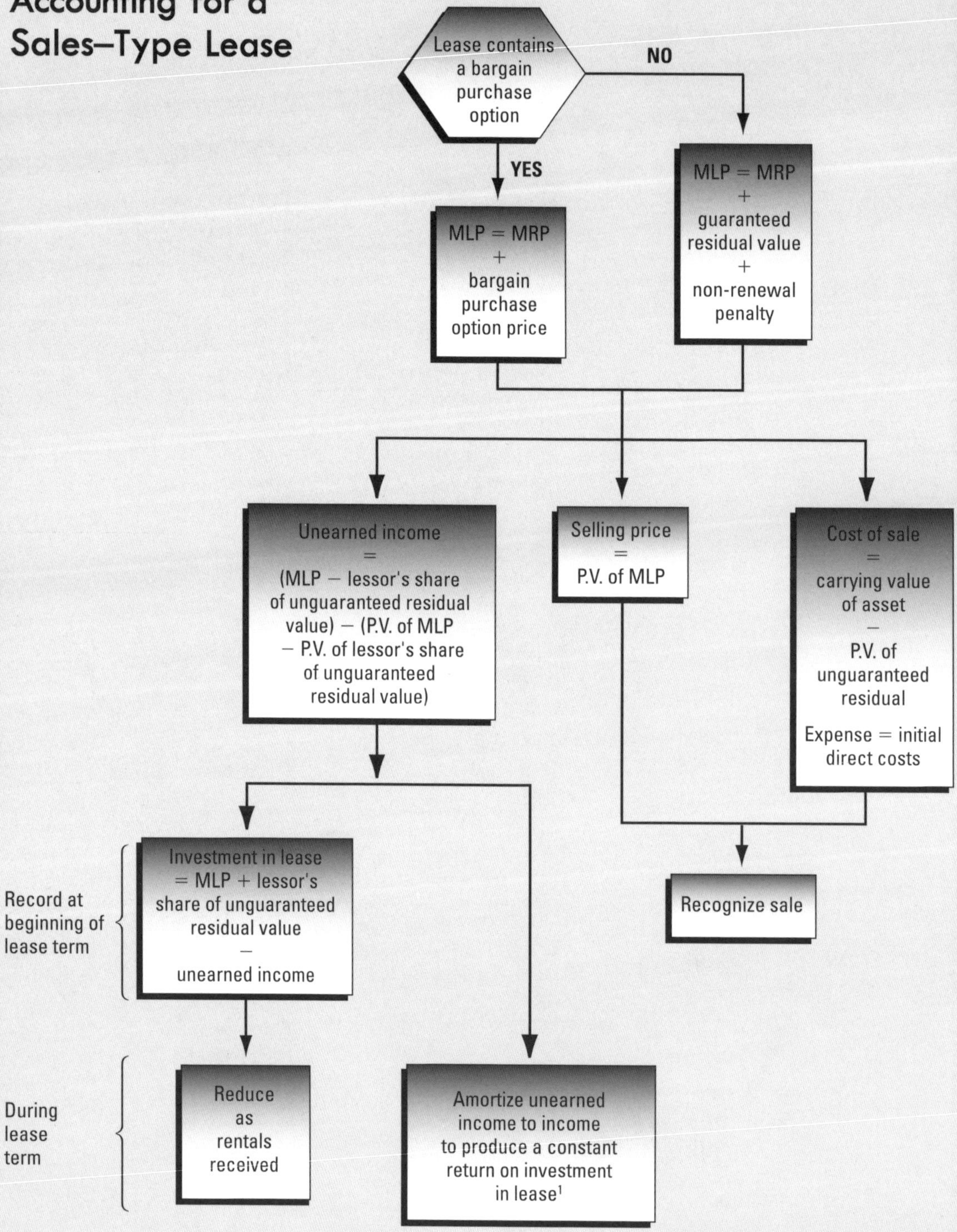

MLP = Net minimum lease payments
MRP = Net minimum rental payments called for over the lease term
P.V. = Present value

[1]Investment in lease for purposes of income recognition:

(a) when income tax factors taken into consideration for accounting purposes = MLP + lessor's share of unguaranteed residual value − unearned income − deferred taxes − investment tax credit; or

(b) when income tax factors not taken into consideration for accounting purposes = MLP + lessor's share of unguaranteed residual value − unearned income.

Accounting for a Direct Financing Lease

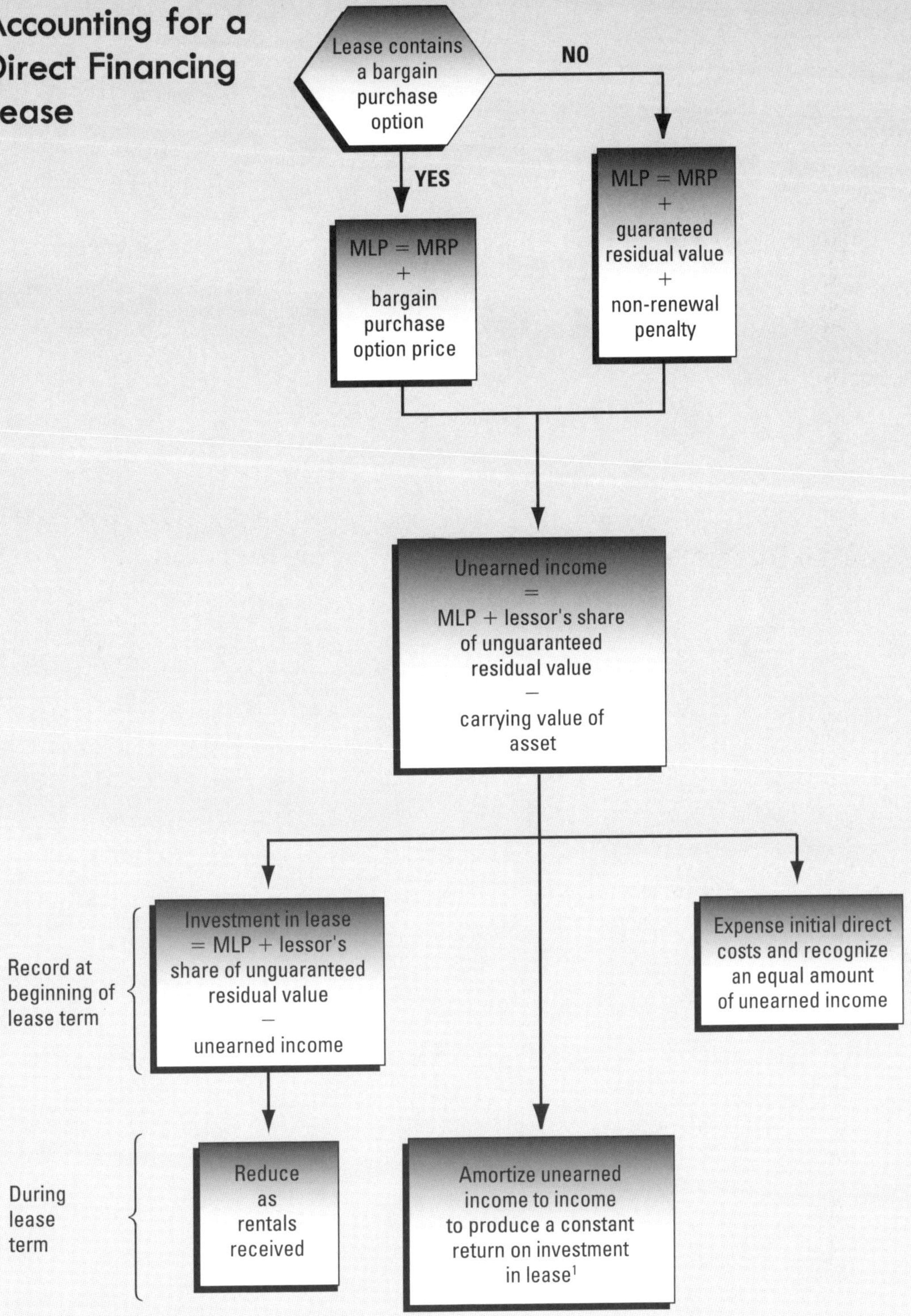

MLP = Minimum lease payments
MRP = Minimum rental payments called for over the lease term

[1]Investment in lease for purposes of income recognition:

(a) when income tax factors taken into consideration for accounting purposes = MLP + lessor's share of unguaranteed residual value − unearned income − deferred taxes − investment tax credit; or

(b) when income tax factors not taken into consideration for accounting purposes = MLP + lessor's share of unguaranteed residual value − unearned income.

DEFINITIONS

These definitions are central to qualitative analysis of financial reporting issues. To that extent this chart should be referred to and used when doing case analysis or analyzing issues. Ideally, these concepts/criteria and definitions should be committed to memory as they form the core of intermediate accounting.

	Reference	Definition	Recognition—General Rule	Measurement General rule*
ASSETS	HB 1000.29-.31	• **future benefit** • entity **controls** access to benefit or has **risks and rewards** of ownership • **transaction or event has occurred**	• meets definition AND • **probable/likely** AND • **measurable**	• at historical cost with write down if impairment in value (see Subsequent Revaluation of Assets) • see also industry practice
LIABILITIES	HB 1000.32-.34	• **obligation**/duty to pay • little or **no discretion to avoid** • **transaction or event obligating entity has occurred**	• meet definition AND • **probable/likely AND** • **measurable**	• at transaction cost or best estimate
EQUITY	HB 1000.35-.36	• **ownership** interest in net assets	• **transaction has occurred AND** • **measurable**	• at transaction cost
REVENUES	HB 1000.37 HB 3400.03	• **increases in economic resources** (from **ordinary operations**)	• **performance/risks and rewards** of ownership passed • reasonable assurance as to **measurement** • reasonable assurance as to **collectibility**	• at transaction cost
EXPENSES	HB 1000.38	• **decreases in economic resources** (from **ordinary operations**)	• if asset **no longer has future benefit**, OR • expense (not linked to specific revenues) **occurred in period** OR, • in order to **match** with revenues	• at transaction cost or best estimate
GAINS	HB 1000.39	• **increases in net assets** from **peripheral/incidental** transactions	• when **realized**	• at transaction cost
LOSSES	HB 1000.40	• **decreases in net assets** from **peripheral/incidental** transactions	• when **likely/** measurable	• at best estimate
CONTIN-GENCIES	HB 3290	• **existing condition involving uncertainty as to possible gain or loss that will be resolved by future event**	• loss-when likely and measurable • gain-may not recognize even if likely	• at best estimate

STUDY GUIDE TO ACCOMPANY

INTERMEDIATE ACCOUNTING

VOLUME 2

FIFTH CANADIAN EDITION

Irene Wiecek

UNIVERSITY OF TORONTO

John Wiley & Sons Canada, Ltd

Toronto • New York • Chichester • Weinheim • Brisbane • Singapore

Permission Acknowledgements

Extracts from Strategic Management 1 examinations published by the Certified General Accountants Association of Canada. ©1993-1996, reprinted by permission.

Excerpts reprinted, with permission from CICA Uniform Final Exams, 1995-1996, The Canadian Institute of Chartered Accountants, Toronto, Canada. Any changes to the original material are the sole responsibility of the authors and / or publisher and have not been reviewed by or endorsed by the CICA.

Extracts from CMA Exams published by the Society of Managerial Accountants. © 1994-1996, reprinted by permission.

Canadian Cataloguing in Publication Data

Wiecek, Irene

Study guide to accompany Intermediate Accounting, fifth Canadian edition

ISBN 0-471-64214-2 (volume one)
ISBN 0-471-64264-9 (volume two)

I. Accounting—Problems, exercises, etc.
I. Kieso, Donald E. Intermediate Accounting
II. Title

HF5635.I573 1997 Suppl. 657'.044 C97-931722-3

Production Credits

Acquistions Editor: John Horne
Developmental Editor: Karen Staudinger
Publishing Services Director: Karen Bryan
Assistant Editor: Michael Schellenberg
Design: Christine Kurys, RGD
Electronic Assembly: Vesna Mayer
Copy Editor: Tracy Wolgemuth
Printing and Binding: Webcom Limited

Printed and Bound in Canada
10 9 8 7 6 5 4 3 2

About the Author

Irene Wiecek is Assistant Director of the Master of Management and Professional Accounting Program at the University of Toronto where she is also a full-time faculty member, lecturing primarily in Financial Reporting at both the undergraduate and graduate levels.

A profilic case writer, Irene has won case competitions for writing and presenting cases as well as leading and coaching student teams. She has had several cases published in accounting journals and is one of the authors contributing financial reporting material for the Kieso text on the Wiley Web site.

At the professional level, Irene is involved in an educational capacity with both the Canadian and Ontario Institute of Chartered Accountants as well as the Society of Management Accountants.

Prior to working at the University of Toronto, Irene worked for KPMG as a public accountant for eight years and as a consultant in private industry. Irene obtained her Chartered Accountancy designation in 1981.

CONTENTS

Introduction

HOW TO GET THE MOST OUT OF USING VOLUME TWO

This book is the **second volume of a two volume set** that comprises the **Study Guide** for Kieso's *Intermediate Accounting, Fifth Canadian Edition.* The book is structured in the same manner as the first volume of the Study Guide. Each chapter has the following components:

- **Perspective/insights** into what makes the topic interesting and challenging from a learning perspective
- **Study steps** to enhance the learning process including

  1) Emphasis on the **business transactions**

  2) Analysis of key **recognition, measurement and disclosure** issues

  3) In–depth look at **calculations** and methods used to account for the topics
- **Multiple choice questions**, including questions from the CA, CMA, and CGA exams
- Quantitative **problems** with worked-out solutions
- **Cases** and solutions

Reference should be made to the chapter on **case analysis** at the beginning of volume one of the Study Guide to assist in your case analysis. Furthermore, I have added some additional charts for the **TOOLKIT** in this volume. The TOOLKIT in volume one includes basic material for accounting issues analysis such as charts, and frameworks covering basic principles, definitions, criteria and concepts.

GOOD LUCK with your accounting course and I sincerely hope that this Study Guide enhances your learning experience.

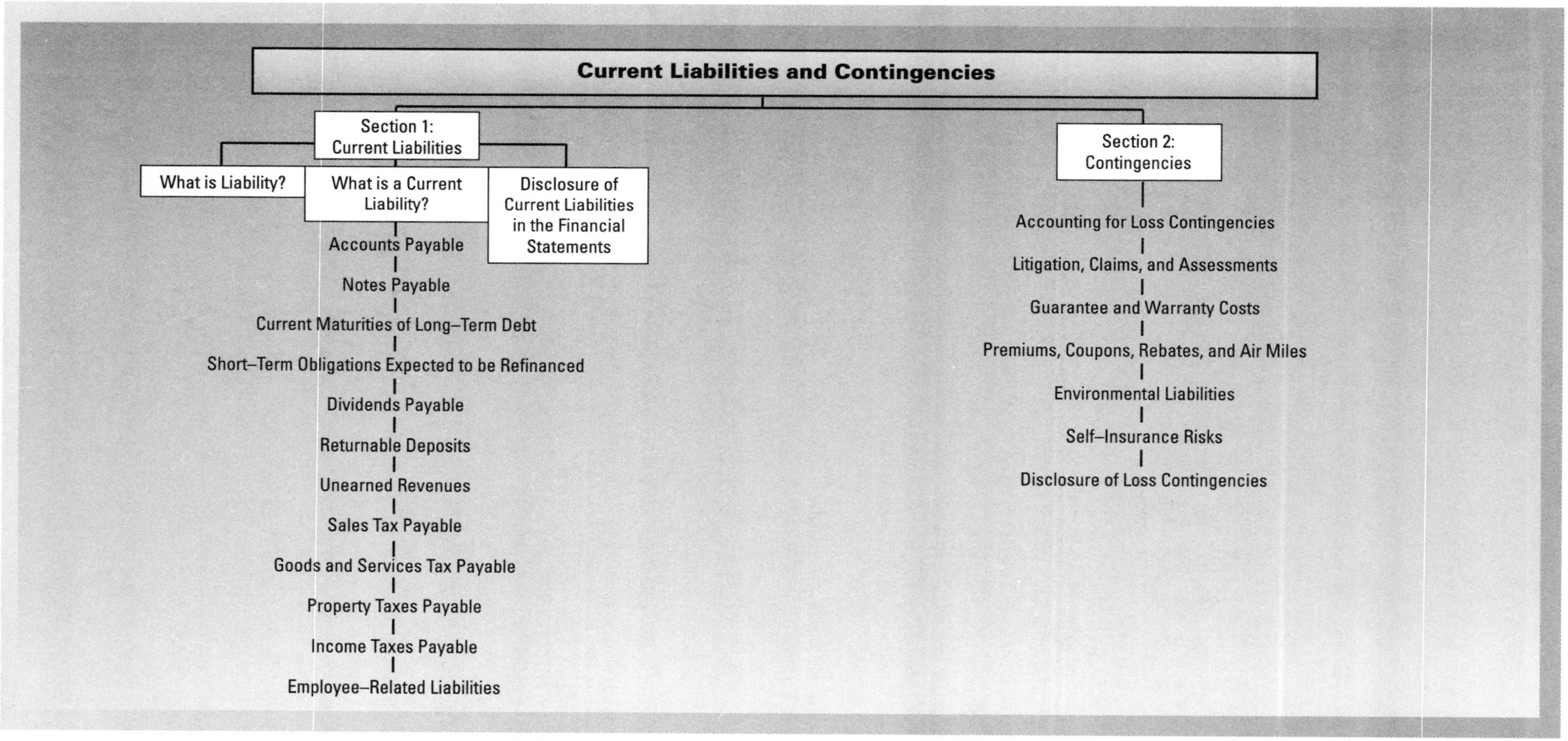
Current Liabilities and Contingencies
Section 1:
Current Liabilities
What is Liability?
What is a Current Liability?
Disclosure of Current Liabilities in the Financial Statements
Accounts Payable
Notes Payable
Current Maturities of Long–Term Debt
Short–Term Obligations Expected to be Refinanced
Dividends Payable
Returnable Deposits
Unearned Revenues
Sales Tax Payable
Goods and Services Tax Payable
Property Taxes Payable
Income Taxes Payable
Employee–Related Liabilities
Section 2:
Contingencies
Accounting for Loss Contingencies
Litigation, Claims, and Assessments
Guarantee and Warranty Costs
Premiums, Coupons, Rebates, and Air Miles
Environmental Liabilities
Self–Insurance Risks
Disclosure of Loss Contingencies

chapter 14

CURRENT LIABILITIES AND CONTINGENCIES

PERSPECTIVE

The most difficult issue relating to this topic is discerning when there is a liability and hence, when to record it (recognition). Certain liabilities are obvious (i.e., if inventory is purchased, a liability to pay the supplier arises), but what about a pending lawsuit or environmental liabilities?

In order to assist in the decision, GAAP provides a definition of a liability; however, although this definition helps, it is still subject to interpretation and judgement. Often the decision about whether to record a liability is a function of uncertainty (i.e., uncertainty with respect to the outcome [lawsuit] or the amount [warranty costs]). The greater the uncertainty, the less likely that a liability is recorded.

Certainty with respect to outcome and $	**Record liability**
↓	
Extreme uncertainty	**Note disclosure or do nothing**

This chapter will review the definition of a liability and review GAAP with respect to contingencies. These areas are perhaps the most difficult due to the amount of interpretation and judgement required.

INSIGHTS

- *A fundamental concept to internalize is the definition of a liability. This definition will be at the heart of many issues and analyses.*
- *Criteria for recognition of contingencies should also be memorized. This is also an issue that arises time and time again.*

STUDY STEPS

1. Understanding the Nature of Liabilities

Liabilities

Liabilities represent claims upon the company. By definition (HB Section 1000), they have the following characteristics:

CICA HANDBOOK

Liabilities defined:

They embody a **duty or responsibility** to others.

The responsibility **cannot be avoided** (i.e., if the employee has earned vacation pay by law or under the employment arrangement, the company must pay it).

The underlying **event that caused the duty to arise has already occurred** (i.e., the act of the employee working causes the vacation pay obligation to arise).

Tip! **Liabilities need not be legally enforceable to be considered a liability. They may arise out of moral or ethical obligations.**

Tip! **Often, the key to the analysis is determining the "event" that gives rise to a liability.**

Tip! **A current liability is an obligation that must be discharged within a year or the current operating cycle of business (HB Section 1510.)**

CICA HANDBOOK

Contingencies

Contingencies defined:

Existing conditions involving **uncertainty** (as to possible gain or loss) that will be resolved in the future by the occurrence of a confirming event.

Tip! **It is very important to focus on the uncertainty surrounding a possible liability. The more uncertain, the less likely it is that a liability and, therefore, loss will in fact be realized.**

Tip! **It is also important to focus on the fact that the condition causing possible loss already exists and that the future event is really just a confirming event and not the event itself.**

2. Understanding How the Transaction Fits into the Financial Reporting Model and the Conceptual Framework—Analysis and Critical Thinking

Since the issue of whether a liability exists or not and when to recognize it is so fundamental to the analysis of many issues, this part of the analysis is shown in the TOOLKIT under "Definitions".

Where there are conditions of uncertainty, the analysis falls under the contingency heading. This analysis is also in the TOOLKIT under "Definitions". A decision tree for uncertainties is shown in Exhibit 14-1. Note that contingent gains as well as losses are shown here.

Exhibit 14-1

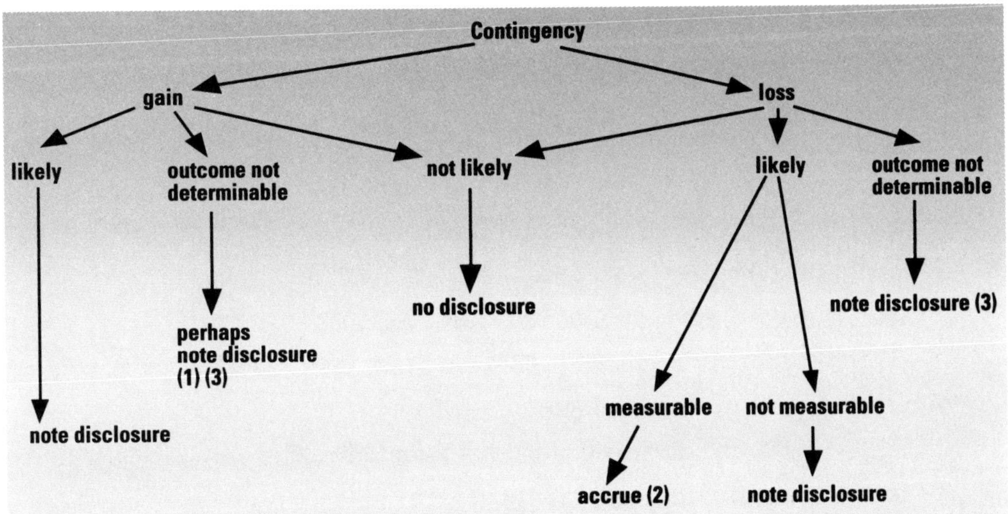

(1) Contingent gains are not recognized due to the realization principle, even though it may be likely that they will occur.
(2) Contingent losses are accrued due to the conservatism principle, even though they are only likely, but have not yet occurred. Note here that the underlying event giving rise to the liablility has not occurred yet it is likely to.
(3) Note disclosure would seem prudent since there is a 50/50 chance or greater that the confirming event will occur.

Prepared by Irene Wiecek

MULTIPLE CHOICE QUESTIONS

The following relates to Multiple Choice questions (1) and (2):

It is mid-February 1996, and you are the senior in charge of the December 31, 1995 year-end audit of Defy Co. You learn that two lawsuits are pending against Defy Co. One was initiated in February 1996 by an employee who was fired in October 1995. He believes that he was wrongfully dismissed and is claiming $500,000 in pain and suffering. The client has stated that the company is unlikely to have to pay that much but that a settlement of at least $100,000 will be made. The second lawsuit concerns a worker injured by a Defy Co.'s truck in January 1996. The employee is suing for $250,000, but management has informed you that the company will have to pay at least $75,000 to the employee in settlement. The company's lawyer has confirmed both of these assessments.

How should Defy Co. report the outstanding law suits in their financial statements in order to receive an unqualified audit opinion?
(CICA—Uniform Final Exam September 1996)

1) With respect to the wrongful dismissal,
   a) accrue $100,000 and disclose that the suit is for $500,000.
   b) accrue $100,000 with no other disclosure.
   c) disclose that the range is $100,000 to $500,000, with no accrual.
   d) disclose that the suit is for $500,000, with no accrual.

2) With respect to the injured employee,
   a) accrue $75,000 and disclose that the suit is for $250,000.
   b) accrue $75,000 with no other disclosure.
   c) disclose that the range is $75,000 to $250,000 and the nature of the event with no accrual.
   d) disclose that the suit is for $250,000, with no accrual.

3) A company is about to be sued for producing and selling an unsafe product. Attorneys for the company cannot predict the outcome of the litigation, but they state that the lawsuit may be filed in the $80 million to $120 million range. In its financial statements, the company should
   a) make the following journal entry and disclose the existence of the lawsuit in a footnote:

      Estimated loss from litigation $100,000,000 dr.

      Estimated liability from litigation loss $100,000,000 cr.
   b) disclose the existence of the lawsuit in a footnote without making a journal entry.
   c) neither make a journal entry nor disclose the lawsuits in a footnote because bad publicity will hurt the company.
   d) make the following journal entry and disclose the existence of the lawsuit in a footnote:

Cost of goods sold....$120,000,000 dr.

Estimated liability from litigation loss....$120,000,000 cr.

(CMA entrance examination—June 1996—adapted)

4) Debt that is currently due but that is expected to be refinanced through long-term debt may be classified as long-term if which of the following set of conditions holds: (Assume that the company in question poses a high audit risk.)

   a) There is a non-cancellable agreement (that extends beyond one year) with a financially solvent lender. The company is not in violation of any of the terms of the contract.

   b) The company fully intends to refinance and has contacted several interested parties—all financially solvent.

   c) There is a signed agreement to refinance the loan through a demand loan facility with a financially solvent lender. The company is not in violation of any of the covenants under the agreement.

   d) The company fully intends to refinance and has a verbal agreement with a financially solvent party. The company is not in violation of any terms of the agreement. Under the terms of the contract, the company may cancel the agreement at any time.

5) The cash basis method for recording warranty liabilities is acceptable except:

   a) when the costs are likely to be incurred and estimable.

   b) when the liability cannot be reasonably estimated.

   c) for income tax purposes.

   d) when warranty costs are immaterial.

6) A company lacks fire insurance. Which of the following statements is true.

   a) This represents a loss contingency and should be provided for in the financial statements if estimable and note disclosed if not.

   b) This constitutes an uncertainty as to amounts and timing of losses; however, it should not be recorded since no impairment of an asset or incurrence of a liability can exist prior to the event (the fire).

   c) This represents a contingent loss where the outcome is not determinable and therefore should be disclosed.

   d) This represents a condition involving uncertainty where it is unlikely that a future event will confirm that an asset has been impaired or liability incurred; however, note disclosure is required.

7) The definition of a liability includes all but which of the following:

   a) an obligation or duty to another party.

   b) little or no discretion to avoid.

   c) legally enforceable.

   d) the transaction or event giving rise to the obligation has occurred.

8) Apex Company Limited (ACL) recently had a policy meeting with its top management and Board of Directors and concluded, among other things, that the company would initiate a new policy, whereby any waste water would be neutralized prior to being pumped into a nearby lake. As part of the policy, they also agreed to spend $500,000 on cleanup of the lake over the next five years. How should the $500,000 be treated in the financial statements?

   a) Accrue the full amount as a liability since it meets the definition of a liability.

   b) Disclose the amount in the notes to the financial statements as it is a future commitment.

   c) Do not accrue the amount nor disclose in the notes to the financial statements as it is not legally enforceable.

   d) Do not accrue, but disclose on the basis that this type of policy would be viewed as favourable to potential investors.

9) Vega Corporation (VC) sells computer games on disk. VC has recently begun a promotional campaign, whereby customers collect five coupons and get a free game if they mail in the coupons along with $1. The games cost $2 each to produce. One coupon is packaged with each game. During 1998, the first year of the promotion, VC sold 100,000 games and estimates that 60% of the coupons issued will be redeemed. As of year-end, 40,000 coupons had been redeemed. What is the amount of the outstanding liability that VC should record on the balance sheet at year-end?

   a) $12,000

   b) $7,200

   c) $4,000

   d) $20,000

10 Assuming the same information as 9, what expense would be booked for premium expense for the year?

   a) $8,000

   b) $12,000

   c) $4,000

   d) $24,000

SOLUTIONS TO MULTIPLE CHOICE QUESTIONS

1) a) Defy Co. must accrue since a loss is likely and there is an exposure in excess of the loss accrued. Also, the condition existed at year–end; therefore, type 1 subsequent event.
2) c) No accrual is necessary since the event occurred after year-end. Since the event will have a significant effect on assets and liabilities in the future period, it should be disclosed.
3) b) Since the outcome is not determinable, only note disclosure is warranted.
4) a) is the best answer since neither party may get out of the agreement and it provides for long-term financing. B) is based on intent and does not provide sufficient assurance. C) is a demand loan which is technically another current liability. D) allows the company to back out of the agreement.
5) a) If the loss is likely and estimable, the accrual method must be used. If the amounts are immaterial or the period short, then the cash basis may be used. The cash basis must be used for tax purposes.
6) b) HB Section 3290 states that acts such as fires are random in occurrence and unpredictable. Therefore, note disclosure is not required (although it may be desirable) since the event giving rise to a potential loss has not yet happened nor may ever happen.
7) c) The transaction need not be legally enforceable to be an obligation.
8) a) This is a very interesting question. This represents a liability under HB Section 3060 as site restoration costs. The key thing here is that the company has established a policy to restore the site and has thus created a non-discretionary obligation.
9) c) [($100,000 X 60%—40,000) /5] X ($2-$1) = $4,000.
10) b) ($100,000 X 60%/5)—($2-$1) = $12,000

SHORT PROBLEMS

1) Purpose: To illustrate accounting required for compensated absences.

Denzel Morton Limited (DML) has been in operation for 30 years and employs approximately 200 employees. Recently, the company applied for a loan from the bank, which required that DML produce audited financial statements for the year ended December 31, 1998. This is the first year that audited statements will be prepared. Previously, the company followed tax accounting because DML is private.

Among other things, DML found that they might have to change the way they account for their vacation and sick leave. The following is a description of the company's policies with respect to these issues:

Vacation:

Employees are entitled to three weeks per year. If not taken in the year, the employee can carry it forward to subsequent years. Employees must take time off and are never paid out in cash unless the employees quit or are fired.

Sick days:

Employees are entitled to five sick days a year but lose entitlement to take them if they have not done so by year-end.

Up to this point, all of the above have been expensed in the year that the employee either takes the sick days or the vacation. There are numerous instances where the full sick days and vacation entitlements are not taken by year-end. On January 1, each year, pay raises are announced.

Required

Prepare the journal entries for recording these costs for the year ended December 31, 1998. Discuss the treatment.

2) Purpose: To illustrate accounting for warranty and guarantee costs.

Denzel Morton Limited (DML) (see 1 above) also accounts for warranty costs on a cash basis. That is, when a product is sold, there is no accrual for estimated warranty costs even though all products are covered by a comprehensive five-year warranty. If a customer subsequently has problems with a product that they have purchased under the warranty, DML will fix it and expense the costs in the period that the product is fixed. In the past, annual warranty costs have been as high as 1% of sales although over the past two years, this has been reduced significantly due to new product design and enhanced quality control. In fact, last year, the amount spent to honour the warranties was less than 1/8 of 1%.

The auditors of the company have decided to look at the past 10 years to get a rough idea of the warranty cost as a percent of sales and have concluded that warranty costs of approximately 1% of sales should be accrued to be on the safe side.

Required

Discuss the auditor's position.

3) Purpose: To discuss treatment of long-term liabilities that are currently due, but that are expected to be refinanced.

The loan that DML has applied for from the bank (see 1 above) is to replace existing long-term debt that is currently due. The bank has agreed, in principle, to provide the financing as long as the financial statements of the company look fine. The tentative terms are that the new loan will be a demand loan; however, the understanding between the bank and DML is that the loan will not be called unless DML's financial position deteriorates significantly. As at year-end, the agreement has not been finalized, since the bank is waiting for the signed, audited statements before the financing goes through.

Required

Discuss the classification of the existing long-term debt that is currently due for repayment.

SOLUTIONS TO SHORT PROBLEMS

1) Vacation:

This is perhaps the easiest to deal with since the amount earned during the period is known. The vacation accrues as the employees provide services to the company. Therefore, it should be booked at that time, and not when the employees actually take the vacation. The only issue is whether the employee earns the vacation at the current or the future pay rate. For practical purposes, the amount is usually booked at the current rate. Therefore, at year-end, the following entry should be made:

dr. payroll benefits
    cr. accounts payable

Sick days:

There is no entry required here since if the employees lose the days if they are not taken in that period. They are not cumulative.

2) A warranty expense must be booked in the year of the sale since it is a cost of sales and, therefore, must be matched with revenues. The problem is that there is uncertainty with respect to the measurement of the amount.

From the auditor's perspective, 1% of sales would not seem unreasonable since, historically, this has been the amount spent per year. The auditors might lean towards being more conservative since they know that the bank will rely on the financial statements.

On the other hand, DML management might just as equally argue that this is overly conservative since it gives undue weight to past circumstances, which are no longer relevant. Due to the increase in quality control and the decrease in the expense over the past few years, a case may be made for accruing only 1/8 of 1%.

Lastly, DML management might argue that no adjustment is needed since they are already expensing warranty costs, albeit one year after the sales. But as long as sales have not changed dramatically, net income is not overstated in any given year under the cash method except the first year. The only problem is that accruals have been understated. The auditors must assess whether the amount is material.

3) The issue is whether the debt should be classified as long-term, since it will probably not be repaid out of the working capital of the company, or whether it should be treated as a current liability, since it is due within the year.

Normally, long-term liabilities that become due within the year following the balance sheet date must be classified as current liabilities. This gives users of the financial statements predictive information about cash flows of the company and also cash flow requirements.

However, in this case, the financing will be replaced by long-term financing and will not be paid out of the working capital of the company. Therefore, does it make sense to show it as a current liability? Section 1510 of the CICA Handbook states that obligations of this sort may be excluded from current liabilities if contractual arrangements have been made to settle the debt with funds other than current assets.

In this case, it is questionable whether there is a firm contractual agreement since the refinancing is contingent on acceptance of the financial statements by the bank. If the financial statements show that DML is financially sound, even though the bank has not formally approved them, this might be sufficient. It would be wise for the auditors to see a letter of intent from the bank or something in writing regarding the tentative agreement. They might wish the bank to review the draft financial statements for acceptance.

Furthermore, the issue arises as to whether the new debt is long-term or current. Technically, it is currently payable at any time since the terms are that it is a demand loan. That means that the bank may demand payment at any time. On the other hand, it is not the intention of the bank to demand payment unless the financial position of the company deteriorates. Therefore, a case may be made for considering the new debt as long-term as long as the financial position of the company is sound. The auditors might wish to discuss these points specifically with the bank and to disclose the exact terms in the notes to the financial statements.

Note disclosure of the intended financing would also be prudent.

CASES

1) Envirocompany Limited

Environmental accounting is one of the most controversial current trends in accounting. It is not controversial in the sense that professionals disagree as to whether it is important; rather, it is controversial because implementation of any environmental accounting model requires us to go outside the traditional GAAP model. It essentially involves a form of social accounting whereby an attempt is made to measure the impact on the environment (usually negative) of running a business. What is the cost of polluting the air and water or of destroying rain forests?

Envirocompany Limited (EL) is a pulp and paper company that has been in operation for 50 years. Its shares trade on a major stock exchange. It is situated in a small town in Northern Ontario and employs thousands of people. In fact, the town exists primarily because of the jobs created by EL. Its equipment is fairly antiquated and pollutes the surrounding water and air with chemicals that have been shown to be carcinogens. The old equipment is part of the reason for the "success" of the company since it is all paid for and requires little maintenance. For the employees, the pollution is tolerated because EL provides them with jobs and keeps the local economy going.

Last year, a new Chairman of the Board of Directors was appointed to EL. Charles Champion first became aware of the extent of the pollution prior to being appointed to the Board and felt that he would like to do something about it. He took this mission as a personal challenge and in the first year of his appointment, commissioned several in-depth studies as to how EL might reduce or eliminate the pollution. He wanted to be careful to protect himself and the other members of the Board because directors were increasingly held personally liable for the actions of companies.

Most studies pointed to the old machinery and recommended that it be replaced by new state-of-the-art equipment. Cost estimates ran into the millions of dollars and the Board of Directors felt that the company would not be able to survive that type of expenditure. One study proved that the company should not even be in business any more given the cost of new environmentally friendly equipment, declining demand for unrecycled newsprint, and increasing competition from abroad. That study was quickly shelved.

Recent environmental studies had shown that the pollutants were seeping into the water table and finding their way south to where major cities were situated. The studies showed that there were increasing incidences of birth defects in animals and humans in the areas in question, including increases in sterility for certain aquatic and marine life. This caused a number of politicians to start grandstanding and calling for tighter pollution controls and steep fines.

Recently, there had been reports of a local tribe of Indians downstream getting sick, apparently from the chemical pollutants from EL. One had threatened to sue, and EL's lawyers were privately acknowledging the potential for a class action suit. EL has insurance that would cover up to $1 million in damages.

Meanwhile, the accountants were struggling with how to account for the problem for the year-end statements. Charles has requested that two sets of financial statements be drafted. He would like to know how the problem should be reflected for the external statements that will be presented at the shareholders' meeting and he would also like a set of financial statements that looks at the problem from a broader, all-encompassing perspective, for management decision making. Specifically, he wants to know if there is a liability, exactly what it is, and when it arose (or arises), if at all.

REQUIRED

Analyse the issue. Adopt the role of the company controller for the external financial reporting and the role of a university professor for the other analysis.

2) CANADIAN AIRLINES—www.cdnair.com

According to the web page of Canadian Airlines (CA), CA carried more than 11.9 million passengers to over 160 destinations in 17 countries in 1996. CA is the descendant of several predecessor companies, including CP Air and Pacific Western Airlines. The amalgamated company was created in 1987. In the years that followed, the world airline industry slumped, resulting in many airline companies going bankrupt and/or suffering severe financial hardship. CA weathered the storm by undergoing a significant restructuring, part of which included employees of the company taking share options as part of their remuneration. The latter resulted in the employees investing $200 million in the company.

In 1996, still suffering losses ($187 million and $194 million in 1995), the CEO announced a new restructuring plan aimed at countering the continuing losses (resulting partly from increased competition and falling seat prices). The plan focused on three areas: improved network profitability, decreased overhead costs, and decreased labour costs. In regard to the latter, employees were asked to accept reduced wages over a four year period.

As always, the company is now concerned with increasing market share and maintaining customer loyalty. On the company's web site, the company has the following advertisement:

> "Fly 5, fly free—Fly five times with Canadian Airlines and its worldwide partners and earn a free trip. The more you fly, the more the world is within reach"

Free flights have been offered by CA in the past through its well-publicized "Frequent Flyer Program" under which customers earn points for flying with CA. The points are accumulated and then may be used to take free flights. In the notes to the financial statements, CA notes that the incremental costs of Frequent Flyer Points are accrued as the entitlements to free flights are earned. The accrual is included as part of accrued liabilities.

Excerpts from the 1996 financial statements follow (in millions of $):

Total assets (including current assets of $456.5 million)	$1866
Current liabilities	765
Long-term debt	841
Preferred shares	289
Common shares	407
Deficit	(436)
Total liabilities and equity	$1866

REQUIRED:

Adopt the role of company management, and discuss the treatment of the "Fly 5, Fly Free" program for financial reporting purposes.

SOLUTIONS TO CASES

1) ENVIROCOMPANY LIMITED

Overview

Two sets of statements are required, one for public presentation and one for management decision making. The information content of each will differ since they will be used for different decisions, and since different roles will be adopted for each.

EXTERNAL FINANCIAL STATEMENTS:

These will be seen by **shareholders** who may not want the problem overemphasized since it might drive the stock price down. **Employees** will likely feel the same way since they could lose their jobs if the company were forced to close. **Management** might be reluctant to disclose too much for the same reasons, especially until they figure out a plan of action. Furthermore, any negative disclosures reflect poor **stewardship**. **Potential investors**, on the other hand, would want **full disclosure** in order to **assess the risks** before investing. Whatever is disclosed could be used against the company by the public "at large" in an effort to protect themselves and the environment.

Other users would be the **government environmental agencies** who might use the information against EL. The **Board of Directors** might resist disclosures that imply negligence or guilt since they might be held personally liable.

In all likelihood, the financial statements will likely play the problem down and not overemphasize it even though this is a short-term solution. Traditional **GAAP** will be a constraint since the company is public.

INTERNAL STATEMENTS FOR DECISION MAKING:

These will be seen only by the Board and will be used to assess the situation and the **true costs of running the business**. These statements will disclose the full extent of the problem and attempt to grapple with the liability from a broader perspective, ignoring the political implications of any disclosures since the financial statements will not be publicly released. Traditional GAAP will not be a constraint.

Analysis and Recommendations

EXTERNAL FINANCIAL STATEMENTS:

Technically (and based on a traditional interpretation of GAAP), there is no liability here until the company is sued. EL has no **duty or responsibility** to the person suing the company until it is proven in a court of law that EL is guilty. Likewise, until the person actually sues the company, and a court rules against the company, there is a chance to avoid the potential obligation (i.e., hire good lawyers, present a good defence). The **event** that potentially obligates the entity may be the act of polluting, or the act of the person getting sick and, therefore, this may have already happened. However, as noted above, the obligation has not yet been established.

Therefore, if anything, this could be construed as a **contingent liability**, given that there is **uncertainty (as to possible loss)** that will not be resolved until some **future confirming event** happens (i.e., lawsuit lost). Note that, at this time, the outcome of the situation is unknown. Will EL be sued? If sued, will they lose? If they lose, what will the cost be?

At most, **note disclosure** might be prudent; however, given that the person has only threatened to sue and has not actually done it, traditionally this would not be disclosed, as it is difficult to assess the probability that the person or others will actually sue. What about potential investors? Does management in all good conscience have to warn them? Given the increasing onus on Boards of Directors to take full responsibility for the actions of the company, should they disclose the problem in order to protect themselves?

Regarding the specific lawsuit threat, it is likely unnecessary to disclose it for the above-noted reasons (primarily the uncertainty and the fact that the loss from a potential lawsuit is **not measurable**). However, regarding the larger problem (i.e., the inescapable fact that the pollution is harmful), it could be argued that they should. However, since the information will already be in the newspapers (i.e., the environmental studies are likely public and politicians are involved) and since the problem is industry-wide, chances are that there is no additional need to disclose anything further.

No disclosure is required since, at best, the threatened lawsuit is a contingent liability and it could be argued that it is unlikely that the company will suffer a **material loss** from it, especially since EL's insurance will cover up to $1 million. There is no reason to alarm people unless there is a real problem and no reason to overemphasize this episode to the point of putting the company out of business.

Analysis and Recommendations

INTERNAL FINANCIAL STATEMENTS:

Since the traditional GAAP constraint may be relaxed, the issue may be looked at from a broader perspective. The following is a time line that may be used to establish if and when a liability arose.

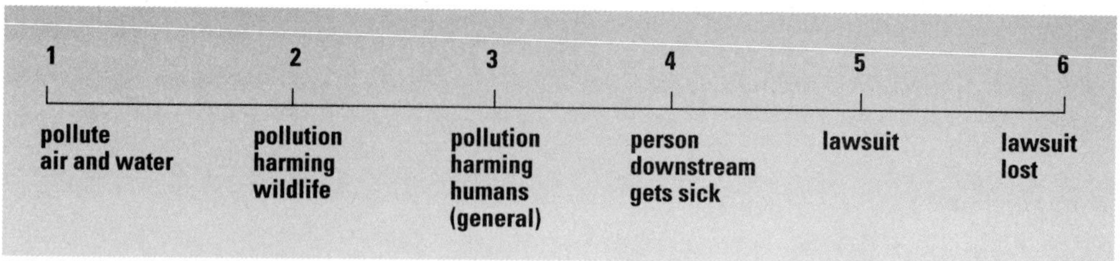

Traditionally, as shown by above analysis for external financial statements, in this type of situation, a potential liability is not usually recognized until there is a lawsuit or a fine. Even then, a liability is only acknowledged if the company is likely to lose, or the outcome is not determinable (meaning that there is a 50/50 chance of suffering a loss). The reasoning behind this, as it relates to polluting the environment, is that (a) the issue has in past, never been taken seriously by most people and (b) it is difficult to attribute air or water pollution to any one company since most companies and people do in fact pollute the environment.

If we examine the time line more closely, it may be argued that a liability exists at point 4. At this point, it might be argued that there is a direct relationship between EL polluting the surrounding area and a person in close proximity (i.e., downstream from the company) getting sick. Does EL owe that person anything? That is a matter of opinion, but as times change, it is becoming more acceptable to acknowledge that pollution is harmful to life and that the offending parties must somehow be held accountable. Therefore, as long as it can be established that EL is the offending party, then it can be argued that they have a duty to compensate individuals who are harmed by their actions. It is only a matter of time until they do get sued and over time, after a few precedent cases, it will become likely that these lawsuits will indeed result in a loss. Therefore, the critical matter becomes linking damage done by the pollution directly to the company.

Taking this a bit further, perhaps a liability exists at point 3. Maybe it is acceptable to harm wildlife but not humans and, therefore, anytime that a company undertakes actions that harm humanity in general, it must be held accountable. The link that must be made is whether EL pollutes the environment in such a way as to harm individuals in general. Environmental studies have shown that the pollutants released by EL do affect humanity (e.g., birth defects) so this link has perhaps already been established.

It is not out of the question to assume that if wildlife is being harmed then human beings are also being harmed since we are all linked by the food chain. Therefore, we might argue that 2 is the point where liability arises.

Finally, we might just as well acknowledge that any pollutant will affect the environment in a negative way by definition and, therefore, why wait until it has been proven that specific wildlife or humans have been harmed? The act of polluting creates a liability. And that brings us to point 1. Perhaps in reality, the real liability arises once a company takes it upon itself to disturb the ecosystem and place the natural order of the environment in jeopardy.

If this is so, perhaps this whole issue is a question of **cost versus benefit**. Does the benefit of having EL produce paper outweigh the costs to society as a whole including the deterioration of the ecological environment? What exactly are the costs to society? What are the benefits? How can they be measured? Who should measure them? Should these costs be accrued on the income statement and **matched** against revenues as ongoing costs of doing business?

It might be easy to measure damages that a court may award to one person who has suffered an illness as a direct result of pollution from a company. But what about those that do not take the company to court? What does the company owe them? What does the company owe society at large if it pollutes the water or cuts down irreplaceable rain forests, etc.? These costs become extremely difficult, if not impossible, to measure.

CONCLUSION

In all reality, a liability to society probably exists at point 1. However, it is impossible to measure the costs to society of polluting the environment. Therefore, it is impossible to prepare financial statements that reflect this cost. These costs cannot be ignored, however. If EL acknowledges responsibility for polluting the environment to the point where it is contributing to the deterioration of the ecosystem, then this factor must be considered in any decision about the company's future, even if it cannot be quantified. It should be considered along with declining prices and demand for the product, the jobs that are at stake, and the invested funds. Perhaps EL should be looking at gradually shifting over to recycling newspaper using newer methods that do not pollute the environment, etc. At this stage, the case moves beyond financial accounting.

2) CANADIAN AIRLINES

Overview

The company is in a highly competitive and risky industry. The economic environment over the past few years has caused many airlines to restructure or fold in the face of declining sales, increased competition and falling seat prices. CA has held its own by undergoing two restructurings, the most recent of which revolves around increases in network profitability and cutting costs. Even so, the company is in a very precarious position with a debt to equity ratio of 3.2 to 1 and a current ratio of .6 to 1. Losses for the past two years have been significant at close to $200 million.

Users of the statements will be existing **creditors** and **shareholders** who will be monitoring the **liquidity** of the company given the ratios identified above. Employees, who are also shareholders will be watching the statements for information about financial and job stability. **GAAP** is a constraint due to the fact that the shares are publicly traded.

Management would be concerned with **full disclosure** of the situation, due to the liquidity issues which are apparent in the statements and yet will also be concerned with assuring the stakeholders that the company will continue to operate.

Analysis and Recommendations

The issue here is accounting for the free flights. As already noted, these flights are similar to the Frequent Flyer Points, the cost of which is accrued in the financial statements as part of accrued liabilities.

One option is to treat them the same as the Frequent Flyer Points since they are, in **substance**, the same i.e., the more you fly, the more free flights you earn. In this case, the company assumes that there is a cost to providing these free flights, which must be **accrued** and **matched** with the revenues. The revenues would be the revenues from the paid flights that would be recorded in the current period. The cost of the free flights should be tied to the current revenues as they are seen as an inducement to buy tickets and are therefore **like advertising costs**. Also, the program creates a **liability** to the customers since, as the customers fly more, CA has a **duty to them** that they **cannot avoid** and the

event obligating the company is the fact that the customers have taken the flight. There is a **measurement issue** here since not all customers will complete the requirement for a free flight i.e., 5 flights and, even if they do, not all customers will indeed take the free flight.

Another option is to **note disclose** the program only. This option would be based on the fact that there is **no incremental cost** for free flights. The plane will be flying anyway. The only possible cost might be if a paying customer is bumped. Given increased competition, it is unlikely that the planes will always be full and CA might protect itself against this by only allowing the free flights on certain flights that might not normally ever reach capacity. Note, however, that part of the latest restructuring strategy is to increase network profitability, which means filling up each plane. This might result in paying passengers being bumped in the future and therefore a real cost.

The accrual option **increases the current liabilities**, which **worsens the current ratio**—a very sensitive ratio for the company at this time.

Finally, note that the company's policy of accruing for incremental cost really leaves the door open for either treatment. They might concur that a liability is created in principle, but if there is no incremental cost, i.e., if the planes are not full, then the accrual would be zero. **In practice**, different companies use different methods for accounting for free flights so there is really no GAAP. As management, this leaves a bit of maneuvering room. The policy itself is a **conservative** one, yet the measurement of the cost is left open to **judgement**. **Conservative** accounting in this situation, along with **full disclosure**, would be prudent for the company.

SELECTED SOLUTIONS FROM THE TEXTBOOK

EXERCISE 14-5 (25-30 MINUTES)

(a) To accrue the expense and liability

Year	for compensated absences:		
1997	Wages Expense	6,912	
	Vacation Wages Payable		4,320 (See 1 below)
	Sick Pay Wages Payable		2,592 (See 2 below)
1998	Wages Expense	8,064	
	Vacation Wages Payable		5,040 (See 4 below)
	Sick Pay Wages Payable		3,024 (See 5 below)

Year	To record payment for compensated time used by employees		
1997	Sick Pay Wages Payable	1,728 (See 3 below)	
	Cash		1,728
1998	Wages Expense	792	
	Vacation Wages Payable	3,888 (See 6 below)	
	Sick Pay Wages Payable	2,376 (See 7 below)	
	Cash		7,056 (See 8 below)

(1)	9 employees x $6.00/hr. X 8 hrs./day x 10 days	=	$4,320.	
(2)	9 employees x $6.00/hr. X 8 hrs./day x 6 days	=	$2,592	
(3)	9 employees x $6.00/hr. X 8 hrs./day x 4 days	=	$1,728.	
(4)	9 employees x $7.00/hr. X 8 hrs./day x 10 days	=	$5,040.	
(5)	9 employees x $7.00/hr. X 8 hrs./day x 6 days	=	$3,024.	
(6)	9 employees x $6.00/hr. X 8 hrs./day x 9 days	=	$3,888.	
(7)	9 employees x $6.00/hr. X 8 hrs./day x 6-4 days	=	864.	
	9 employees x $7.00/hr. X 8 hrs./day x 5-2 days	=	$1,512. =	$2,376.
(8)	9 employees x $7.00/hr. X 8 hrs./day x 9 days	=	$4,536.	
	9 employees x $7.00/hr. X 8 hrs./day x 5 days	=	2,520. =	$7,056.

NOTE: Vacation days and sick days are paid at the employee's current wage.

(b) Accrued liability at year-end.

	1997		1998	
	Vacation Wages Payable	Sick Pay Wages Payable	Vacation Wages Payable	Sick Pay Wages Payable
Jan. 1 balance	$ 0	$ 0	$4,320	$ 864
+ accrued	4,320	2,592	5,040	3,024
- paid	(0)	(1,728)	(3,888)	(2,376)
Dec. 31 balance	$4,320 (1)	$ 864 (2)	$ 5,472 (3)	$ 1,512 (4)

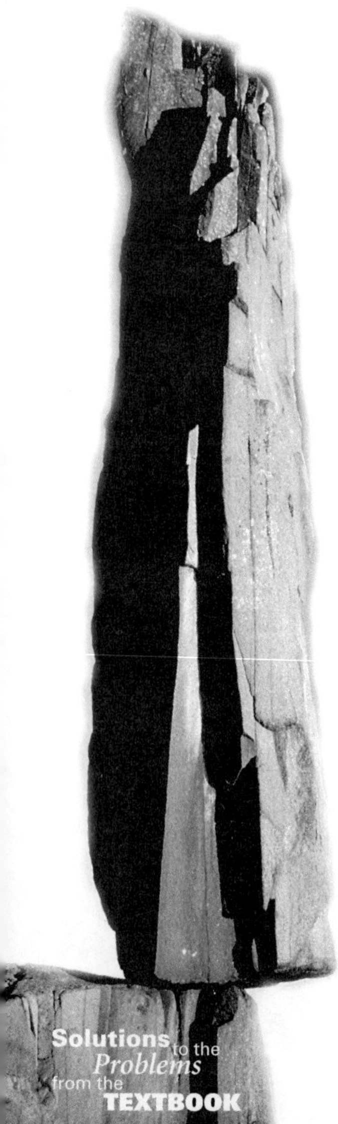

(1)	9 employees x \$6.00/hr. X 8 hrs./day x 10 days	=	\$ 4,320	
(2)	9 employees x \$6.00/hr. X 8 hrs./day x (6-4) days	=	\$ 864	
(3)	9 employees x \$6.00/hr. X 8 hrs./day x (10-9) days	=	\$ 432	
	9 employees x \$7.00/hr. X 8 hrs./day x 10 days	=	+5,040	
				\$5,472
(4)	9 employees x \$7.00/hr. X 8 hrs./day x 10 days	=	\$1,512	

EXERCISE 14-13 (15-20 MINUTES)

Inventory of premiums (8,800 x \$.88)	7,744	
Cash		7,744
Cash (110,000 x \$3.30)	363,000	
Sales		363,000
Premium Expense	3,872	
Inventory of Premiums ([44,000 ÷ 10] x \$.88])		3,872
Premium Expense	1,936 *	
Estimated Liability for Premiums	1,936	

*([110,000 x 60%] - 44,000) ÷ 10 x \$.88 = \$1,936

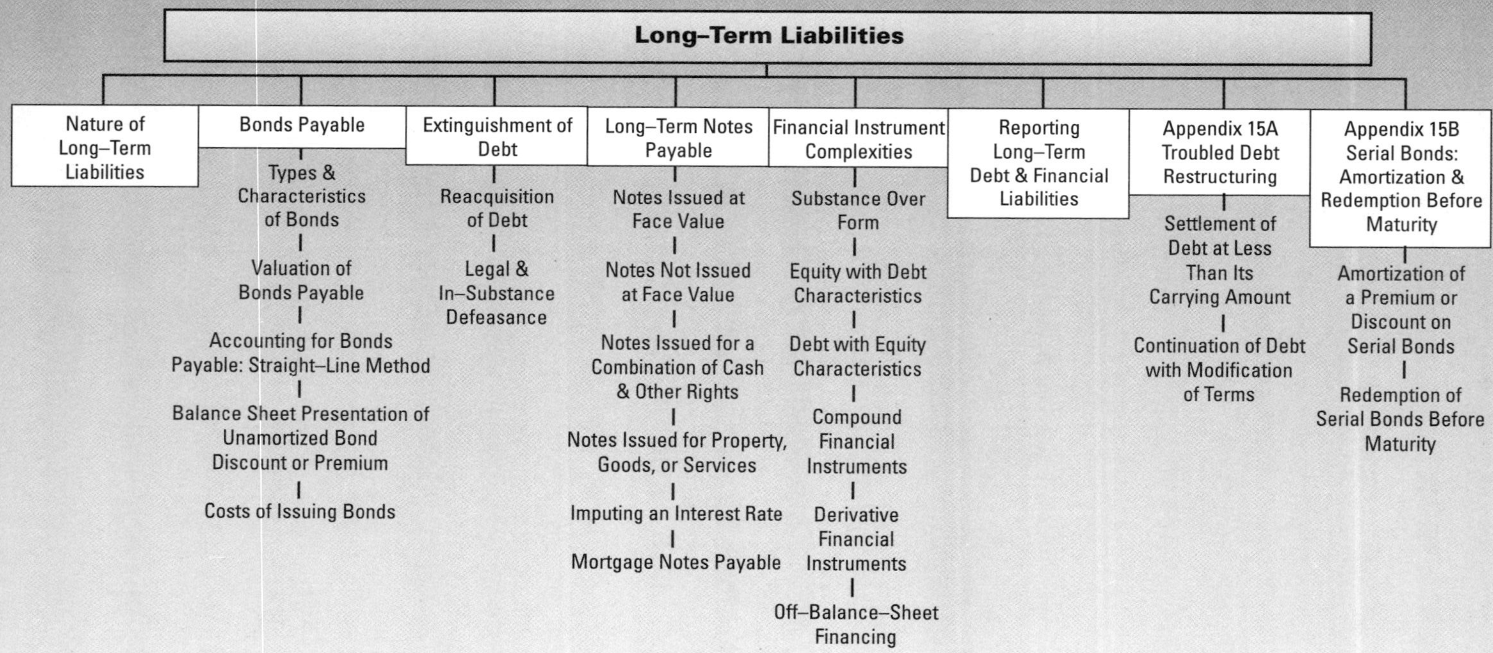

Long–Term Liabilities
Nature of Long–Term Liabilities
Bonds Payable
Types & Characteristics of Bonds
Valuation of Bonds Payable
Accounting for Bonds Payable: Straight–Line Method
Balance Sheet Presentation of Unamortized Bond Discount or Premium
Costs of Issuing Bonds
Extinguishment of Debt
Reacquisition of Debt
Legal & In–Substance Defeasance
Long–Term Notes Payable
Notes Issued at Face Value
Notes Not Issued at Face Value
Notes Issued for a Combination of Cash & Other Rights
Notes Issued for Property, Goods, or Services
Imputing an Interest Rate
Mortgage Notes Payable
Financial Instrument Complexities
Substance Over Form
Equity with Debt Characteristics
Debt with Equity Characteristics
Compound Financial Instruments
Derivative Financial Instruments
Off–Balance–Sheet Financing
Reporting Long–Term Debt & Financial Liabilities
Appendix 15A Troubled Debt Restructuring
Settlement of Debt at Less Than Its Carrying Amount
Continuation of Debt with Modification of Terms
Appendix 15B Serial Bonds: Amortization & Redemption Before Maturity
Amortization of a Premium or Discount on Serial Bonds
Redemption of Serial Bonds Before Maturity

chapter 15

LONG–TERM LIABILITIES

PERSPECTIVE

This topic, while previously being thought of as almost introductory and mechanical in nature (the study of bond accounting), has become very complex and sophisticated with the onslaught of ***financial instruments*** *and financial instrument accounting. Although the term "financial instruments" includes most monetary assets and liabilities on the balance sheet, as well as some other items, the larger issues are often dealt with in the long-term debt chapter of books since many of the more complex financial instruments are related to long-term debt.*

This area of study is also very interesting since it deals not only with ***recorded*** *obligations, but also those that are* ***not recorded*** *on the balance sheet (****off-balance sheet financing****). The basics of liabilities were covered in Chapter 14.*

INSIGHTS

- ***Bond accounting*** *in itself is not complex and lends itself to* ***self-study****. The secret is to do as many problems as possible. A number of multiple choice questions have been added to this edition to assist with this.*
- *The term "financial instruments" includes most debt/financing arrangements.*
- *Accounting for the more complex financial instruments and other transactions involving debt or financing (both on the books and off) is not so straight forward and is often not covered in the CICA HB. This results in* ***significant professional judgement*** *being used.*
- ***Presentation and disclosure*** *issues* ***for financial instruments are discussed in HB 3860; however, recognition and measurement issues are not****. Sound reporting practices should rely on HB 1000, definitions in HB 3860, and* ***basic principles****. However, current practice for accounting for these items is widespread with little or no consensus.*

STUDY STEPS

STUDY STEPS

1. Understanding the Business Transactions

Bonds

Bonds are instruments used to raise financing. They are considered liabilities of the company as they generally require repayment along with interest on the principal. Bonds usually have a **face value** (i.e., the value at which the bonds will be redeemed at maturity) and a **stated interest rate**. If the **market interest rate** (i.e., the current interest rate for similar bonds with similar risk) is the same as the stated rate on the bond, the bond trades at face value (e.g., a bond with a face value of $100 and a stated interest rate of 10% will be bought and sold for $100 assuming that current market interest rates were at 10%).

If market interest rates are lower than the stated rates, the bond becomes more valuable to investors and therefore would trade at a **premium** (would be bought and sold for greater than $100 in the example). Likewise, if the market interest rate is higher, the bond would trade at a **discount**.

Tip! **The market value of a bond varies with demand and current market interest rates and, therefore, it is rare that a bond's market value would be the same as its face value or carrying value.**

Tip! **Bond premium is the excess value attributed to the bond, often primarily due to the fact that the stated interest rate on the bond exceeds the market interest rate.**

Tip! **Bond discount is the decrease in value (from face value), often primarily due to the fact that the bond's stated interest rate is less than the market rate.**

Extinguishment of Debt

Extinguishment of debt involves **paying off debt before it becomes due**. This assumes that the debt agreement allows for early repayment.

Often, early repayment is not an allowable option under the terms of the agreement or there are stiff **penalties** for early repayment. One way around this is by entering into a **transaction/business arrangement** called **debt defeasance**. Here we'll look at the business transaction and later we'll look at how to account for it.

Defeasance occurs when the company takes the funds that it would have otherwise used to extinguish the debt, if it could, and puts them in investments that are then held to be used solely to pay off the debt. In other words, the investment and the return on the investment may only be used to make the scheduled repayments on the old debt as they come due.

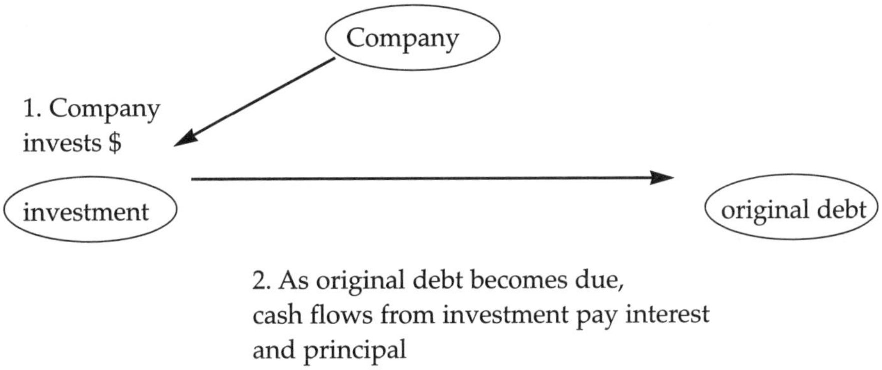

Legal defeasance occurs when the company gets the creditors (from original debt) to agree to this arrangement and to **release the company from further liability**. The creditors would want to ensure that the investment funds will be used only for repayment and, therefore, they would normally require that the funds be placed in trust.

In-substance defeasance occurs when the creditors **do not agree to release the company from any further liability relating to the debt** or they do not know about the defeasance arrangement.

> **The difference between legal and in-substance defeasance is primarily that with legal defeasance, the creditors give up their legal claim on the company, and look solely to the trust for repayment.** *Tip!*

Financial instrument complexities

Most debt instruments are considered to be "financial instruments". In 1995, the CICA issued a new HB section on financial instruments (CICA HB 3860) to deal with these and more complex arrangements. Financial instruments are defined according to CICA HB 3860 as:

> **Financial instruments** are contracts that give rise to both a **financial asset** of one party and a **financial liability** or **equity instrument** of another.

CICA HANDBOOK

> **Most liabilities are part of a broader category called financial instruments.** *Tip!*

> **All financial instruments have two parties to the arrangement, e.g., for accounts payable, the other party would be the company who holds the accounts receivable.** *Tip!*

CICA HANDBOOK

A **financial liability** is any liability that is a contractual obligation (i) to deliver cash or another financial asset to another party or (ii) to exchange financial instruments with another party under conditions that are potentially unfavourable.

Tip! **The main aspect of this definition for most non-complex financial instruments is that a liability is a liability if there is a contractual obligation to deliver cash.**

Tip! **It is easier to understand this HB Section if you look first at the simpler financial liabilities, i.e., accounts payable, bonds, and mortgages payable.**

CICA HANDBOOK

A **financial asset** is any asset that is (i) cash, or (ii) a contractual right to receive cash or another financial asset from another party, or (iii) a contractual right to exchange financial instruments with another party under conditions that are potentially favourable, or (iv) an equity instrument of another entity.

Tip! **Simple examples of financial assets are cash, accounts receivable, and notes receivable.**

CICA HANDBOOK

An **equity instrument** is any contract that evidences a residual value in the net assets of a company.

Tip! **A simple example of an equity instrument is common shares.**

Tip! **CICA HB 3860 deals only with presentation and disclosure issues and not measurement and recognition issues. The latter have not yet been agreed upon.**

All financial instruments have financial risks associated with them. They allow companies to transfer risks to the other party (the counterparty) and often result in the company taking on additional risk. The main risks are as follows:

- **price risk**: the risk that the value of the instrument will change due to changes in market values, interest rates or foreign currencies
- **credit risk**: the risk that the counterparty will not deliver under the contract (i.e., pay up)
- **liquidity risk**: the risk that the company will not be able to deliver under the contract (i.e., pay up)

- **cash flow risk**: the risk that the amounts required to be paid out (or received), i.e., future cash inflows and outflows under the contract, will fluctuate.

Information about financial risks is important to users and should therefore be disclosed in the financial statement notes. This is required disclosure under CICA HB 3860. **Tip!**

Next, let us look at some instruments that are more complex:

Hybrid securities are securities or financial instruments that have some debt characteristics and some equity characteristics. Two examples mentioned in the text are **term preferred shares** and **perpetual bonds**. Review the description of these in the text. Term preferred shares are shares (equity) that have a maturity date (debt-like). Perpetual bonds are bonds (debt) that do not have a maturity date and hence are more like permanent financing (equity-like).

Compound instruments are securities or financial instruments that have **both** a debt component and an equity component. That is, the economic substance is that they have two parts to them, an equity part and a debt part. An example of a compound instrument is **convertible debt**. Convertible debt is a liability with an option to buy shares. Options to buy shares are normally considered to be equity.

Derivative financial instruments are a special type of instrument that **derive** their **value** from an underlying instrument or item such as the US dollar, a stock index, an interest rate, a common share, etc. They generally **transfer risk** from one party to another and **do not necessarily result in the physical transfer of the underlying instrument/item either at inception of the contract or on settlement**. However, their market value will fluctuate with the value of the underlying instrument/item, such that the holder will benefit from and is at risk for changes in value. Examples are forwards contracts and options. These instruments are very common.

Financial instruments transfer risk from one party to the other. Knowledge and understanding of these risks is important to users and therefore the risks should at least be disclosed if not accounted for. **Tip!**

Off-balance-sheet financing

Off-balance sheet financing entail a company obtaining some sort of financing without recording debt on the balance sheet. Indeed, often the sole purpose of these arrangements is to avoid recording debt. For example, if a company needs cash, there are many creative ways to obtain financing without actually borrowing the funds. They could sell their inventory for cash up front and agree to buy it back over time. They could transfer their receivables while retaining the risks and rewards of ownership or they could finance the purchase of equipment through a lease, etc. There are several other examples in the text.

Exhibit 15-1: Long-Term Liabilities
Relevant criteria, definitions and issues

	How it relates to LTD	Relevant criteria/definitions	Topic specific analysis-how it should be	What makes the analysis challenging–how it is
Hybrid securities e.g., term preferred shares—shares that must be redeemed.				
Presentation	• how should the term preferred shares be classified on B/S	**definition of liability** • HB 1000.33 • HB 3860.05c **definition of equity** • HB 1000.35 • HB 3860(d) **economic substance over legal form** • HB 3860.18 **full disclosure**	Term preferred shares have a maturity date that obligates the entity to pay out cash. Therefore economic substance is debt. On the other hand, the legal form is equity, dividends paid.	• company bias towards not recognizing liability since it affects debt/equity ratio and net income • may cause company to review legal form prior to issue • what about shares that are redeemable only if certain conditions occur (see HB 3860.22 and .23)
Compound instruments e.g., convertible debt—debt that carries an option to convert to common shares or equity				
Measurement	• **how much** should be recorded as debt and how much as equity	• PJ-not dealt with in HB 3860	• consider options pricing models, see also Ch 18	• many ways of assigning value between debt and equity that are verifiable. Therefore, open to PJ.
Presentation	**classify** as debt or equity or both	**verifiability definition of liability** • HB 1000.33 • HB 3860.05c **definition of equity** • HB 1000.35 • HB 3860 (d) **economic substance over legal form** HB 3860.24 **full disclosure**	Legal form is debt. However, economic substance is that part of the value of the debt is attributable to the option to convert thus, part is equity (normally, $ paid for options are classified as equity) • HB 3860.24—show parts separately	
Derivative instruments—e.g., forwards, futures and options, etc.				
Recognition	• should derivatives be recognized in the f/s	• not covered in HB • open to PJ • **definition of liability** (see above) • **definition of equity** (see above) • **economic substance**	• should recognize if an obligation or asset	• often dealing with very large amounts • recording would throw off key ratios
Measurement	• how should they be measured if recognized?	• not covered in HB • open to PJ	• generally FMV would be the most appropriate since most have values tied to FMV and are settled in short term	
Presentation	• how to classify? • disclosure	• **full disclosure** • required disclosures under CICA HB 3860 • consider offsetting HB 3860.34—intent and legal right to offset must be present	• since risks and transfer of risks are key—disclosure of risks mandated by HB • if contract will be settled on a net basis, makes sense to show net = economic substance of exposure	
Off–balance–sheet financing				
Recognition	• should these transactions be recorded in f/s?	• not covered in HB • open to PJ • **definition of liability** (see above) • **definition of equity** (see above) • **economic substance**	• should recognize if an obligation or asset	• reluctance to include as impacts debt/equity ratios
Defeasance				
Recognition	• should the original debt be de-recognized? • does a liability still exist?	• **economic substance** • legal defeasance vs. in-substance • **definition of liability** (see above) • HB 3860.41—on offsetting	• for legal defeasance— yes since creditors have given up claim on the liabilities • for in-substance defeasance, argue that economic substance is that debt repaid versus argue that original creditors still have claim on company (consider likelihood of having to pay out additional $ due to poor returns on investment, etc.)	• tendency would be to remove debt under either legal or in-substance

Prepared by Irene Wiecek

Always scrutinize complex business arrangements that are entered into for the purposes of raising funds. **Tip!**

2. Understanding How the Transaction Fits into the Financial Reporting Model and Conceptual Framework—Analysis and Critical Thinking

STUDY STEPS

See exhibit 15-1.

3. Becoming Proficient in Related Calculations and Accounting Skills

STUDY STEPS

Bond accounting

If the bond is issued at a premium, the issuing company gets more than the face value in cash and would record the bond as follows:

Assume face value $100, issue price $104, stated interest 10%, market interest 9%, 5-year bond.

dr. cash	104	
cr. deferred premium		4
cr. bond payable		100

The premium would be amortized to income as an adjustment to the interest expense over the life of the bond. This makes intuitive sense since, in the above case, the stated interest rate was greater than the market interest rate. Investors paid $104 for the bond but will only get interest based on $100 ($10 interest/$104 paid = 9% yield or market interest rate). Conversely, from the perspective of the issuer, the amortization of the premium will reduce the interest expense otherwise recorded such that the yield reflects market rates. **Tip!**

Note that $104 is calculated as follows:

Present value $100, 5 years 9%	= $65.00
+ present value annuity $10, 5 years 9%	= 39.00
	$104.00

The $104 would be the starting point on the amortization table under the principal column and the table would calculate interest at 9% or the market rate at the issue date. At the end of year 1, the interest expense would be calculated as follows:

$104 x 9% = $9.36

The actual interest paid would be the 10% on the face value of $100 = $10. The difference ($10—$9.36 = $0.64) would be the amortization of the premium and the following entry would be booked:

dr. interest expense	9.36	
dr. deferred premium	0.64	
cr. cash		10.00

Date	Payment ($100 x10%)	Interest Principal (@ 9%)		Principal Reduction
				$104.00
12/31	$10.00	$9.36	$0.64	$103.36

The interest expense divided by the book value of the obligation or $9.39/$104 produces a 9% yield, which is the market interest rate at the time of the bond issue. Therefore, the bond was priced to yield 9%.

The scenario above uses the effective interest method to amortize the premium.

Tip! **The effective interest method is the most commonly used method and provides a constant return on the declining book value (or 9%).**

MULTIPLE CHOICE QUESTIONS

1) On July 1, 1999, Denim Limited issued 500 of its 6%, $1,000 bonds at 99 plus accrued interest. The bonds are dated April 1, 1999 and mature on April 1, 2009. Interest is payable semiannually on April 1 and October 1. What amount did Eagle receive from the bond issuance?

(a) $502,500

(b) $495,000

(c) $500,000

(d) $507,500

2) Offsetting assets and liabilities results in the assets and liabilities being netted against each other to show a net asset or a net liability. The full asset and full liability would not be shown separately. Offsetting requires that certain conditions be present. Which of the following represents those conditions?

(a) Management intends to realize the asset and settle the liability separately.

(b) Management intends to settle the transaction on a net basis.

(c) There is a legal right of offset.

(d) Management intends to settle on a net basis and there is a legal right of offset.

3) Defeasance is a transaction that allows a company to set aside funds (often in a trust) and effectively prepay / repay debt up-front. Accounting for this transaction / arrangement sometimes results in the debt being removed from the financial statements or the investment and debt being offset. The key condition which would clearly allow the debt to be taken off the balance sheet is as follows:

   (a) the funds must be set aside in an irrevocable trust.

   (b) the funds must be deposited in interest bearing, risk-free securities.

   (c) the creditor must accept the assets of the trust as settlement of the debt.

   (d) the likelihood of the company having to pay out additional funds beyond the amount set aside up-front is unlikely.

4) Lima Corporation issues 10% bonds when the market rate is 12%. Would the bonds be Issued at a discount or premium and would the yield be higher or lower than the stated interest rate?

	Premium / discount	yield
a)	premium	higher
b)	premium	lower
c)	discount	higher
d)	discount	lower

5) Zenon Limited issued 10 year bonds at a discount and is trying to determine whether they should amortize the discount using the straight-line method or the effective interest method. If the effective interest method is used to amortize the discount, which of the following is true in the first few years of the bond?

   a) The interest expense would be the same under both methods.

   b) The interest expense would be higher under the effective interest method.

   c) The interest expense would be lower under the effective interest method.

   d) The interest expense would be less than the actual interest payment.

6) Assume the same question as 5. Which of the following is true over the life of the bond?

   a) The interest expense would be the same under both methods.

   b) The interest expense would be higher under the effective interest method.

   c) The interest expense would be lower under the effective interest method.

   d) The interest expense would be less than the actual interest payment.

The following applies to both question 7 and 8.

On June 30, 1998, Binford Tools issued 200, $1,000 bonds at 102. Interest on the bonds is 11% and market rates are 10%. Premium / discount is amortized using the effective interest rate method.

7) At December 31, 1998, what is the book value of the bond including any premium/discount?

a) $203,200

b) $204,000

c) $202,400

d) $204,800

8) What is the amount of the bond interest expense at December 31, 1999?

a) $10,200

b) $20,400

c) $22,000

d) $20,320

9) Fox Company sold its shares in Rabbit Company for $200,000 and took back a note receivable that will be repaid over the next year. The risk that Rabbit Company will not be able to repay the note is known as:

a) liquidity risk

b) credit risk

c) price risk

d) solvency risk

10) Fox Company also borrowed funds from the banks. The borrowings are long-term and significantly increase the debt to equity ratio. The risk that Fox Company will not be able to repay the debt is known as:

a) liquidity risk

b) credit risk

c) price risk

d) cash flow risk

SOLUTIONS TO MULTIPLE CHOICE QUESTIONS

1) a) Bond issue price plus accrued interest since issued after April 1.
= (500 X $1,000 X 99%) +($500,000 X 6% X 3/12)
= $495,000 + 7,500
= $502,500

2) d) There must be both intent and legal right of offset to allow the amounts to be recorded net.

3) c) The creditor must give up their legal claim on the company and look only to the trust fund or investment to settle the debt. Therefore, the company would no longer have the obligation to pay them.

4) c) The bond would be issued at a discount since it is not worth as much if the interest being paid on it is less than market. Since there is a discount, the yield would be higher than the stated rate (i.e., the amount paid for the bond is less and therefore the actual return is higher).

5) c) The interest expense would be lower in the earlier years of the bond since the principal amount of the loan is the lowest in the earlier years. As the discount is amortized, the interest, as calculated under the effective interest method, rises. The interest expense will always be higher than the payment since the bond is issued at a discount to yield a higher rate of return to the purchaser.

6) a) By the end of the bond, the total interest will be the same no matter which amortization method is used (= actual interest paid plus the discount).

7) a) At issue, the bonds are worth $204,000 (200 X $1000 X 102). After six months, $800 of premium would be amortized as follows: interest paid = $200,000 X 11% X6/12 = $11,000; interest expense = $204,000 X 10% X 6/12 = $10,200; the difference is $800 which is deducted from the book value.

8) d) At December 31, 1998, the book value would be $203,200. Therefore, interest would be $203,200 X 10% = $20,320.

9) b) The risk in question is a credit risk. This is the risk that the counterparty will fail to pay. This risk is present whenever another party owes the company money.

10) a) This risk is known as liquidity risk. Any time that a company commits itself to pay money out, this increases liquidity risk or risk that the company will not be able to honour their part of the arrangement.

SHORT PROBLEMS

1) Purpose: To illustrate accounting for bonds issued at discount (bond issue costs).

Bondex Limited (BL) issued redeemable, secured bonds with a face value of $2,000,000 on January 1, 1998. The bonds are interest bearing at 10% interest and pay interest annually on December 31. The bonds mature on December 31, 2007. Assume that the market interest rates at the time of issue are 11% and that issue costs are $200,000.

REQUIRED

a) Calculate the price that the market would pay for these bonds today given that the market interest rates are greater than the stated rate on the bond.
b) Prepare the journal entries to record the bond issue and the entries for accounting for the bond for the year ended December 31, 1998.

2) Purpose: To demonstrate accounting for early debt retirement.

BL sold off some real estate in 1999 and generated sufficient cash to repay the bond issue from 1. Since the bonds are redeemable, BL paid the bondholders out on May 31, 1999. The bonds were retired at 97 plus accrued interest.

REQUIRED

Prepare the journal entry to record the retirement.

3) Purpose: To demonstrate the difference in accounting if the bonds retired in 2 were replaced by new debt.

Assume the same information as in 1. In 1999, interest rates dipped sharply and analysts were predicting that they would stay low for the short- to mid-term. Since BL's bonds were at 10%, management at BL felt that they would be paying too much for the financing over the next few years. Management decided to redeem the bonds and to issue new ones at a lower interest rate. The bonds were retired at 97 plus accrued interest.

REQUIRED

Prepare the journal entry to record the retirement of the old bonds.

4) Purpose: To demonstrate accounting for a situation where there was defeasance.

Assume the same information as in 1 except that the bonds were not redeemable unless a very prohibitively high penalty was paid. Shortly after the bond issue, BL was offered $4,000,000 for some vacant land that they had been trying to get rid of. This resulted in a situation where there was excess cash sufficient to repay the bond. However, since the cost of early retirement was prohibitive, they decided to enter into the following transaction. The amount of $1,773,990 was put on deposit at BL's bank at 12%. The amount deposited generated a sufficient return such that there was enough to pay the interest on the debt each year and to repay the bond holders at the maturity date. The transaction was not discussed with the bondholders.

REQUIRED

a) Show the calculations to prove that the amount deposited will indeed be sufficient to meet the commitments on the bonds. For simplicity, assume that the amount was deposited on January 1, 1998.

b) Record the journal entries relating to the new investment for 1998.

c) Given that the company has provided for the repayment of the bond and the related interest, is it necessary to continue to show the bond liability on the balance sheet?

d) If the bondholders had agreed to accept the investment as settlement of the obligation, this would be legal defeasance. Show the journal entries to account for the transaction if there was legal defeasance.

SOLUTIONS TO SHORT PROBLEMS

1) (a) Since the market rate is greater than the stated interest rate on the bond, prospective purchasers of the bonds would find them less desirable. They could presumably get a better rate on their investment by investing in another type. However, everything has a price. Prospective investors would invest if they could achieve an overall yield of 11% based on the purchase price and the interest at 10%. Since the interest is fixed at 10%, they will likely offer to pay less up-front for the bond. Exactly how much should be paid up-front in order to give an overall yield of 11%?

This can be determined by discounting the stream of payments under the bond at 11% as follows:

Present value $2,000,000, 10 years @11%	
= $2,000,000 x 0.35218	= $ 704,360
+ Present value annuity $2,000,000 x 10%	
10 years @11%	
= $200,000 x 5.88923	= 1,177,846
	$1,882,206

The discount is $2,000,000—1,882,206 = 117,794 and it will be amortized over the 10-year life of the bond.

To prove that this will give an annual yield of 11%, the book value of the bond will now be $1,882,206 for the investor and in year 1 the return will be $200,000 or 10% of $2,000,000 plus the amortization of the discount or $7,042. Therefore:

$207,042 / $1,882,206 = $11%

There are other factors that affect the pricing of bonds, but the relationship between the stated interest rate and the market interest rate is key.

(b) January 1, 1998—to record bond issue at discount:

dr. cash	1,682,206	
dr. deferred discount	117,794	
dr. deferred issue costs	200,000	
cr. long-term bonds payable		2,000,000

December 31, 1998—to record payment of interest:

dr. interest expense	207,042	
cr. deferred discount		7,042
cr. cash		200,000

The discount amortization comes from the amortization table below.

Date	Payment ($2 millx10%)	Interest (@11%)	Principal change/amort	Principal
				$1,882,206
12/31	$200,000	$207,042	$7,042	1,889,248

The table uses the market interest rate since the bond was priced by discounting the stream of payments at the market rate in order to give a yield of 11%. Gradually, the principal value will increase until it is equal to the face value. The starting principal balance on the table is equal to the face value minus the discount from the first journal entry, even though these are booked in separate general ledger accounts and may be shown separately on the financial statements.

December 31,1998—to record amortization of the issue costs:

dr. finance expense	20,000	
cr. deferred issue costs		20,000

($200,000/10 years)

These have been amortized using the straight-line method. This is a matter of judgement and it could have easily been amortized using the effective interest method. The straight-line method is generally used due to its simplicity.

2) May 31, 1999—to record the retirement of the bonds:

dr. long-term bonds payable	2,000,000	
dr. interest expense	86,590 (See 2 below)	
dr. finance expense	8,333 (See 1 below)	
dr. loss on disposition	219,162 (See 5 below)	
cr. cash		2,023,333 (See 4 below)
cr. deferred discount		110,752 (See 3 below)
cr. deferred issue costs		180,000 (See 1 below)

(1) deferred issue costs $200,000/10 x 5/12 = $8,333; 200,000—$20,000= $180,000

Date	Payment ($2 millx10%)	Interest (@11%)	Principal change/amort	Principal
				$1,882,206
12/31	$200,000	$207,042	$7,042	1,889,248
05/31	83,333	86,590	3,257	1,892,505

(2) interest $1,889,248 x .11 x 5/12 = $86,590
(3) deferred discount $2,000,000—1,889,248 = $110,752
(4) $2,000,000 x .97 = $1,940,000 plus accrued interest of $83,333 on the face value of $2,000,000 x .10 x 5/12 = 83,333; $1,940,000 + 83,333 = $2,023,333.
(5) The loss occurs because the bonds were redeemed at 97 when their book value was at 94.6 (or $1,892,505/2,000,000) and the remaining issue costs had to be written off. $1,940,000—1,892,505 + 171,667 = $219,162

3) The journal entry would be the same as for 2; however, there might be a case for deferral of the loss on disposition. If deferred, the loss would be written off over the life of the new debt. The argument for deferral would be that, in substance, there had been no real change in the financing (i.e. still outstanding) and, therefore, it would not make sense to recognize the loss. Rather, the loss would be assumed to be part of a larger transaction (i.e., the refinancing). The case for deferral would be strengthened if the new bond issue was for the same term and had similar attributes.

4) (a) The amortization table for the investment is as follows:

Date	Payment on bond	Interest on inv. (12%)	Principal	Balance
01/98				$1,773,990
31/98	$200,000	$212,879	$12,879	1,786,869
31/99	200,000	214,424	14,424	1,801,293
31/00	200,000	216,155	16,155	1,817,448
31/01	200,000	218,094	18,094	1,835,542
31/02	200,000	220,265	20,265	1,855,807
31/03	200,000	222,697	22,697	1,878,504
31/04	200,000	225,420	25,420	1,903,924
31/05	200,000	228,470	28,470	1,932,394
31/06	200,000	231,887	31,887	1,964,281
31/07	2,200,000	235,714	1,964,286	5 (rounding)

(b) January 1, 1998—to record the investment:

dr. investment	1,773,990	
cr. cash		1,773,990

December 31, 1998—to record the interest on the investment:

dr. cash	212,879	
cr. investment income		212,879

(c) It might be argued that the liability has already been settled, since the company has already provided for the settlement and the income and principal from the investment will be sufficient to settle the debt. However, we must examine the substance of the arrangement. Has BL actually settled the obligation, or are they still responsible? What if something happens to the investment? Would BL still have to settle the obligation? Factors that influence the answer are as follows:

Remove the obligation:

- if investment is held in trust for the benefit of the bondholders only.
- if the investment is in no-risk or low-risk investments.
- if the bondholders agree to accept the trust and the income from the trust as settlement.

In this case, insufficient information is given. However, since the bondholders have not agreed to the transaction, this is, at best, in-substance defeasance. Chances are that the substance is that the liability to the bondholders still exists until it is proven in hindsight that the investment is sufficient. This position is supported by the HB Section 3860 on Financial Instruments in the paragraphs that deal with offsetting.

(d) January 1, 1998—to record the investment:

dr. investment	1,773,990	
cr. cash		1,773,990

January 1, 1998—to record the legal defeasance:

dr. long-term bonds payable	2,000,000	
dr. loss	91,784	
cr. investments		1,773,990
cr. deferred discount		117,794
cr. deferred issue costs		200,000

There is a loss on booking the defeasance. This occurs because the net liability has been settled for more than the net book value. Often there is a gain, and there would have been here since BL has invested in an investment with a higher interest rate than the debt resulting in a lower present value for the investment than the debt ($1,773,990—1,882,206 = 108,216 gain). However, since the issue costs must also be written off, this turns it into a loss ($108,216—200,000 = 91,784).

Both the investment and the liability would be removed from the balance sheet. Likely, there would be note disclosure of the transaction.

CASES

1) LEVERAGED LTD.

Leveraged Ltd. (LL) is in the construction business and has borrowed heavily from its bank, Money Bank, to finance a recent construction project. As is the case with the real estate industry, funds are often loaned on reputation and since LL has always had an excellent financial track record, it has been easy for them to borrow funds. Although Money Bank was eager to lend the money to LL, they included several restrictive covenants in the loan agreement.

The agreement requires that audited financial statements of LL be presented to the bank within 60 days of the year-end and that the debt/equity ratio not exceed 2:1 or the loans will be called immediately. This would obviously be undesirable since LL would have to sell the property under construction in order to repay the loan. Since the building would not yet be finished, they would not be able to get their money back.

Close to year-end, LL went to the market to raise funds since they felt that they could get financing at a lower rate. They issued two different instruments as follows:

> Term preferred shares-$10 million: The shares were repayable after 10 years and bore cumulative dividends at 10% per annum. The shares ranked in preference over all other outstanding classes of shares.
>
> Bonds-$6 million: The bonds had no specified repayment date and were secured by the assets of the company. The interest was variable having a fixed minimum component of 5% plus a variable component that was based on net income. This was attractive to the investors since their return would increase in good years. LL had had increasing profits over the past 10 years.

After the issue, Rita Rahemtulla, the controller of LL, prepared a rough calculation of the debt/equity ratio for the bank as follows:

> Debt (including the new bonds) = $36 million
> Equity (including the new shares) = $18 million
> debt:equity = 36:18 = 2:1

Rita was thankful that the debt covenant had not been breached. Earnings had not been as high as originally projected and had caused equity to be lower than anticipated. The preliminary calculations were sent to the bank, which was happy to see that the covenant had not been violated. The bank eagerly awaited the audited financial statements.

REQUIRED

Adopt the role of the auditor and analyze the treatment afforded the bonds and the shares.

2) Dura Pharmaceuticals—www.durapharm.com

Dura Pharmaceuticals Inc., ("DPI") is a U.S. based company whose shares are publicly traded. Its main business is in the pharmaceuticals industry, developing and marketing/distributing drugs related primarily to respiratory ailments. During 1994, the company signed several deals to arrange financing for expansion on several strategic fronts. Specifically, DPI signed an agreement with Drug Royalty Corporation, a Nevada Corporation, under which DPI would receive funding ($2 million in 1994 and 1995) to expand its sales force in specified territories. In return, DPI would be required to pay royalties on net revenues in the specified territories. DPI accrued $400,000 as contract revenues under the deal in 1994.

According to the annual report of Drug Royalty Corporation, the company notes the following with respect to the arrangement and others similar to it.

" Pharmaceuticals companies are willing to pay royalties to Drug Royalty to acquire capital and expertise needed to develop emerging and existing products and technologies. At a time when lack of financing is a critical issue in the industry, Drug Royalty offers non-recourse financing, the opportunity to avoid equity dilution, and valued industry knowledge and expertise..."

DPI had suffered losses of $8 million for the year ended December 31, 1993 ($7 million in 1992) and showed a profit of just under $2 million for 1994. Revenues have been increasing significantly.

Required:

Discuss the treatment of the $400,000 accrued under the agreement, noting possible alternative treatments.

SOLUTIONS TO CASES

1. LEVERAGED LIMITED

Overview

Since the financial statements must be audited as part of the loan arrangement with the bank, **GAAP** is a constraint. The **debt/equity ratio** is critical since there is a debt covenant that stipulates that the ratio cannot fall below 2:1 or the loan will be called. Therefore, classification of the new financing is very important. **Management** of the company is happy with the way the financing has been classified at present and would be reluctant to change. However, as **auditor**, knowing that the bank will rely on the statements and is concerned about the company taking on additional debt, it is important that an objective, defensible analysis be made. This is of high risk to the auditor.

Analysis and Recommendations

The issue is how the shares and debt should be calculated. Presumably the choices are either debt or equity. It is worthwhile to examine all options since the client is presently planning to classify the shares as equity and debt as debt.

Term preferred shares:
Support for equity:

- Legally shares.

Support for debt:

- CICA HB 3860 says **economic substance over legal form** .
- Meets the definition of a financial liability since there is a **contractual obligation to repay**—since the equity is repayable after 10 years, it has a **maturity date**. This is more like debt than equity, which is usually only distributed upon liquidation of the company.
- The dividend rate is cumulative (which means it must be paid) and is stipulated as a fixed amount regardless of income. This is more like interest on debt.

Bonds:
Support for equity:

- CICA HB 3860 calls for **economic substance over legal form.**
- No repayment date makes this more like **permanent financing** and hence, more like equity.
- The return on the financing as a function of net income rather than being a fixed percentage and bond holders sharing in net income makes it more like equity than debt.

Support for debt:

- Legally debt.

- It is secured by the assets of the company.

Other

- If the debt and equity were reclassified based on economic substance (versus legal form), then the debt covenant would be breached as follows:

  Debt:equity = $40 million:$14 million = 2.86:1
- Also, the company would be reluctant to change the statements and the calculation since they have already given it to the bank.
- As auditor, however, if it is misleading and the bank is relying on it, it is risky not to reclassify it no matter if management objects.

Recommendation

The issue is whether these instruments should be classified according to legal form or economic substance. CICA HB 3860 clearly states that **economic substance prevails over legal form** and therefore both instruments must be reclassified regardless how management may object.

Full disclosure should be made of the details of the instruments (such as interest rates etc.) due to the **materiality** of the instruments and, therefore, this will at least give the **bank** and other users all of the details.

2) Dura Pharmaceuticals

Overview

As noted, the company is in the pharmaceuticals industry which is a very risky industry. Large amounts of funds are required for continued research and development and success is not always guaranteed. Due to the riskiness of the industry, the market is very sensitive to changes in net income. The amount in question is **material**, being 20% of net income.

DPI has been steadily expanding but has suffered losses up to this point, showing a net income for the first time in three years in 1994.

U.S. GAAP is a constraint since the company has shares that trade on U.S. stock markets.

Since the company is always looking for new funding, and due to the riskiness of the industry, there may be pressure on the company to report more favourable financial statements. Users will be **existing creditors** and **shareholders** as well as **potential investors,** who will be assessing the financial position of the company for cash flow potential.

Analysis and Recommendations

The issue as identified, is the treatment of the funds receivable from Drug Royalty under the terms of the agreement. To begin with, the **legal form** of the arrangement must be identified.

Royalties on net revenues in specified sales territories

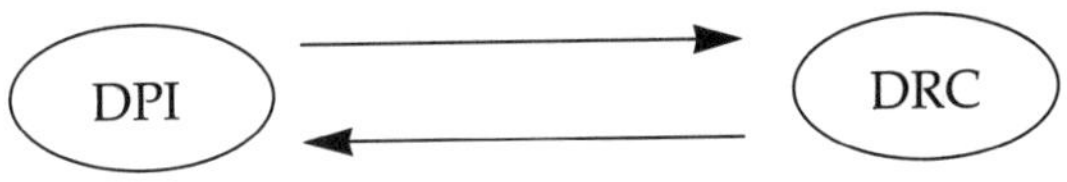

$2 million to expand sales force in specified sales territories

On the one hand, the company has recorded the amounts as contract **revenues**. This is presumably supported by the fact that under the terms of the agreement, the funds were given to them to expand sales forces in specified territories. DPI might argue that they have **performed** this duty or service and, therefore, as specified under the contract, they have **earned** the money and the **earnings process is substantially complete**. Under the terms of the agreement, they must pay royalties on the sales in those territories. Normally, royalties are paid when a company sells a product that is owned by another company. In this case, one might argue that Drug Royalty owns the sales territories or part of them since they funded their development and therefore if DPI wants to use those territories as distribution channels, then they must pay for that use—through the royalty fee.

On the other hand, one might argue that since they have to pay a certain amount back, that this is some sort of **financing arrangement**. Does this represent a liability? Does DPI have an obligation to repay Drug Royalty? What is the transaction or event, if any, that gives rise to the liability?

Given the industry, and the constant need for raising capital, the **economic substance** of this transaction might be seen as a form of funding or financing. One might argue that DPI does have an **obligation to "repay"** Drug Royalty for the funding through the royalty fee. However, since the royalty would only be paid if there are sales in the territory, there is a certain amount of **uncertainty** regarding any "repayment". If there are no sales in the territories, then no amount will be paid back.

This could be viewed as a **contingent liability** with the event being the receipt of the funds up-front. If it is probable that the amounts would be paid (albeit through the "royalty" payment), then it would be recorded as a liability. Management would probably argue that the sales territories will be successful and generate revenues and hence royalties.

The decision as to whether a liability exists boils down to what the **event** is, if any, that obligates the entity. Is it the signing of the deal up-front or is it future sales in the designated territories? Either is supportable. Finally, the question arises as to whether the liability, if indeed one does exist, is **measurable** given that it is not tied to the $2,000,000.

In conclusion, either position is supportable.

SELECTED SOLUTIONS FROM THE TEXTBOOK

EXERCISE 15-3

(a)

1.

	June 30, 1998		
Cash		3,225,690	
Bonds Payable			3,000,000
Premium on Bonds Payable			225,690

2.

	December 31, 1998		
Bond Interest Expense			
($3,225,690 x 12% x 6/12)			193,541.40
Premium on Bonds Payable			1,458.60
Cash ($3,000,000 x 13% x 6/12)			195,000.00

3.

	June 30, 1999		
Bond Interest Expense*		193,453.88	
Premium on Bonds Payable			1,546.12
Cash			195,000.00

* ([$3,225,690 - $1,458.60] x 12% x 6/12)

4.

	December 31, 1999		
Bond Interest Expense*		193,361.12	
Premium on Bonds Payable			1,638.88
Cash			195,000.00

* ([$3,225,690 - $1,458.60 - $1,546.12] x 12% x 6/12)

(b) Long-term Liabilities:

Bonds payable, 13% (due in 2018)	$ 3,000,000.00
Unamortized Bond Premium*	221,046.40
Book value of bonds payable	$ 3,221,046.40

*($225,690.00) - ($1,458.60 + $1,546.12 + $1,638.88) = $ 221,046.40

(c)

1. Interest expense for the period from January 1 to June 30, 1999 (from (a) 3, above)	$ 193,453.88
Interest expense for the period from July 1 to December 31, 1999 (from (a) 4, above)	193,361.12
Amount of bond interest expense reported for 1999	$ 386,815.00

2. The amount of bond interest expense reported in 1999 will be greater than the amount that would be reported if the straight-line method of amortization were used. Under the straight-line method, the annual amortization of bond premium is $11,284.50 ($225,690 ÷ 20). Bond interest expense for 1999 is the difference between the amortized premium of $11,284.50 and the actual interest paid $390,000 ($3,000,000 x 13%). Thus, the amount of bond interest expense is $378,715.50, which is smaller than the bond interest expense under the effective interest method.

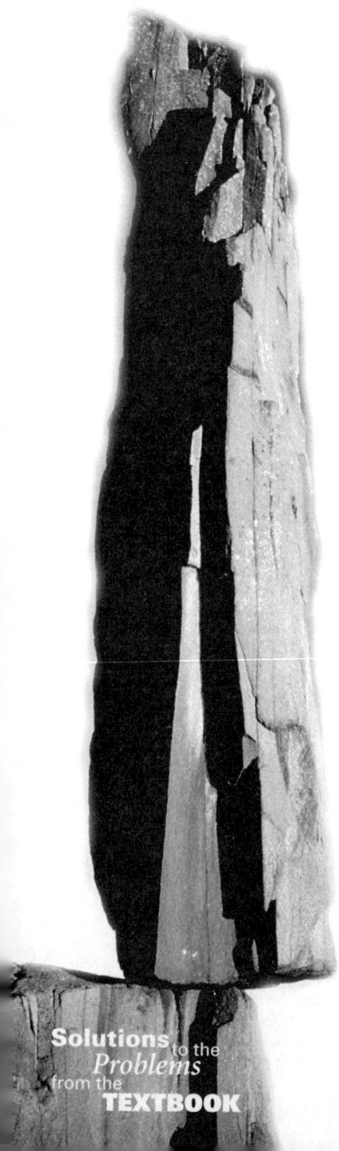

3. Total interest to be paid for the bond

$3,000,000 x 13% x 20 =	$ 7,800,000
Principal due in 2018	3,000,000
Total cash outlays for the bond	$10,800,000
Cash received at issuance of the bond	3,225,690
Total cost of borrowing over the life of the bond	$ 7,574,310

4. It will be the same as under the effective interest method.

Exercise 15-5

1. Using the straight-line basis:

March 1 (issuance):

Cash ($462,414 + $6,667)	469,081	
Discount on Bonds Payable	37,586	
Bonds Payable		500,000
Interest Expense ($500,000 x .08 x 2/12)		6,667

The remaining life of the bonds is 58 months (5 years less 2 months). Therefore, the straight-line amortization of the discount is $648.03 per month ($37,586 ÷ 58).

June 30 (interest date):

Interest Expense	22,592.12	
Discount on Bonds Payable ($648.03 x 4)		2,592.12
Cash ($500,000 x .08 x 6/12)		20,000.00

December 31 (interest date):

Interest Expense	23,888.18	
Discount on Bonds Payable ($648.03 x 6)		3,888.18
Cash		20,000.00

2. Using the effective interest method:

March 1:

Cash 469,081		
Discount on Bonds Payable	37,586	
Bonds Payable		500,000
Interest Expense		6,667

June 30:

Interest Expense	22,047	
Discount on Bonds Payable		2,047
Cash		20,000

*Present value of bond payments for 9 periods from June 30 to maturity, discounted at 5%:

Principal: $500,000 x .64461 (Table A-2)	$ 322,305
Interest: $20,000 x 7.10782 (Table A-4)	142,156
	$ 464,461
Issuance proceeds March 1	462,414
Change in present value = 4 months discount amortization	$ 2,047

Account	Debit	Credit
December 31		
Interest Expense		
[($462,414 + $2,047) .10 x 6/12]	23,223	
Discount on Bonds Payable		3,223
Cash		20,000

EXERCISE 15-8

(a)

June 30, 1998	Debit	Credit
Bonds Payable 700,000		
Loss on Redemption of Bonds	35,700	
Discount on Bonds Payable		
(.02 x $700,000 x 11/20) 7,700		
Cash ($700,000 x 104%)		728,000
Cash ($800,000 x 102%)	816,000	
Premium on Bonds Payable		16,000
Bonds Payable		800,000

(b)

December 31, 1998	Debit	Credit
Bond Interest Expense	39,600	
Premium on Bond Payable (1/40 x $16,000)	400	
Cash (.05 x $800,000)		40,000

*EXERCISE 15-16

Part I

(a) Toshiba Co. Ltd.'s entry:

Account	Debit	Credit
Notes Payable 180,000		
Accrued Interest Payable	19,800	
Property	75,000	
Gain on Property Disposition ($120,000 - $75,000)		45,000
Gain on Restructuring [($180,000 + $19,800) - $120,000]		79,800

(b) Zimmer Inc.'s entry:

Account	Debit	Credit
Property	120,000	
Allowance for Doubtful Accounts	79,800	
(or Loss on Investment in Note Receivable)		
Notes Receivable		180,000
Interest Receivable		19,800

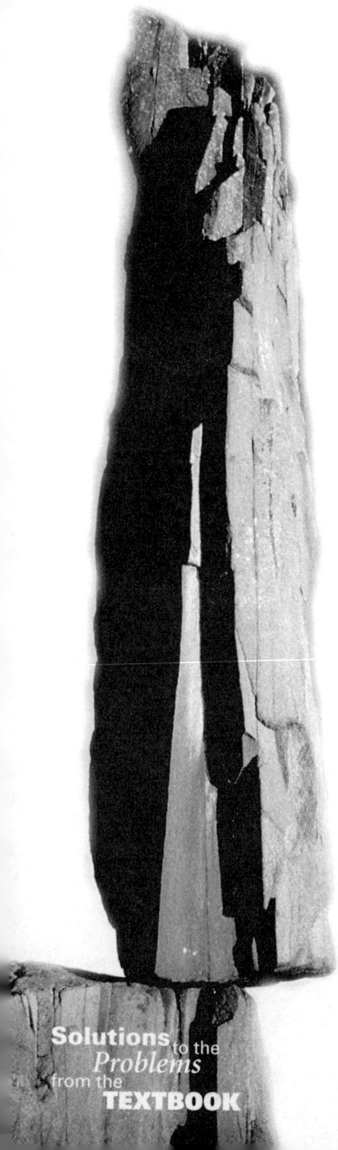

Part II

(a) Eaton Corp.'s entry on December 31, 1998:

Account	Debit	Credit
Interest Payable	24,000	
12% Note Payable	200,000	
Discount on 5% Note Payable	17,355	
5% Note Payable		200,000
Gain on Restructuring of Debt		41,355

Present value of future payments under the restructure arrangement:

Principal of \$200,000 discounted for 2 years at the 10% prevailing rate \$200,000 x .82645 (Table A-2)	\$165,290
Interest of 5% for 2 years discounted at 10% \$200,000 x .05 x 1.73554 (Table A-4)	17,355
Present value	\$182,645

Therefore, the discount is \$17,355 (\$200,000 - \$182,645)

(b) Eaton Corp.'s entry on December 31, 1998:

Account	Debit	Credit
12% Note Payable	200,000	
Interest Payable	24,000	
Discount on Note Payable	23,662	
Gain on Restructuring on Note		47,662
5% Note Payable		200,000

Present value of the restructured liability:

PV of principal (2yrs, i=12%) \$200,000 x .79719 (Table A-2)	\$159,438
PV of interest (\$200,000 x .05) x 1.69005 (Table A-4)	16,900
	\$176,338

SOLUTIONS TO PROBLEMS

PROBLEM 15-7

May 1, 1997	Debit	Credit
Cash (\$700,000 x 105% + \$28,000)	763,000.00	
Bonds Payable		700,000.00
Premium on Bonds Payable		35,000.00
Interest Expense (\$700,000 x 12% x 4/12)		28,000.00

December 31, 1997	Debit	Credit
Interest Expense		84,000.00
Interest Payable (\$700,000 x 12%)		84,000.00
Premium on Bonds Payable	2,413.79	
Interest Expense (\$35,000 / 116 = \$301.724/month) (\$301.724 x 8 = \$2,413.79)		2,413.79

*(12 x 10) - 4 = 116 months from issuance to maturity.

January 1, 1998

Interest Payable		84,000.00
Cash	84,000.00	

April 1, 1998

Interest Expense		12,600.00
Interest Payable ($420,000 x .12 x 3/12)		12,600.00
Premium on Bonds Payable	543.10	
Interest Expense [($301.724 x 3) x 420,000 / 700,000]		543.10
Bonds Payable 420,000.00		
Premium on Bonds Payable*	19,008.62	
Interest Payable (see above)	12,600.00	
Cash [($420,000 x 1.02) + $12,600]		441,000.00
Gain on Retirement of Bonds		10,608.62

* 60% of Premium: ($35,000 - 2,413.79) x 60% - 543.10 = $19,008.62

Reacquisition price ($420,000 x 102%)		$428,400.00
Net carrying value of bonds redeemed:		
Par value	$420,000.00	
Unamortized premium ($35,000 x [$420,000 / $700,000] x 105/116)	19,008.62	(439,008.62)
Gain on redemption		$(10,608.62)

December 31, 1998

Interest Expense ($280,000 x .12)	33,600.00	
Interest Payable		33,600.00
Premium on Bonds Payable	1,448.28	
Interest Expense		1,448.28

Amortization per year on $280,000
($35,000 x 12/116 x 40%*) = $1,448.28
*($700,000 - $420,000) / $700,000 = 40%

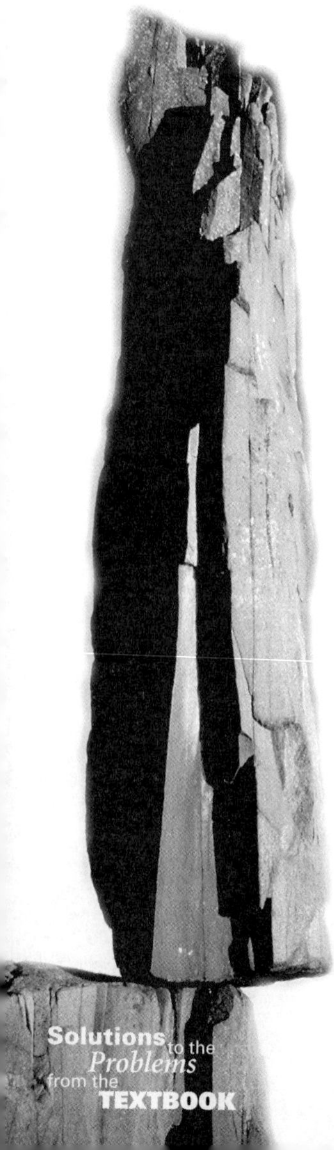

PROBLEM 15-11

(a) December 31, 1997

Computer Equipment	273,204	
Discount on Notes Payable	126,796	
Notes Payable		400,000
(Computer capitalized at the present value of the note—$400,000 x .68301 from Table A-2)		

(b) December 31, 1998

Depreciation Expense [($273,204 - $40,000)/5]	46,640.80	
Accumulated Depreciation—Computer		46,640.80
Interest Expense	27,320.40	
Discount on Notes Payable 27,320.40		

Schedule of Note Discount Amortization

Date	Debit, Interest Expense Credit, Discount on Notes	Carrying Value of Note
12/31/97	—	$273,204.00
12/31/98	$27,320.40	300,524.40
12/31/99	30,052.44	330,576.84
12/31/00	33,057.68	363,634.52
12/31/01	36,365.48*	400,000.00

*2.03 adjustment due to rounding.

(c) December 31, 1999

Depreciation Expense	46,640.80	
Accumulated Depreciation—Computer		46,640.80
Interest Expense	30,052.44	
Discount on Notes Payable		30,052.44

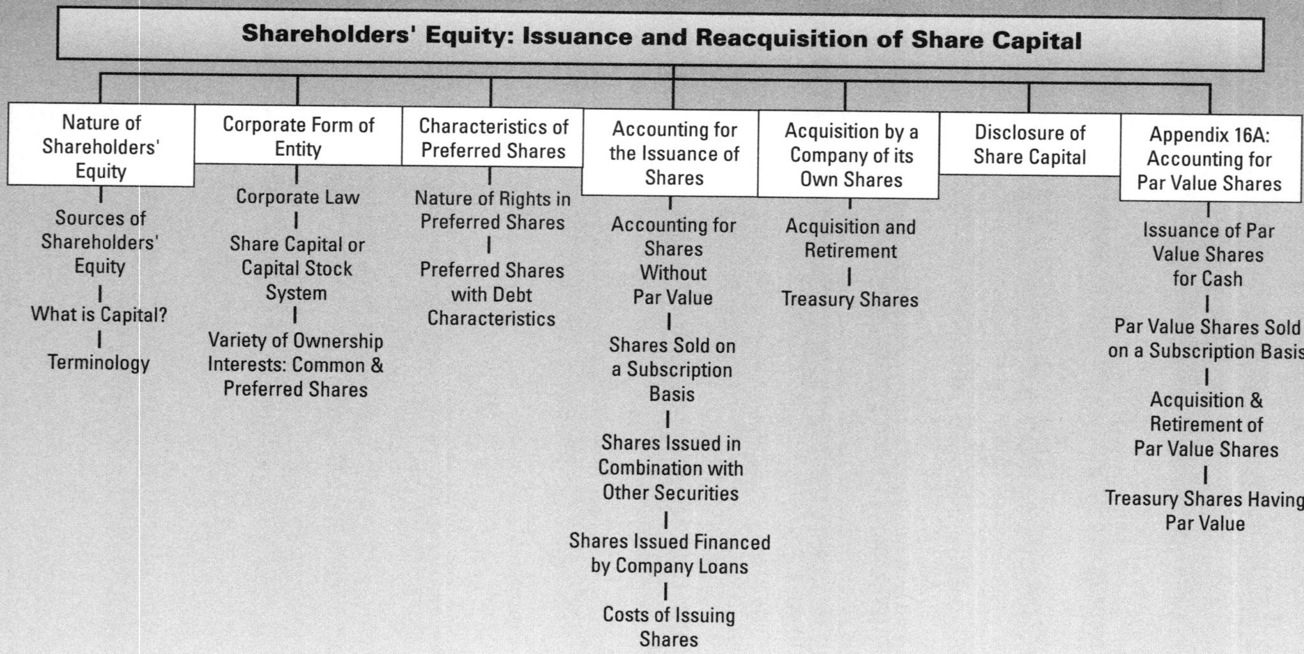
Shareholders' Equity: Issuance and Reacquisition of Share Capital
Nature of Shareholders' Equity
Sources of Shareholders' Equity
What is Capital?
Terminology
Corporate Form of Entity
Corporate Law
Share Capital or Capital Stock System
Variety of Ownership Interests: Common & Preferred Shares
Characteristics of Preferred Shares
Nature of Rights in Preferred Shares
Preferred Shares with Debt Characteristics
Accounting for the Issuance of Shares
Accounting for Shares Without Par Value
Shares Sold on a Subscription Basis
Shares Issued in Combination with Other Securities
Shares Issued Financed by Company Loans
Costs of Issuing Shares
Acquisition by a Company of its Own Shares
Acquisition and Retirement
Treasury Shares
Disclosure of Share Capital
Appendix 16A: Accounting for Par Value Shares
Issuance of Par Value Shares for Cash
Par Value Shares Sold on a Subscription Basis
Acquisition & Retirement of Par Value Shares
Treasury Shares Having Par Value

chapter 16

SHAREHOLDERS' EQUITY: ISSUANCE AND REACQUISITION OF SHARE CAPITAL

Perspective

This chapter in the text deals with numerous aspects of shareholders' equity including the legal form of entities and capital. This is interesting background reading and it is important to know; however, since it is relatively straightforward, it will not be reviewed in great detail here.

The focus of the material will be on financial statement disclosure and the fundamentals of accounting for share issuance and reacquisition.

Insights

- *This topic is not difficult to study and there are no complex calculations.*
- *The text provides excellent background material regarding corporate structure and different types of shares. This material will be reinforced through the multiple choice questions in this Study Guide.*

Study Steps

1. Understanding the Nature and Purpose of Equity

STUDY STEPS

A company is financed using either debt or equity. Ideally, this is recorded on the balance sheet, although off-balance-sheet financing, where the financing is not recorded on the balance sheet, has become more and more common as discussed in Chapter 15.

The different types of financing carry **different rights and claims** on the company. Debt holders usually have the greatest rights. Generally, they have preferential treatment with respect to a return on their investment (interest) after a specified period of time or on liquidation of the company.

Most preferential treatment

Secured debt	**preferred treatment i.e., fixed return (interest), secured by assets – first priority on liquidation**
Preferred shares	**fixed return, next in line after interest or debt is paid and next in priority on liquidation**
Common shares	**entitled to residual earnings after interest and other dividends – last in line on liquidation**

Least preferential treatment (i.e., gets whatever is left)

All forms of financing fit somewhere on the spectrum noted above. Common shares are **residual** in nature in that these shareholders get whatever is left after other claims on the company are settled. Further, the common shares carry the **votes** and therefore the right to make decisions for the company. Common shareholders are therefore seen to have **the risks and rewards of ownership**.

Tip! Common shares are often called **residual ownership** shares since they get the "residue" or whatever is left after other investors and creditors have had their share in earnings and net assets.

Tip! Since the common shareholders are at risk with respect to their original investment and return on that investment, they have the **risks of ownership.** Note that they also have **rewards of ownership** since they also stand to gain more and have control over the company through the voting provisions in the shares.

The shareholders' equity section on the balance sheet has two basic types of equity included in it: **earned** equity and **contributed** equity. Contributed equity is the amount invested in the company by the shareholders or contributed to the company and earned equity is the amount that has been earned by the company itself (i.e., through net income). These will be covered in the next chapter.

Tip! Remember that equity may be **earned or contributed.**

There are numerous disclosures required by Section 3240 of the CICA Handbook. Basically, all details about the shares including their characteristics and changes during the year must be disclosed.

2. Understanding How Issues Relating to Shareholders' Equity Fit into the Financial Reporting Model and Conceptual Framework—Analysis and Critical Thinking

STUDY STEPS

There are no significant issues here that need to be analyzed within the framework. Hybrid, compound securities and other more complex transactions are dealt with in Chapter 15 and 18 of the Study Guide.

3. Becoming Proficient in Related Calculations

STUDY STEPS

There are no significant calculations or methods that need be mastered here. The par value method of accounting for shares is common in the United States; however, in Canada, most companies would not issue shares with par value since it is not permitted by law (CBCA and most provincial Acts). The journal entries for acquisition of shares and subsequent sale/cancellation may be tricky and a number of the multiple choice questions and problems below focus on this.

MULTIPLE CHOICE QUESTIONS

1) Manny Company issued preferred shares in 1999. Under the terms of the shares, the shares may be redeemed at the option of the holder. Therefore, the shares may be described as being:

   a) redeemable.

   b) callable.

   c) cumulative.

   d) retractable.

2) Basic Limited issued cumulative preferred shares with a 5% dividend rate. By the end of the second year following the issue, the company had not paid nor declared dividends on these shares. How should this be accounted for, if at all?

   a) two years' worth of dividends should be accrued and recorded as a liability in the current year since "cumulative" means that the company has an obligation to pay.

   b) The company should record each year's dividend in the relevant year i.e., one year's worth in both year one and year two, since the nature of the "cumulative" provision would infer that the dividend is due whether paid or not.

   c) The company should do nothing since a dividend has not been declared yet and therefore no liability has been incurred.

   d) The company should not record a liability since a dividend has not been declared yet and therefore no liability has been incurred. The company should disclose this information, however.

3) The term "pre-emptive right" refers to which of the following:

a) the company's right to offer shares for sale to the public without offering the existing shareholders a chance to increase their shareholdings and therefore remain undiluted.

b) the shareholder's right to acquire additional shares of any new issue of shares in proportion to their existing holdings.

c) the right of another company to acquire controlling interest in the company without being hindered by the existing shareholders.

d) the shareholder's right to purchase all new shares offered by the company.

4) There are many different names and attributes of shares; however, the main factor that differentiates common shares from other shares is:

a) the fact that common shares are entitled to residual profits through dividends.

b) the fact that common share dividends are not fixed as a % of share value.

c) the fact that dividends on common shares are not cumulative.

d) the fact that common shareholders have voting rights.

5) Nina Limited issued cumulative 4% preferred shares that are obligatorily redeemable in the year 2005. In the balance sheet, these share should be classified as:

a) equity, since they are shares and, traditionally, shares have been classified as equity—consistency.

b) equity, since legal form takes precedence over economic substance.

c) liability, since they are mandatorily redeemable, meaning that they have a maturity date.

d) neither equity nor liability, since they do not meet the definition of either debt or equity.

6) Costs of issuing shares should be afforded which of the following treatments according to GAAP:

a) record as a debit in the equity section of the balance sheet.

b) record as a reduction of the amounts paid in and show share capital net.

c) record as a deferred cost and amortize.

d) charge directly to retained earnings.

7) Corporations incur ongoing costs annually to maintain shareholder records and handle ownership transfers. These costs should be accounted for as follows:

a) capital transactions—charged against share capital.

b) capital transactions—charged against contributed surplus.

c) expensed.

d) charged to retained earnings.

8) Company A acquired some of its own shares on the open market. How would these shares be treated for financial statement purposes?

a) as an investment with any dividends being shown as income.

b) as an investment however, dividends would not be paid by the company to itself and therefore there would be no income.

c) as a reduction of shareholders' equity, with dividends being credited to contributed surplus.

d) as a reduction of shareholders' equity; however, dividends would not be paid by the company to itself.

9) Company B has repurchased some of its no par shares on the open market. Assume that they are allowed by the Act that they are incorporated under, to hold these shares and are not required to cancel them. Assume further that they subsequently resold the shares for a higher amount and that they use the single transaction method. Note how the shares would be recorded prior to the sale and where the gain/loss would be booked on resale.

	Share Purchase Prior to Sale	Gain/Loss on Sale
a)	debit share capital	retained earnings
b)	debit treasury shares (contra equity account)	retained earnings
c)	debit treasury shares (contra equity account)	contributed surplus
d)	debit share capital	contributed surplus

10) Company C acquired and immediately cancelled some of its no par shares. The shares were acquired at a cost in excess of original issue price. There was no contributed surplus related to these shares. The transaction should be accounted for as follows:

a) the cost would be (1) debited to share capital at an assigned value equal to the average per share amount for that class of share and (2) the excess debited to retained earnings.

b) the total cost would be debited to share capital.

c) the total cost would be debited to treasury shares—a contra account to share capital

d) the cost would be (1) debited to share capital at an assigned value equal to the average per share amount for that class of share and (2) the excess debited to contributed surplus.

SOLUTIONS TO MULTIPLE CHOICE QUESTIONS

1) d) Retractable refers to the right of the holder to redeem the shares. Redeemable or callable generally refers to the right of the company to redeem the shares.

2) d) These would be known as dividends in arrears, and although no liability technically exists until a dividend is declared, a commitment still exists to the shareholders to pay the cumulative amount.

3) b) "Pre-emptive rights" protect existing shareholders from involuntary dilution of ownership interest through new shares issues.

4) d) Voting rights are the most critical determining factor since they signal the risks and rewards of ownership (which may lead to significant influence or control of the other company). Note that some preferred and other shares may share in residual profits and some preferred shares are not cumulative either.

5) c) HB Section 3860 requires that financial and equity instruments be classified according to their economic substance. In this case, the shares have overwhelming debt-like characteristics; they must be redeemed, meaning that the company has a non-discretionary obligation to repay the shareholders.

6) b) HB Section 3610 includes these as capital transactions and, therefore, they should be shown as part of equity. Traditional treatment is to show share capital net of these costs. Note that while other methods might exist in practice, the CICA HB recommendations should prevail.

7) c) These costs should be expensed since they are considered to be part of the costs of operating and running the business. These costs are not referred to in HB Section 3610, and, since they do not result from issue, redemption, and changes in shares capital, they are not considered to be capital transactions.

8) d) HB Section 3240.09 states that "it is an economic and legal fact that a company cannot own part of itself". Therefore, this would not be shown as an asset. Dividends would not be paid on company-owned shares and these shares would be excluded in EPS calculations. Generally, under the Canada Business Corporations Act, these shares would be cancelled and perhaps restored to the status of authorized but unissued shares.

9) c) On purchase, the shares would be shown as a deduction from total shareholders' equity (HB 3240.10 and .11) and since they resold the shares for a higher amount, there is a gain. Gains are credited to contributed surplus (HB Section 3240.20).

10) a) The cost would be debited to share capital, and not treasury stock, since these shares are also being cancelled. Further, since there is no contributed surplus related to these shares, the excess cost is debited to retained earnings.

SHORT PROBLEMS

1) Purpose: To illustrate accounting for share issuance.

Capital Ltd. (CL) issued 10,000 Class A voting shares for $1,000,000. CL's articles of incorporation showed 30,000 shares authorized for issue. At the same time, the company issued subscriptions to purchase an additional 10,000 of the same shares. The subscription required $50 per share payment immediately and $50 in three months. As part of the arrangement, if the second payment was not made, the first would be forfeited to the company. The cost of issuing the shares and subscriptions was $45,000.

Required

(a) Prepare the journal entries to record the share issue and the subscription issue. Show how this would be presented on the balance sheet.

(b) Assuming that all subscriptions were paid up in three months, prepare the journal entry to record the receipt of the funds three months after the subscription issue.

(c) Assume that half of the subscribers to the subscription issue did not make the second payment. Prepare the journal entry required at that time.

2) Purpose: To illustrate the journal entries required for shares issued in a noncash transaction.

Investment Company Limited (ICL) purchased 100,000 shares or 10% of the shares of Investee Limited (IL). As consideration, ICL issued 3,000 new preferred shares. The net book value of IL according to the audited financial statements was $56,890,000 and the shares of IL were actively traded on the stock exchange for $70 per share.

The preferred shares issued by ICL were part of a new class of shares that had not previously been offered by ICL.

Required

(a) Prepare the journal entry to record the investment and share issue on the books of ICL.

(b) Calculate the book value per share of IL shares. Give one reason why the book value per share of IL shares is different from the trading price.

(c) How would the transaction be valued if the IL shares were not traded on a stock exchange and if the fair value of these shares was not known?

3) Purpose: To demonstrate accounting for share reacquisition.

In 1999, Buyback Limited (BL) purchased and cancelled 20,000 of its own shares in the open market for $735,000. Prior to the share repurchase, the shareholders' equity section of the balance sheet was as follows:
Buyback Limited
Shareholders' equity

Common stock (500,000 shares authorized, 250,000 issued and outstanding)	$4,500,000
Contributed surplus	450,000
Retained earnings	1,980,000
Total shareholders' equity	$6,930,000

The common stock is no-par value and the contributed surplus arose several years ago when BL reacquired and cancelled 50,000 of its shares for $9 per share.

Required

(a) Recreate the journal entry required when the 50,000 shares were reacquired several years ago.

(b) Prepare the journal entry to record the more recent reacquisition of the 20,000 shares.

SOLUTIONS TO SHORT PROBLEMS

1) (a) To record share and subscription issue:

dr. cash	1,455,000 (See 1 below)	
dr. subscriptions receivable	500,000	
cr. capital stock		977,500 (See 2 below)
cr. capital stock subscribed		977,500

(1) $1,000,000 + 500,000—45,000
(2) $1,000,000—(45,000/2)

Partial balance sheet:

Shareholders' equity		
Share capital		
Class A voting shares, 30,000 authorized 10,000 issued		$977,500
Class A shares subscribed	$977,500	
Less: subscriptions receivable	(500,000)	477,500
Total share capital		$1,455,000

The share issue costs have been deducted from the amount of the share capital. The subscriptions could have been accounted for differently, being shown as an asset instead of a reduction of the share capital account.

(b) To record the second instalment received on the subscription:

dr. cash	500,000	
cr. subscriptions receivable		500,000
dr. capital stock subscribed	977,500	
cr. capital stock		977,500

This results in the full amount of the subscription being shown on the balance sheet as share capital. The shares would be issued once the second payment was made.

(c) To record the second instalment under the subscription where only half of the subscribers make the second payment.

dr. cash	250,000	
cr. subscription receivable		250,000
dr. capital stock subscribed	977,500	
cr. capital stock		488,750
cr. contributed surplus		488,750

The amount initially contributed by the subscribers who defaulted has been forfeited under the arrangement. And since it is non-refundable and did not result in any shares being issued, it has been booked as contributed surplus.

2) (a) To record the purchase of IL shares:

dr. long-term investment	7,000,000	
cr. capital stock-preferred shares		7,000,000

The investment and the preferred shares have been valued at $7,000,000, which is calculated as follows:

100,000 shares x $70

The fair market value of the IL shares has been used to value the transaction, since the fair value of the shares issued by ICL is not known. Normally, we would use the fair value of either the item purchased or the shares issued in consideration, whichever is more clearly determinable.

(b) The book value per share of IL's shares is $56.89 or $56,890,000/1,000,000 shares. Often the book value of a company's shares differs from the fair value of the shares. One reason is that the book value of the shares comes from the financial statements with the book value being calculated as assets minus liabilities. Since the financial statements are based on historical cost, the assets values will be outdated. Therefore, this is one reason that the book value of a company's shares is often lower. Also, the trading price of a share

will reflect up-to-the-minute information about the company such as new technological developments or the impact of a change in top management. Trading prices are also a function of the volume of shares purchased and sold that day (e.g., if many were purchased, this would tend to drive the share price up).
(c) If the fair value of either the IL shares or the ICL shares were not known, then, ICL would likely hire an outside consultant to calculate a fair value of one or the other or both. The valuation of IL would consider the underlying assets of the business, as well as, future projected cash flows, among other things.

3) (a) To record the first reacquisition of 50,000 shares for $9 per share:

dr. common stock	900,000 (See 1 below)	
cr. cash		450,000 (See 2 below)
cr. contributed surplus		450,000 (See 3below)

(1) The amount of the debit to common stock is calculated by determining the average book value of the outstanding shares. This is calculated as follows: $4,500,000/250,000 shares = $18 per share assigned value. This assumes that there have been no other share issues since the first reacquisition. If the shares were par value shares then the debit would have been 50,000 X par value.

(2) 50,000 X $9

(3) to balance the entry

The contributed surplus account now relates to the common shares.

(b) To record the second reacquisition of 20,000 shares for $735,000:

dr. common stock	360,000 (See 1 below)	
dr. contributed surplus	375,000 (See 2 below)	
cr. cash		735,000 (See 3 below)

(1) $4,500,000/250,000 = $18; $18 x 20,000

(2) $735,000—360,000. Normally with no-par stock, the debit would be booked to retained earnings since there would not likely be contributed surplus relating to the shares. However, since this contributed surplus does relate to these shares (i.e., it was created when the earlier reacquisition occurred for less than the book value of the shares), the debit is booked to contributed surplus.

CASES

1) Gibbins Development Corporation

Gibbins Development Corporation (GDC) is the principal operating subsidiary of Gibbins Realty Holdings Limited (GHL). The 1998 consolidated balance sheet of GDC is divided up into the following classifications:

December 31, 1998
(in thousands)

Assets	$4,962,916
Liabilities	3,025,716
Preference shares of subsidiaries	308,000
Capital base	1,629,200
	$4,962,916

The "capital base" referred to above is made up of the following:

Secured capital loans	$1,566,960
Shareholders' equity	62,240
	$1,629,200

The "secured capital loans" consist of a secured capital loan facility (the "facility") granted by BDE Inc. (BDE) and Colchina Developments Limited (Colchina). According to the notes to the 1998 financial statements, advances under the facility are secured by charges on substantially all of the company's assets. The facility bears interest at variable rates with the interest rate fluctuating with market rates.

Originally, the facility was to mature on July 15, 1998; however, prior to the issuance of the 1998 financial statements, it was agreed that the maturity date would be deferred to April 30, 2000. The deferral was conditional on BDE and Colchina receiving satisfactory evidence that GDC's other creditors would continue to support GDC, including deferring enforcement of any claims during this period. The notes to the statements further state that if the other creditors do not abide by these terms, BDE and Colchina are "entitled to take such actions as necessary to protect their secured capital loans, including the commencement of realization or other enforcement proceedings."

At the time of the financial statement issue, certain of the other creditors had initiated actions against the company but neither BDE nor Colchina had enforced their rights. Colchina and BDE made it known that they intended to work with GDC with a view to helping it.

The agreement allowing the extension of the maturity date on the facility also provides for the advances under the facility to be applied to the purchase of GDC's common shares, subject to receipt of all the requisite regulatory and other approvals. That is, the amounts owing under the facility will be converted to common shares. If the common share issue is not completed by April 30, 2000, the credit facility becomes due.

All of these were disclosed either in the notes to the 2000 financial statements or in the annual report. The financial statements were given a clean audit opinion.

Required

Discuss the accounting and the disclosures for the facility arrangement.

2) Canadian Airlines—www.cdnair.com

Canadian Airlines share capital consists of four types of shares as follows:

- voting common shares—trade on Toronto, Alberta, and Vancouver Stock Exchanges
- non-voting shares—trade on the Toronto Stock Exchange only. These shares have identical rights to the common shares except that they are non-voting. Canadian investors may convert these shares to common shares. Non-Canadian investors may convert these shares to common shares; however, non-Canadian shareholders may eventually be limited in their ability to convert if the non-Canadian ownership of the voting common shares of the company in total approaches 25%. The Canadian Transportation Act prohibits non-Canadians from owning >25% of the voting equity of the company and these shares were created to facilitate trading by non-Canadian investors.
- second preferred shares—series Y—one share issued for nominal value and held by the Canadian Airlines Pilot Association to ensure the right to elect one director to the company's Board of Directors.
- second preferred shares— series X—one share issued for nominal vale and held by the Council of Canadian Airlines Employees Limited to ensure the employees' right to elect two directors to the company's Board of Directors.

There are 8 members on the Board of Directors.

Required:

Discuss the nature of ownership of the various share classes. Which shares have the risks and rewards of ownership?

SOLUTIONS TO CASES

1. Gibbins Development Corporation

Overview

This case is based on a real company, although the dates and names have been changed here. GDC, prior to 1998 had been facing financial difficulty and this "facility" and the deferral arrangement were part of a larger financial restructuring. Much of the activity relating to the restructuring was available in the newspapers since the parent company is a public one. Although the shares of GDC are held by GHL, audited financial statements were prepared for issue and a clean audit opinion given.

Given the tenuous financial status of GDC (especially if the facility was called for repayment), management would likely want to have as favourable a position as possible in the financial statements so as not to make things worse. Management would also want to show investors that everything is under control.

Analysis and Recommendation

The main issue is whether the facility should be accounted for as debt or as equity. Keep in mind that GDC has classified it as equity and that the auditors have agreed with this decision.

Debt:

- The **legal form** of the facility appears to be debt. They are even called "loans" in the financial statements.
- The facility is **interest** bearing.
- It is **secured by the assets** of the company.
- It has a fixed **maturity** date-originally due July 15, 1998, but later deferred to April 30, 2000.
- The extension of the facility maturity date is conditional upon the other creditors of GDC deferring any claims against the company. If these conditions are not met, BDE and Colchina are entitled to call the loan. Notwithstanding this, certain creditors have indeed initiated actions against the company; however, BDE and Colchina have not taken any action. Technically, the facility is now due and an argument might be made for even recognizing it as a **current liability**.

Equity:

- The **substance** of the financing appears to be of a more permanent nature (i.e., the **intent** is that the funds will not be repaid, rather that they will be converted to common shares).
- This facility appears to be part of a larger agreement with BDE and Colchina, which includes the equity conversion. Therefore, although accounting for the facility might appear to be the issue, perhaps accounting for the larger restructuring agreement is really the issue.
- Accounting for the arrangement as equity yields a more palatable debt/equity ratio. Note the significance/**materiality** of the facility as compared to the dollar value of the equity.
- It also reflects how management is dealing with the financial crisis.

Conclusion

Although on the surface, the facility would appear to be debt, the larger issue is really how to account for the refinancing arrangement, since the funding is of a more permanent nature. There is some **uncertainty** as to whether the terms of the refinancing arrangement are still valid, since some of the conditions have not been met. However, it would appear that BDE and Colchina are willing to live with the noncompliance. An assessment must have been made about the likelihood of BDE and Colchina calling the loan. This uncertainty puts **management** and the **auditors** in a more **risky** position if something were togo wrong.

This is a good case of accounting for the **economic substance over the legal form**. To protect themselves, and to provide adequate explanation to users of the statements, management and the auditors have included detailed disclosures regarding the arrangement and the situation. Nevertheless, the facility has been accounted for as equity on the face of the balance sheet. And if we subscribe to the theory that users focus more on the key statements than the notes, this would appear to be fairly **aggressive** accounting. Current accounting standards would dictate that economic substance would prevail over legal form.

2) Canadian Airlines

The voting common shares reflect the traditional view of common shares in that they are **residual** and have **voting rights**. Therefore, they carry the risks and rewards of ownership.

The non-voting shares are interesting since they have the same rights as the common shares with the exception of voting power. They are **residual** in nature and they would seem to carry with them the **risks and rewards of ownership**. The fact that they do not have **voting rights** signals that they do not have all the rewards of ownership.

However, in fact, most common shareholders do not own a sufficient number of shares in a company to allow them to influence company decisions. Therefore, in practice, this may be a very small part of the rewards of ownership. Note that the non-voting shares were created solely to facilitate non-Canadian ownership given the legislative restriction on non-Canadian ownership of voting shares. They allow the non-Canadian investors to participate in substantially all risks and rewards without going against the law.

The preferred shares are very interesting. These shares do not have a **return** on them and are indeed just a nominal investment. At first glance, they do not appear to allow holders to participate in the **risks and rewards of ownership**. However, they do allow significant stakeholders in the company, a say in the key decisions. These shares likely have more power than most shareholders of common shares have in that there are only eight directors and these shares have the right to appoint two.

SELECTED SOLUTIONS FROM THE TEXTBOOK

*EXERCISE 16-2

	Debit	Credit
Initially		
(a) Subscriptions Receivable (30,000 x $25)	750,000	
Common Shares Subscribed		750,000
Cash (30,000 x $25 x .40)	300,000	
Subscriptions Receivable		300,000
Six months later		
Cash	450,000	
Subscriptions Receivable ($750,000 - $300,000)		450,000
Common Shares Subscribed	750,000	
Common Shares		750,000

	Debit	Credit
Initially		
(b) Subscriptions Receivable	750,000	
Common Shares Subscribed (30,000 x $10)		300,000
Contributed Surplus—excess over par (30,000 x $15)	450,000	
Cash (30,000 x $25 x .40)	300,000	
Subscriptions Receivable		300,000
Six months later		
Cash	450,000	
Subscriptions Receivable ($750,000 - $300,000)		450,000
Common Shares Subscribed	300,000	
Common Shares		300,000

EXERCISE 16-6

	Debit	Credit
(a) 1. Bond Issue Costs	200,000	
Cash	9,120,000	
Bonds Payable		5,000,000
Common Shares		4,320,000

Assumes bonds are properly priced and issued at par; residual attributed to common shares, which have a weak measure of market value.

Investment broker costs 400 @ $950 = $380,000; allocate 5/9.5 to debentures and 4.5/9.5 to common shares. Bond portion is bond issue cost; common portion is treated as a reduction of proceeds from sale of common shares. The $180,000 of broker's costs applicable to the common shares could alternatively be set up as Share Issue Costs (or Organization Costs) resulting in Common Shares being credited for $4,500,000.

2.			
	Cash	9,120,000	
	Bond Issue Costs		211,111
	Bonds Payable	5,000,000	
	Bond Premium		277,778
	Common Shares		4,053,333

Using the market value for a bond of $500 and a share being $40 (therefore 10 shares have a market value of $400) the proportional allocation would be:

10,000 units @ $950 each	=	total value of $9,500,000
$9,500,000 (5/9)	=	$5,277,778 to debentures
$9,500,000 (4/9)	=	$4,222,222 to common shares
$380,000 (5/9)	=	$211,111 to bond issue costs
$380,000 (4/9)	=	$168,889 for share issue costs

Common shares net = $4,222,222 - $168,889 = $4,053,333. Alternatively, the Common Shares could be recorded at $4,222,222 and the $168,889 could be debited to Share Issue Costs (or Organization Costs).

(b) One is not better than the other. This question is presented to stimulate some thought and class discussion. Whichever method is preferred by the student would require some rationale to support the judgemental choice.

SOLUTIONS TO PROBLEM

PROBLEM 16-4

(a)

-1-

Common Shares ($360,000/9,000 x 380)	15,200	
Contributed Surplus—excess of assigned value over acquisition cost		380
Cash (380 x $39)		14,820

-2-

Common Shares [($360,000 - $15,200) / (9,000 - 380)] x 300	12,000	
Contributed Surplus—excess of assigned value over acquisition cost	300	
Cash		12,300

-3-

Cash [(1,000 x $44) - $260]	43,740	
Common Shares		43,740

-4-

Cash [(800 x $45) - $190]	35,810	
Common Shares		35,810

-5-

Common Shares	16,298 *	
Contributed Surplus—excess of assigned value over acquisition cost	80	
Retained Earnings	422	
Cash (400 x $42)		16,800

* ($360,000 - $15,200 - $12,000 + $43,740 + $35,810) x 400
(9,000 - 380 - 300 + 1,000 + 800)

(b)

Jonrowe Corporation
Partial Balance Sheet
At End of 1998 Fiscal Period

Shareholders' Equity:	
Common shares, no-par value, XXX authorized,	
9,720 issued (Note X)	$396,052
Retained earnings	79,598 + NI

	Note X # of shares	$ amount
Opening balance	9,000	$360,000
Add: new shares issued (1,000 + 800)	1,800	($43,740 + $35,810)
79,550		
Less: shares cancelled (380 + 300 + 400)	(1,080)	
($15,200 + $12,000 + $16,298)	(43,498)	
Ending balance	9,720	$396,052

SOLUTION TO CASE

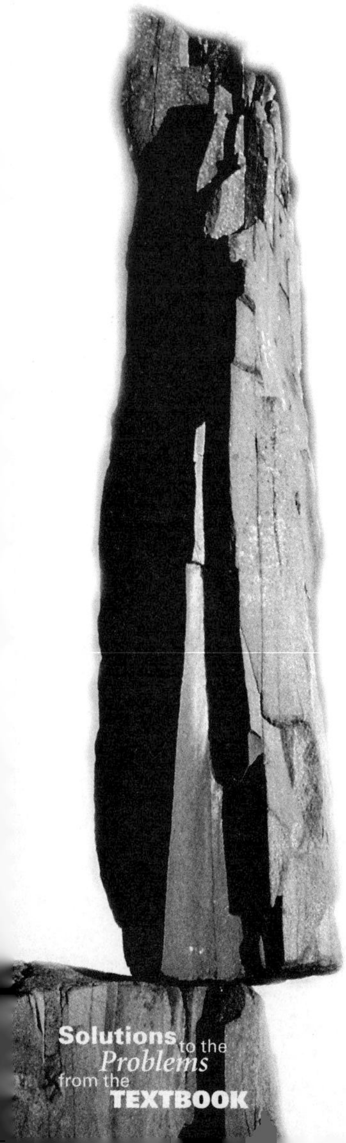

CASE 16-6

(a)1. In a cash transaction, cost is measured by the amount of the cash consideration. In a credit transaction, however, cost is measured by the amount of cash required to settle immediately the obligation incurred. Since the cash payment of $100,000 did not settle the obligation incurred for the purchase of the equipment, the cost of the equipment cannot be $100,000.

2. The amount of cash that would have been required to settle the obligation immediately is $160,000 and, hence, the cost of the equipment is $160,000. There is no reason to presume that the parties were not independent or that they did not bargain at arm's length.

3. Because of the credit nature of the $60,000 balance due on the equipment, the Corporation will have to forego the $80,000 market value of the shares that it transfers to the vendor to settle the obligation over the 4-year period. The additional $20,000, however, is in the nature of an interest cost and should not be a part of the book value of the equipment. Therefore, the cost of the equipment cannot be $180,000.

(b)1. The principal argument for treating the balance as a liability is that the corporation will have to forego assets it otherwise might have acquired by issuing the shares for cash in order to meet the obligation, even though the obligation is expressed in terms of delivery of common shares. Another argument is that the "extra" $20,000 of the market value of the shares to be transferred over the 4 years is really a financing cost on deferred amounts due for the instalment purchase. The liability approach may also be preferable to the shares subscribed approach because it may overcome certain misunderstandings created by the latter approach. The users, under the subscribed approach, may incorrectly assume that delivery of the shares depends upon performance (payment) by the subscriber instead of the passage of time.

2. The principal argument for treating the balance due as common shares subscribed is that the equipment vendor made a contribution to shareholders' equity by selling the equipment for $100,000 cash and the promise of the corporation to delivery the shares of its own capital to make up the balance of the purchase price in accordance with the agreement. Another reason supporting this approach is that the obligation can be discharged only by the transfer of common shares and not by the transfer of assets.

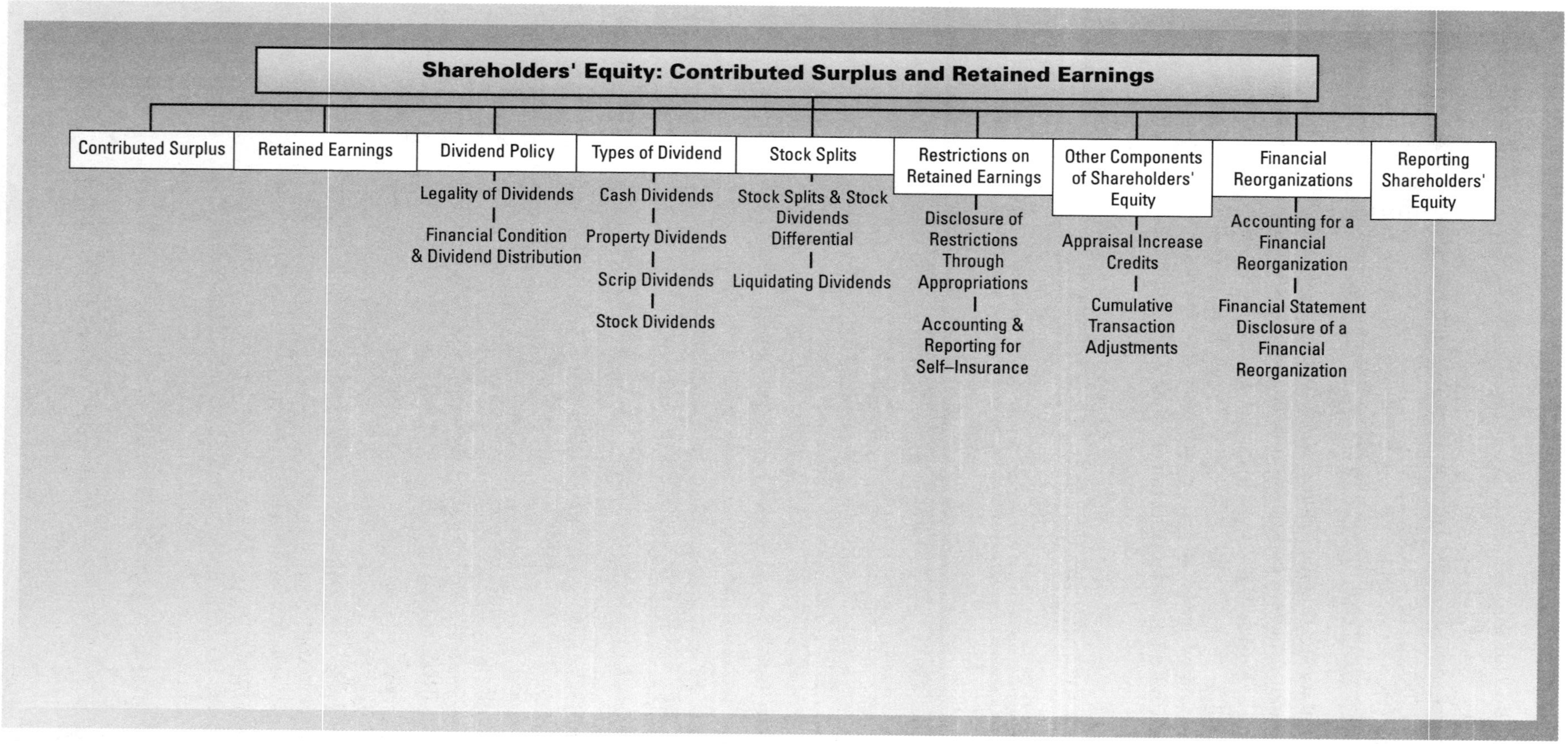

Shareholders' Equity: Contributed Surplus and Retained Earnings
Contributed Surplus
Retained Earnings
Dividend Policy
Legality of Dividends
Financial Condition & Dividend Distribution
Types of Dividend
Cash Dividends
Property Dividends
Scrip Dividends
Stock Dividends
Stock Splits
Stock Splits & Stock Dividends Differential
Liquidating Dividends
Restrictions on Retained Earnings
Disclosure of Restrictions Through Appropriations
Accounting & Reporting for Self–Insurance
Other Components of Shareholders' Equity
Appraisal Increase Credits
Cumulative Transaction Adjustments
Financial Reorganizations
Accounting for a Financial Reorganization
Financial Statement Disclosure of a Financial Reorganization
Reporting Shareholders' Equity

chapter 17

SHAREHOLDERS' EQUITY: CONTRIBUTED SURPLUS AND RETAINED EARNINGS

PERSPECTIVE

This is the second chapter dealing with shareholders' equity. While Chapter 16 covered share capital, this chapter focuses more on contributed surplus and retained earnings.

INSIGHTS

- *Much of the material is straightforward, requiring some memory work.*
- *There are no complex calculations or journal entries. Therefore, the focus points and study questions below will emphasize the basic concepts.*

STUDY STEPS

STUDY STEPS

1. Understanding the Nature of Surplus

Contributed versus earned surplus

Firstly, the distinction between **contributed capital** and **retained earnings** should be recognized. Retained earnings is effectively **surplus net income** that has not yet been distributed to shareholders. It is **earned** by the company. Contributed surplus, on the other hand, is not earned by the company but is **contributed** usually, although not necessarily, by the shareholders. As such, it is not connected with operations or the earnings process of the company. The distinction is not always so clear, however, and requires some judgement.

Both contributed surplus and retained earnings are forms of surplus in the company. One is contributed however, and one is earned. **Tip!**

Dividends

Dividends are charged to retained earnings and effectively represent the distribution of the excess profits of the company to the shareholders.

There are legal restrictions on how much may be distributed. In general, dividends should not be paid if there is a deficit or if it would result in the company going bankrupt. Often there are other restrictions on how much of retained earnings may be distributed. These arise from contractual arrangements entered into by the company, such as covenants on debt obligations or shares.

Although legal restrictions need not be separately disclosed, since it is presumed that this is public knowledge, other restrictions on dividend payout should be disclosed since this is decision relevant to users of the financial statements.

Usually dividends are paid in cash; however, sometimes they may take the form of **property** or **stock**. These are called **dividends in kind** and are valued at the fair value of the property given up.

Tip! **Dividends in kind are nonmonetary and therefore there are measurement issues.**

Liquidating dividends occur when the dividend is paid out of equity other than retained earnings. The implication is that the dividend is a return of capital to the shareholders rather than a distribution of profits (retained earnings).

Appropriations from retained earnings

Appropriations of retained earnings are amounts that have been set aside from retained earnings for some other use. It generally signals management intent and gives information regarding future dividend payout (i.e., the appropriated amounts have been put aside for another purpose and are not presently available for distribution).

Tip! **Appropriations signal management intent; however, they do not necessarily involve cash outlays.**

Financial reorganizations

A financial reorganization occurs when a financially troubled company restructures its debt and equity in agreement with existing creditors and shareholders. Often, existing creditors exchange their debt for equity of the company and, in general, the capitalization and financing of the company is adjusted to place less of a financial burden on it. Control of the company changes as a result of the reorganization.

The restructuring involves a change in ownership or voting control. Often it is the creditors who gain control. **Tip!**

Normally, the assets and liabilities would be revalued and any retained earnings or deficit relating to accumulated net losses would be closed out to either contributed surplus or share capital. This gives the company a new start and allows retained earnings to start from zero.

The removal of any accumulated deficit allows the company to pay dividends again as long as there is retained earnings on a going forward basis. In many cases, the law does not allow a company to pay dividends if it has a deficit. **Tip!**

Because of the significance of the restructuring and the unique accounting allowed (i.e., revaluation of assets) note disclosures are required for three years afterwards showing all details.

2. Understanding How These Specific Issues Relating to Shareholders' Equity Fit into the Financial Reporting Model and Conceptual Framework—Analysis and Critical Thinking

STUDY STEPS

Exhibit 17-1: Financial Reorganizations
Relevant criteria, defintions and issues

	How it relates to financial reorganizaions	Relevant criteria/definitions	Topic specific analysis-how it should be	What makes the analysis challenging–how it is
Presentation	• is the transaction a financial reorg per HB 1625?	• **change in control and new costs measurable**	• there must be new owners in control after the transaction • since assets and liabilities are revalued–must be measurable	• since this allows assets and liabilities to be revalued to FMV, this goes against the HC principle and care should be taken to ensure this happens only in certain situations
Measurement	• assets and liabilities are revalued to reflect up–to–date values	• **relevance** • **FMV** • **verifiable**	• the revaluation is called **fresh start accounting** and is meant to give stakeholders a better idea of the true position and value of the company	• the valuation is a result of PJ and is therefore subjective. In many cases, the parties involved will also be involved with the valuation so that it is fair to all stakeholders • this is a good time for a company to clean out its balance sheet or write off over–valued assets.
Presentation/ Disclosure	• how to present in balance sheet and note disclosures	• **full disclosure**	• date, description, amount of change in each b/s class–all for three years	

Prepared by Irene Wiecek

3. Becoming Proficient in Related Calculations

STUDY STEPS

There are no complex calculations nor accounting methods to master here. The problems review some basic dividend calculations and journal entries.
For **financial reorganizations**, the following chart should assist:

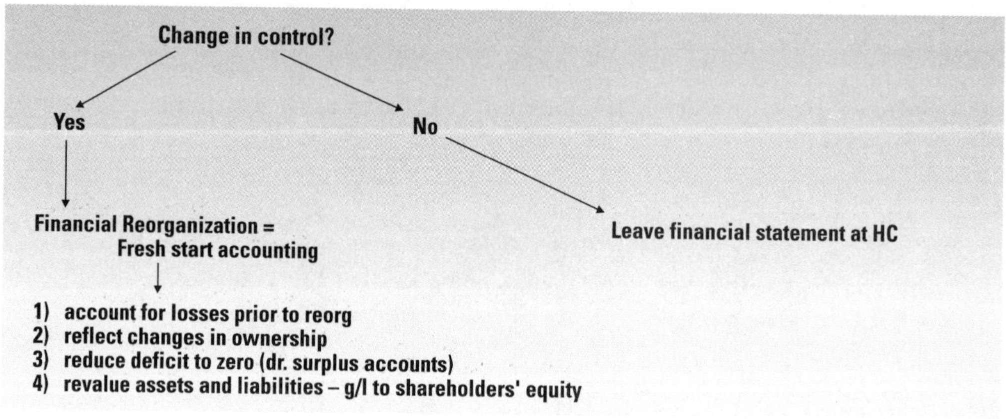

MULTIPLE CHOICE QUESTIONS

1) Dividend payout is a function of several factors. Which of the following should be considered in deciding on whether a dividend should be paid out?
   a) available cash
   b) dividend rights attached to the share
   c) the balance in the retained earnings account
   d) all of the above

2) Dividends in kind are defined as follows:
   a) nonreciprocal, nonmonetary transfers.
   b) reciprocal, nonmonetary transfers.
   c) reciprocal, monetary transfers.
   d) nonreciprocal, monetary transfers.

3) A scrip dividend might be issued under which of the following situations:
   a) the company wishes to capitalize part of its earnings.
   b) the company wishes to spin off nonmonetary assets.
   c) the company wishes to pay a regular dividend.
   d) the company wishes to pay a regular dividend but lacks the cash.

4) Generally, all transactions should be booked through the income statement. There are a few exceptions, however, that allow transactions to be booked through the retained earnings account directly. Which of the following is not allowed to be booked through the retained earnings account and must be booked through the income statement?

a) dividend in kind

b) adjustments due to retroactive application of a change in accounting policy

c) prior period adjustments

d) error corrections

5) Stock dividends are different from stock splits for the following reason (assume a 2 for 1 split):

a) a stock dividend results in an increased number of shares, whereas a stock split does not.

b) a stock dividend results in a decreased number of shares, whereas the stock split does not.

c) a stock dividend results in a decrease in retained earnings and an increase in the dollar value of common stock.

d) a stock dividend results in no change in either the dollar value of retained earnings or common stock.

6) According to generally accepted accounting principles, which of the following situations would not require an adjustment to opening retained earnings on the financial statements?

a) A bond discount of $50,000 arising from a bond issued two years ago that has not been amortized.

b) An allowance for bad debts on accounts receivable has not been recorded in the past. It is estimated that $40,000 of the current accounts receivable balance represents uncollectible accounts from the past five years.

c) A 40% investment in a foreign operation acquired two years ago has been incorrectly accounted for using the cost method.

d) A piece of machinery has been depreciated using the straight-line method over the last three years assuming a ten-year life. It is now estimated that the machinery will have a total useful life of only six years.

(CMA June 1996 - adapted)

7) Fresh start accounting may be used when which of the following occurs:

a) a change in control

b) fair values of assets and liabilities are measurable

c) both a) and b)

d) either a) or b)

8) Appraisal increase credits result from:

a) current revaluation of assets to reflect higher market values.

b) gains relating to revaluation of assets prior to the new HB section 3060 being issued.

c) financial reorganizations.

d) current appraisals of fixed assets to reflect higher values.

The following relates to 9 and 10:

Dino Corporation recently underwent a financial restructuring under which the major creditors of the company gained control of the company. As part of the negotiations, the net assets of the company were valued at $1.2 million higher than their book value. The deficit of the company was $.8 million and contributed surplus was $.5 million. In order to obtain control, the creditors agreed to forgo their prior claims on the company ($1 million in debt).

9) How should the gain on revaluation be accounted for in the financial statements?

a) as a credit to a separately identified account in the shareholders' equity section

b) as a credit to a separately identified account in the shareholders' equity section, or as share capital

c) as a credit to a separately identified account in the shareholders' equity section, as share capital or as contributed surplus

d) as a direct credit to retained earnings

10) What would be the net change to the share capital account assuming that the revaluation amount is credited there as well?

a) $1.9 million

b) 0

c) $1 million

d) $1.5 million

SOLUTIONS TO MULTIPLE CHOICE QUESTIONS

1) d) All of the above factors affect the decision. Note that a dividend may not be paid out (legally) if retained earnings is a deficit.

2) a) Dividends in kind are nonmonetary by definition. Otherwise they would be normal dividends. All dividends are nonreciprocal since they involve a one-way transfer.

3) d) The scrip dividend allows the company to officially declare the dividend but allows the cash payout at some later point in time. The capitalization of earnings would occur with a stock dividend since equity $ remains the same.

4) c) Prior period adjustments are no longer allowed to be booked through retained earnings. HB Section 3600 has been removed from the Handbook.

5) c) All dividends reduce retained earnings, whereas a stock split just affects the number of shares, not the $ value in the equity accounts. Stock dividends also result in an increase in the number of shares outstanding.

6) d) This is a change in estimate, which requires prospective treatment. The others are error corrections which should be booked through retained earnings.

7) c) There must be both a change in control and the costs must be measurable.

8) b) These amounts relate to gains from earlier periods when appraisals were allowed for revaluation of assets to reflect higher values. Currently, revaluations to reflect higher values are not allowed, except in limited circumstances, including financial reorganizations. Gains on financial reorganizations are generally specified in the equity section as a required disclosure.

9) c) HB Section 1625.44 allows a choice.

10) a) All of the other accounts would be closed out against capital stock given the assumptions made. Note also that the debt would be reclassified to capital stock. Therefore, $1.2 +.5 + 1 - .8 = $1.9 million.

SHORT PROBLEMS

1) Purpose: To demonstrate the difference between capital transactions and income items.

The following transactions occurred during the year:

(a) The government expropriated vacant land held by the company and gave the company an amount equal to fair value. This resulted in a gain.

(b) A lawsuit was settled in favour of the company. The lawsuit had been initiated last year but no amounts had been accrued in the financial statements at that time.

(c) The company issued shares, incurring issue costs of $235,000.

(d) The government gave the company a grant to build a new building.

(e) The company's shares were reacquired at a price less than the stated value of the shares, resulting in a gain.

(f) Advance deposits made by shareholders under share subscriptions were forfeited when the shareholders did not make the required subsequent payments for the shares.

Required

Prepare the journal entry for each item and explain why the transaction affects retained earnings (or net income) or contributed surplus (or capital accounts). Explain why the transaction is an income item or a capital transaction.

2) Purpose: To show preferential dividend status of various classes of shares.

Dividendall Limited (DL) declared cash dividends of $380,000 during the year. These dividends were set aside to cover dividend commitments on all shares of the company. The capital structure is as follows:

Series A shares: 5% cumulative, nonvoting	$1,000,000
Series B shares: 6% non-cumulative, nonvoting	$2,000,000
Series C shares: voting	$3,000,000

No dividends had been declared or paid in the past two years.

Required

Calculate how much would be paid in dividends to each shareholder class.

3) Purpose: To illustrate journal entries for various types of dividends.

Assume the same details as in 2.

Required

Prepare the journal entry to book the dividends on the Series C shares, assuming that the dividends take the following forms:

(a) Cash.

(b) Shares of another company that DL had invested in. The book value of the shares according to DL was $80,000.

(c) The dividends were declared liquidating dividends by the Board of Directors.

(d) Stock dividends. Note how many shares would be issued if the market price of the shares was $35 and the book value $25.

SOLUTIONS TO SHORT PROBLEMS

1) The distinction is between income items and capital items. Any transactions that result from the earnings process or operations of the company are income items. Any items that arise due to shareholder transactions are generally capital transactions. There are some items that do not fit neatly into either and judgement must be applied.

(a) This is similar in nature to a sale of an asset and therefore is treated as an income item. The company had to "earn" the funds by giving up the asset.

dr. cash
    cr. fixed asset
    cr. gain or loss on disposal

(b) Although cash inflows due to the lawsuit are not technically "earned," they are related to the earnings process and occurred because of something that happened to the company in the process of carrying on operations. Therefore, they are an income item.

dr. cash
    cr. gain

(c) There are three different views on this in practice. On the one hand, it may be argued that these costs do not relate to operations, but to the capital structure of the company. Therefore, they should be booked as a capital transaction (dr. share capital, cr. cash).

Alternatively, it may be argued that they do relate to operations in that they are similar to debt costs (i.e., the cost of obtaining financing for the company). Therefore, they should be deferred and amortized to net income (dr. deferred assets, cr. cash).

Lastly, it might be argued that they do not fit either category and therefore should be charged to retained earnings (dr. retained earnings, cr. cash).

Normally, the costs are treated as capital transactions and proceeds from the share issue are shown net of the costs.

dr. cash
    cr. common shares

The amount would be the total share issue less the issue costs.

(d) There are differing theoretical views as to how government grants should be treated. One approach is to treat them as contributed capital since they are contributed to the company, rather than being earned, and form part of the permanent financing of the company. Alternatively, since, in most cases, companies must adhere to certain conditions in order to get the grants, it is often argued that they are earned and therefore should be included in income. The CICA Handbook Section 3800 requires that the grants be treated as income either in the current or future periods since they confer a benefit on the company and are not contributed by the shareholders.

In this case, since the grant is for a building, the amount is credited to the fixed asset account and will affect future net income by reducing depreciation charges.

dr. cash
    cr. fixed assets

(e) This is a capital transaction since the transaction is with the shareholders and has nothing to do with operations. The transaction creates a "gain" since the company was able to reacquire the shares at less than the issue price. The share capital account (common shares) is debited with the assigned or average book value of the shares.

dr. common shares
    cr. cash
    cr. contributed surplus

(f) These are capital transactions. They were contributed by shareholders and do not relate to the operating activities of the company.

dr. share capital subscribed
    cr. contributed surplus

2) The Series A and B shares likely rank in preference to the Series C shares since they carry a fixed dividend rate and are nonvoting. The C shares are residual in nature because they are the voting shares and take part in whatever profits are left after the dividend requirements have been satisfied on the other shares.

No dividends have been paid in the last two years. Since none have been declared on the Series B and C shares, and since the B shares are noncumulative, the company owes nothing for these past years. However, since the Series A shares are cumulative and in arrears, these dividends are owed to the shareholders and must be paid prior to the other dividends.

Total available	$380,000
Less: Series A	
– in arrears	$1,000,000
x 5% x 2 years	(100,000)

– current	(50,000)
Series B	
– $2,000,000 x 6%	(120,000)
Amount remaining for Series C	$110,000

3) (a) To record cash dividend:

dr. retained earnings	110,000	
cr. cash		110,000

(b) To record property dividend:

dr. retained earnings	110,000	
cr. investment		80,000
cr. gain		30,000

The investment account is credited with the book value of the investment given up. In this case, the dividend value was stipulated. However, normally, if the shares were being distributed as the dividend, a value would have to be established and the issue would be whether to record the dividend at book value or fair value of the investment. According to CICA Handbook Section 3830 on nonmonetary transactions, nonreciprocal transfers of nonmonetary assets between an enterprise and its owners is valued at fair value of the asset given up. This recognizes the economic worth of the asset given up and the dividend. It is a nonreciprocal transfer because the company is giving something up and getting nothing in return. Interestingly, the gain ultimately increases retained earnings when net income is closed out, thereby offsetting the larger debit to retained earnings for the dividend (i.e., $110,000 vs. $80,000).

(c) To record liquidating dividend:

dr. common shares/contributed surplus	110,000	
cr. cash		110,000

The dividend would be specified as a liquidating dividend by the company to advise the shareholders that this was a return of capital and not a return on capital.

(d) To record stock dividend:

dr. retained earnings	110,000	
cr. common shares		110,000

The stock dividend would result in $110,000/$35 = 3,143 additional shares being issued since it would be based on the market price. Since there are $3,000,000/$25 = 120,000 shares outstanding prior to the dividend, this results in a 2.6% dividend based on the number of shares.

CASE

Overlevered Limited

Overlevered Limited (OL) is a public company that is in the retail grocery business. In the past five years, OL has borrowed heavily in order to expand into the Ontario market. It had previously only operated in Western Canada. After the new stores were set up in Ontario, the industry became highly competitive, with many stores offering products at or near cost to attract customers. Numerous companies in the industry went bankrupt since they could not maintain gross margins high enough to cover their fixed costs.

Unfortunately, OL had borrowed most of the funds for expansion by issuing fixed interest rate bonds at a rate that is now quite high in comparison to market. OL found that the high interest charges were becoming increasingly more and more difficult to meet. In addition, the bonds required partial repayment of principal within the next month. The high interest expense and the losses suffered from the new stores combined to turn retained earnings into a deficit. No dividends had been paid in the past two years and shares were trading at one-quarter of their normal trading price. OL needed cash not only to sustain the new operations but also to pay the interest on the debt and to make the first scheduled repayment instalment on the bonds, which was due within the month.

OL's bank was unwilling to advance funds to meet the upcoming repayment commitment since it felt that the company was overleveraged and the industry was becoming increasingly risky. Despite the immediate cash shortage, however, OL's management felt that the company was on the verge of turning around. Many of the older stores that were not making money had been sold, albeit at a loss, and the newer stores were starting to generate a profit.

OL was planning to have a shareholders' meeting, including the debt holders, to discuss the current cash shortage. The following plan would be presented to the shareholders and debt holders in an attempt to reorganize:

- Existing debt holders would receive new debt to replace the old debt.
- The new debt would bear variable interest at the market rates.
- The interest for the current and perhaps the next year would be forgiven and the principal repayment delayed. In return, the new debt would be convertible into common shares. If converted, the debt holders would receive 49.9% of the voting shares of the company.

The debt holders would only recover their investment on conversion if the shares reached a certain market value, which was much higher than the present value. Management felt that the shares would increase in value once investors saw that the company was on the upswing. As a matter of fact, without the interest burden, management was forecasting a profit within two years.

Once the proposal was accepted, the assets and liabilities would be revalued and the deficit zeroed out. This would result in the company legally being able to pay out dividends. The fair market value of the assets is quite high since OL owns a lot of property that was purchased decades ago.

Part of the proposed arrangement is that a small dividend will be paid out to appease the shareholders, since dividends have not been paid in the last two years. Hopefully, the dividend will be acceptable to the debt holders since it should increase the share price.

Management is worried whether this constitutes a "financial reorganization" within the context of *CICA Handbook* Section 1625, and if not, what the consequences would be.

Required

Adopt the role of the auditor of the company and advise management.

SOLUTION TO CASE

OVERLEVERED LIMITED

Overview

[Note: As a general comment, be careful not to regurgitate the facts when doing case analysis. In this specific instance, however, it is important to recap the background information in order to be able to focus on a solution that makes sense to all parties involved.]

Management is looking for advice as to **how to structure a reorganization** so that the company can have a decent chance at recovery. The shareholders have not been paid dividends for the past two years and have watched their shares drop to one-quarter of their previous value. Debt holders are awaiting interest and principal repayments, both of which are due. The company cannot afford to pay either dividends or interest or repay principal. They feel that the company is on the road to recovery, having sold off much of its unproductive operations. GAAP is a **constraint** since the company is public. **Management** will want the financial statements to portray its efforts to successfully turn the company around. All parties want higher stock prices and presumably, the prices will be affected positively by the financial statements and dividends, although perhaps not.

Analysis and Recommendations

The issue appears to be how to organize the restructuring such that the following goals are met:

- Shareholders and debt holders are appeased.
- It is legally permissible to pay a dividend.
- The financial statements portray a company that is at a turning point.

The shareholders stand to gain by the reorganization since their company will be relieved of the burdensome interest costs and the requirement to pay the instalment on the debt. Likely, the reorganization will result in a share price increase for those reasons. The debt holders stand to gain since they could potentially achieve control of the company. Therefore, from the perspective of the shareholders and debt holders, the proposed reorganization will likely be acceptable.

It will be legally permissible to pay a dividend only if there is no deficit and if the payment would not result in net worth being less than stated capital. It would appear that these two criteria would be met as long as the reorganization would be accounted for as a **financial reorganization** under *CICA Handbook* Section 1625, hence management's concern. In addition, accounting for the reorganization under Section 1625 will allow the **revaluation of the assets** and will make the company look better, reflecting the underlying value of the assets.

Comprehensive revaluation of the assets and removal of the deficit is only allowable under Section 1625 when a financial reorganization has taken place and **control** of the company has shifted to another party. Therefore, the issue would seem to boil down to whether control of the company will change with the reorganization.

[As an aside, the revaluation is only allowable if there is a change in control, but it can be argued that the removal of the deficit is allowable anyway as long as there is a reorganization and the shareholders agree to the removal. See *CICA Handbook* Section 3250.]

Control is defined in *CICA Handbook* Section 1590 as the **continued ability to influence the key decisions of the company**. This would normally result if more than 50% of the voting shares of the company were held. In this case, the requirement would be that they were held by a different party than the original shareholders.

Has control shifted?
No:

- The original shareholders still have control of the company since they own all of the outstanding shares.
- The debt holders still have debt and although it is convertible, it has not yet been converted.
- At this point, it is not economically viable for them to convert since the share price is so low and may not recover. They might be better off retaining their status as debt holders.
- Even if all debt is converted, it will only result in debt holders holding less than 50%, which is not control.

Yes:

- It is irrelevant that the debt holders will not actually convert in the short run. Since they hold the right to convert, they have control since they can easily veto present shareholder decisions by converting.
- Although it may not make economical sense to convert now, management feels that the share price will increase in the short- to mid-term making it more attractive for the debt holders to convert.

- Given that the shares are likely widely held, it might be argued that 49.9% is so close to legal control that it might as well be legal control. It is unlikely that the rest of the shareholders could get together and outvote the debt holders.

Therefore, it might be argued that control has or has not shifted.

If it is determined that control has not shifted, there is a chance that the deficit may not be eliminated since reorganization accounting may not apply and, therefore, there are legal restrictions prohibiting dividends. Furthermore, the assets would not be revalued and the financial statements would not reflect the true economic value of the company. This is undesirable to management since it does not reflect its efforts to turn the company around and might cause share prices to stay depressed.

Recommendations

Since a reasonable case may be made for arguing that control will or will not shift after the reorganization, management might consider making a stronger case for arguing that control has shifted. One way would be to give the debt holders conversion rights that would allow slightly greater than 50% ownership for the debt holders. It likely would not make much difference in reality, but this would at least strengthen the argument for change in control.

Once this is established, the assets may be revalued, the deficit eliminated, and the proposed dividends paid.

SELECTED SOLUTIONS FROM THE TEXTBOOK

EXERCISE 17-4

		Preferred	Common	Total
(a)	One year arrears ($.70 x 20,000)	$ 14,000	$ 14,000	
	Current year, preferred	14,000	14,000	
	Current year, common	210,000	210,000	

> $\frac{\$14,000}{\$200,000}$ (preferred's return) = 7% return on investment (preferred's investment)
>
> Common shareholders get 7% return also: $3,000,000 x 7% = $210,000

	Preferred	Common	Total
Participating feature, preferred	6,000	6,000	

> Dividends declared remaining ($334,000 - $238,000) = $96,000
>
> $\frac{\$200,000}{\$3,200,000}$ (preferred's share capital) x $96,000 = $6,000 (total share capital)

	Preferred	Common	Total
Participating feature, common	90,000	90,000	

> $\frac{\$3,000,000}{\$3,200,000}$ (common's share capital) x $96,000 = $90,000 (total share capital)

	Preferred	Common	Total
	$ 34,000	$300,000	$334,000

(b)	Preferred	Common	Total
Current year, preferred ($.70 x 20,000)	$14,000	$14,000	
Current year, common ($334,000 - $14,000)	$320,000	320,000	
	$14,000	$320,000	$334,000

(c)	Preferred	Common	Total
Current year, preferred ($.70 x 20,000) $14,000	$ 14,000		
Current year, common (10% of common share capital) ($3,000,000 x .10)	$300,000	300,000	
Participating, preferred	1,250	1,250	

> Dividends declared remaining ($334,000 - $314,000) = $20,000
>
> $\frac{\$200,000}{\$3,200,000}$ (preferred's share capital) x $20,000 = $1,250 (total share capital)

Participating, common	18,750	18,750	

> $\frac{\$3,000,000}{\$3,200,000}$ (common's share capital) x $20,000 = $18,750 (total share capital)

	$15,250	$318,750	$334,000

EXERCISE 17-17

(a) Handbook Section 1625 requires that two conditions be met for a company subject to a financial reorganization to have its assets and liabilities comprehensively revalued:

1. The same party does not control the enterprise both before and after the reorganization, and
2. The new costs are reasonably determinable.

In the case of Cognac Corporation, the existing shareholders gave up their interest and the holder of the note becomes the sole shareholder. Therefore, there has been a change in control. The asset and liability values were determined in bargained transactions among the various parties to the financial reorganization.

(b)
Cognac Corporation

Balance Sheet
(Dated immediately after the financial reorganization)

Current Assets:		
Accounts receivable ($320,000 - $80,000)	$240,000	
Inventory ($450,000 - $170,000)	280,000	
Total current assets		$520,000
Long-term Assets:		
Equipment ($860,000 + $100,000)	$960,000	
Less: Accumulated depreciation	525,000	435,000*
Total assets		$955,000
Current Liabilities:		
Bank overdraft	$ 5,000	
Accounts payable (20% x $450,000)	90,000	
Taxes and wages payable	60,000	
Notes payable (50% x $450,000)	225,000	
Total current liabilities		$380,000

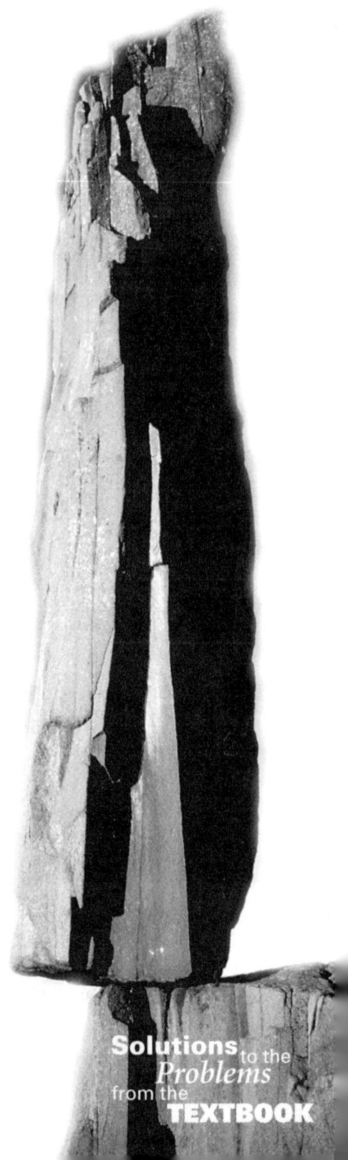

Long-term Liabilities:		
Mortgage payable		150,000
Total liabilities		$530,000
Shareholders' Equity		
Common shares, no-par value, 1,000 issued	$425,000**	
Retained earnings	0	
Total shareholders' equity		425,000
Total liabilities and shareholders' equity		$955,000

* Equally as valid is leaving the equipment at $860,000 and reducing the accumulated depreciation by $100,000 to $425,000, netting to $435,000.
** Required to balance

OR:

Shareholders' equity before reorganization ($50,000 common shares - $135,000 deficit)	$(85,000)	
Revaluation adjustments regarding assets:		
Accounts receivable write-down	$(80,000)	
Inventory write-down	(170,000)	
Intangibles write-off	(80,000)	
Equipment write-up	100,000	(230,000)
		$(315,000)
Realignment of nonequity and equity interests:		
Accounts payable reduction	$135,000	
Elimination of note payable for shares	605,000	740,000
Amount assigned to remaining common shares		$425,000

SOLUTIONS TO PROBLEMS

PROBLEM 17-8

-1-

(a) Fire Loss	54,000	
Building (net)		54,000

Note: As a result of the fire, a portion of the appropriation for fire insurance might be reversed at this point. But, because of the risk of additional uninsured fires, the appropriation may also remain.

-2-

Investments	37,250	
Gain on Appreciation of Securities		37,250
5,000 shares x $16 =		$80,000
Less cost of 5,000 shares (5,000/8,000 x $68,400) =	42,750	
		$37,250

Retained Earnings—Unappropriated	80,000	
Property Dividends Payable		80,000

When paid:

Property Dividends Payable	80,000	
Investments		80,000

Note: This transaction is a partial distribution, and the entry represents a revaluation of only the 5,000 shares distributed of the total of 8,000 on hand. Some might argue for recognizing appreciation on the entire 8,000 shares, but that would result in carrying the remaining investment account at an amount greater than historical cost.

-3-

Preferred Shares (800 / 2,000 x $200,000)	80,000	
Loss on Redemption of Preferred Shares*	16,000	
Cash ($120 x 800)		96,000

*This is recorded as a loss because they are classified as a financial liability.

-4-

Retained Earnings—Unappropriated	57,500	
Common Stock Dividend Distributable		57,500
(50,000 x 5% = 2,500 shares @ $23 = $57,500)		
Common Stock Dividend Distributable	57,500	
Common Shares		57,500

-5-

Land	36,000	
Contributed Surplus—Donated Land		36,000

-6-

Dividend Expense	7,200	
Cash ($6 x 1,200 shares)		7,200

Note: If the company accrued the dividend expense each month, the following entry would have been made:

Dividend Payable		7,200
Cash	7,200	
Retained Earnings-Unappropriated	80,000	
Retained Earnings Appropriated		
for Fire Insurance	95,000	
Retained Earnings Appropriated for Contingencies		25,000
Retained Earnings Appropriated for Plant Expansion		150,000

(b)

Timothy Corporation
Shareholders' Equity
December 31, 1998

Contributed Capital		
Share Capital		
Common shares, no par, 100,000 shares authorized, 52,500 shares issued		$ 657,500
Contributed surplus - donation of land		36,000
		$ 693,500
Retained Earnings		
Unappropriated ($304,000 - $80,000 - $57,500 - $80,000 + $74,500)	$161,000	
Appropriated for contingencies ($75,000 + $25,000)	100,000	
Appropriated for plant expansion	150,000	411,000
Total Shareholders' Equity		$1,104,500

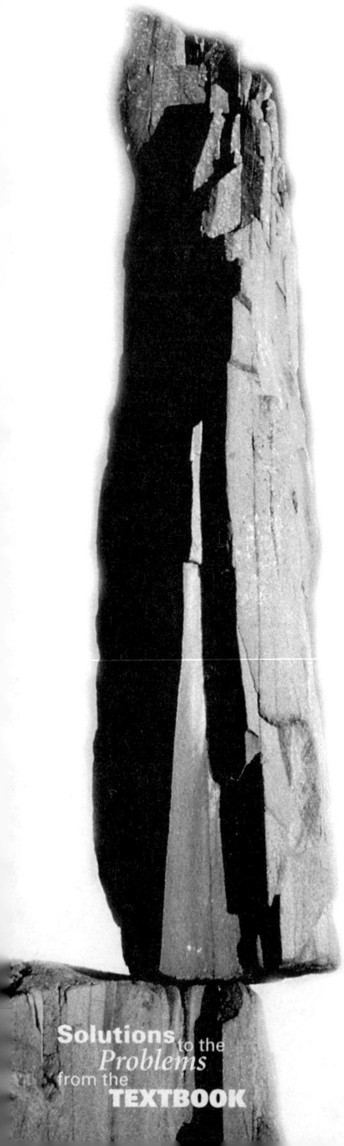

PROBLEM 17-10

(a)

	Dec. 15, 1997	
Unappropriated Retained Earnings	90,000	
Retained Earnings Appropriated for Plant Expansion		90,000
	Dec. 31, 1997	
Income Summary	525,000	
Unappropriated Retained Earnings		525,000
	Nov. 1, 1998	
Factory Building (Plant & Equipment)	322,500	
Cash		322,500
	Dec. 14, 1998	
Retained Earnings Appropriated for Plant Expansion	360,000	
Unappropriated Retained Earnings		360,000
Unappropriated Retained Earnings (25,000 x $46)	1,150,000	
Common Stock Dividend Distributable		1,150,000
	Dec. 31, 1998	
Income Summary	600,000	
Unappropriated Retained Earnings		600,000

Jan. 23, 1999		
Common Stock Dividend Distributable	1,150,000	
Common Shares		1,150,000

(b)

Malaga Corporation
Shareholders' Equity
December 31, 1998

Share Capital	
Common shares, no-par value, 300,000 authorized, 200,000 issued and outstanding	$5,600,000
Common stock dividend distributable 25,000 shares	1,150,000
Total share capital	$6,750,000
Retained Earnings*	2,135,000
Total shareholders' equity	$8,885,000
*Unappropriated retained earnings	
Balance Dec. 15, 1997	$1,800,000
Add: Returned from appropriated retained earnings	360,000
Income, 1997	525,000
Income, 1998	600,000
	$3,285,000
Deduct: Stock dividend in 1998	1,150,000
Balance, Dec. 31, 1998	$2,135,000

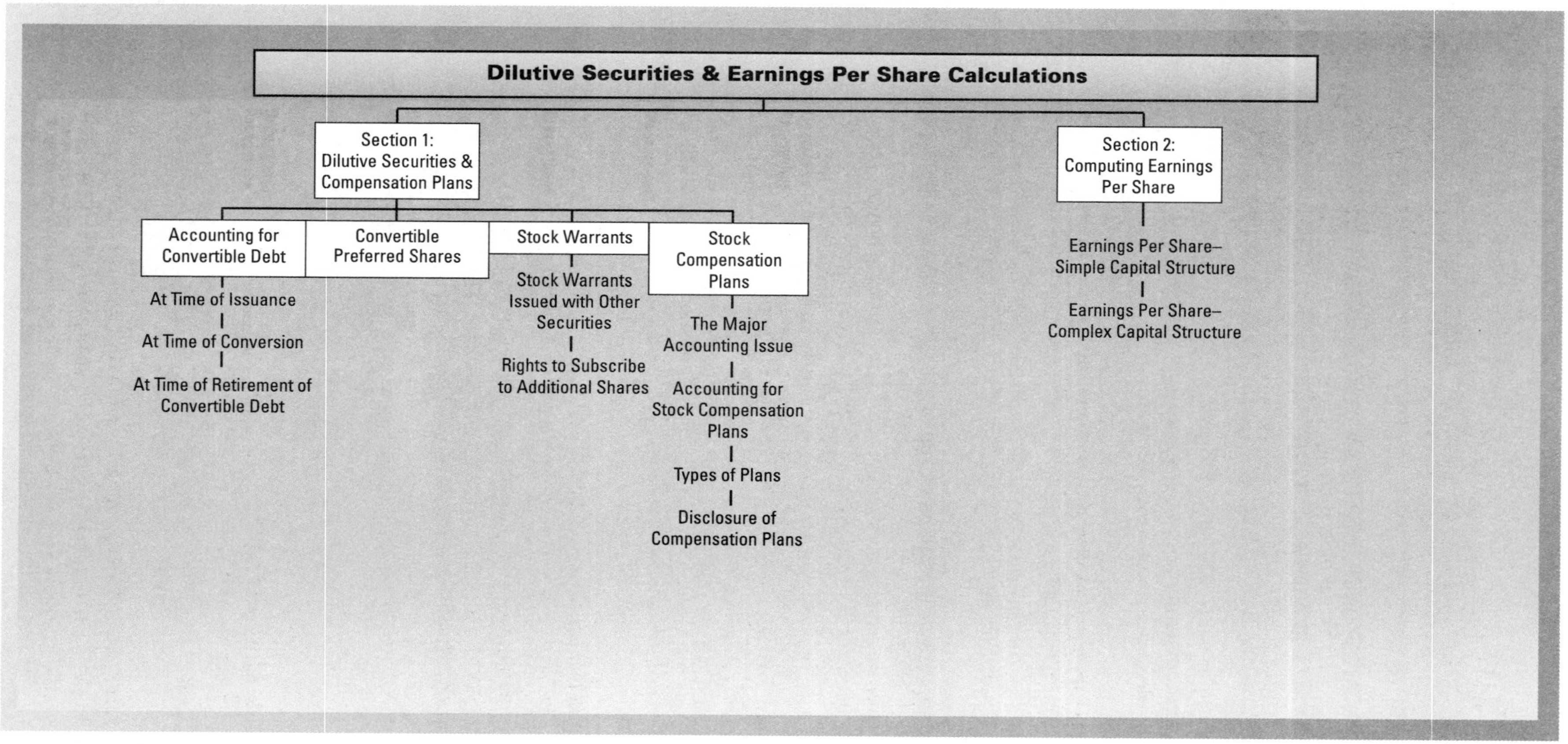
Dilutive Securities & Earnings Per Share Calculations
Section 1: Dilutive Securities & Compensation Plans
Accounting for Convertible Debt
At Time of Issuance
At Time of Conversion
At Time of Retirement of Convertible Debt
Convertible Preferred Shares
Stock Warrants
Stock Warrants Issued with Other Securities
Rights to Subscribe to Additional Shares
Stock Compensation Plans
The Major Accounting Issue
Accounting for Stock Compensation Plans
Types of Plans
Disclosure of Compensation Plans
Section 2: Computing Earnings Per Share
Earnings Per Share–Simple Capital Structure
Earnings Per Share–Complex Capital Structure

chapter 18

DILUTIVE SECURITIES AND EARNINGS PER SHARE CALACULATIONS

PERSPECTIVE

This topic is one that has challenging judgemental issues, as well as, technically complex calculations. The first part, which includes dilutive securities and stock option plans, does not present any real challenges in terms of calculations and journal entries; however, it has some interesting conceptual and implementation issues. Note that many of the issues here are discussed in the long-term debt chapter since dilutive securities and options are also considered to be financial instruments. The second part, which examines earnings per share, is calculations-oriented. Both will be covered here.

INSIGHTS

- *EPS accounting is an area that has technically complex calculations. For that reason, it lends itself to* ***self-study*** *once the material has been mastered.*
- *Accounting for compensatory stock option plans is an example of using management intent and* ***economic substance over legal form*** *to determine accounting treatment. At present, in Canada, there are no clearly defined GAAP.*

STUDY STEPS

1. Understanding the Underlying Business Arrangement Relating to Dilutive Securities and Compensation Plans

STUDY STEPS

Tip!

Dilutive securities are securities, such as convertible debt or preferred shares, options or warrants, which, if exercised, will result in more common shares being issued and, hence, dilute the existing shareholder holdings.

Convertible securities

A convertible security is a security or instrument that is issued by the company to an investor, e.g., convertible debt or convertible preferred shares.

What makes convertible securities unique is that they carry with them the **option to convert to common shares**. The instrument allows the holder to have **limited risks** in that the main instrument is a debt instrument or preferred share instrument. Both the debt and the preferred shares receive a stable fixed return on their investment that ranks in priority (in terms of pay out) to dividends on common shares. Furthermore, if the company went bankrupt, secured creditors and preferred shareholders would get their money out first.

The convertible feature on the preferred shares or debt, however, allows the holder to also participate in the **rewards of owning common shares**. It allows the holder to share in rewards of ownership of the company since the holder has the option to convert the security to common shares. The option would only be exercised if it was favourable to the holder.

Tip! **Convertible securities offer holders greater choice and therefore are generally more valuable.**

Stock warrants or options

These are instruments that give the holder the right to buy shares at a certain price (**exercise price**) over a certain period (**exercise period**) no matter what the market value of the shares is. The purchaser pays money up-front for the option.

Why does a warrant have value? It has value because it provides the **opportunity** to buy the shares at a pre-specified price even if the market price changes. Thus, if an investor pays $1 for an option to buy a share of a company at $10 and the market price of the share goes up to $20, the investor need only pay $10 to acquire the share (plus the price of the option—$1). Therefore, he has paid $11 for a $20 share.

If the market price of the share decreases (e.g., to $5), the option is worthless. But the investor is not committed to buying the shares and therefore only loses $1 (a limited down-side risk). So the warrant allows the investor to benefit from increases in value but limits the exposure to decreases in value to the cost of the warrant.

Stock option plans (SOPs) may be **compensatory** or not. That is, the intent of top management in setting up the plans may be either to **raise money** or to **compensate** their employees. Management **intent** is a critical deciding factor in this issue (i.e., whether the plan is compensatory or not) but factors such as who the options are issued to, the discount on the exercise price, and the exercise period would be considered. Generally, the deeper the discount and the more limited the issuance, the more likely it is that it is to be compensatory in nature. Stock option plans are fairly common for senior executives. They are a benefit awarded to employees for doing a good job, and therefore, form part of the **remuneration** for the employees.

Stock option plans are put in place for one of two main reasons: i) to raise capital and ii) to provide another source of compensation to management. **Tip!**

Management intent often determines whether a stock option plan is compensatory or not; however, the terms of the arrangement must also be reviewed. **Tip!**

Stock appreciation rights plans, sometimes called "phantom" stock plans or SARs, award the employee with increases in stock prices even though the employee does not own the shares. They are, therefore, always compensatory. For instance, an executive might be enrolled in one of these plans as part of his remuneration package. The more productive he is, hopefully, the better the company will do and, hence, the higher the share price will be. The plan would entitle him to the increase in the market price of the company's shares (above the exercise or base price) times a notional number of shares or the number of SARs held.

Benefit on exercise of SAR = # of SARs X (market price of CS—exercise/base price)

The shares are not actually owned by him and have nothing to do with shares he may already own. The notional number of shares or number of SARs held are merely for calculation purposes and may reflect his status in the company (i.e., a more senior executive would presumably have more notional shares). The plans are often in effect for a limited time.

The employee may exercise the right to the increase in price at any time during a prespecified period (i.e.b collect the difference in cash or other).

Stock appreciation rights plans are always compensatory. **Tip!**

2. Understanding How These Arrangements Fit into the Financial Reporting Model and Conceptual Framework—Analysis

STUDY STEPS

Convertible securities—see exhibit #1 in Chapter 15 on long-term debt

As mentioned in Chapter 15, the main issues with convertible securities are measurement issues. Since they are seen as compound financial instruments, they are felt to have two distinct components and, therefore, part is booked as debt or preferred shares and part as a warrant or option to purchase a common share. The measurement issues are currently under discussion by the CICA. Suggested approaches include using options pricing models to value the option and using discounted cash flows to calculate debt portion.

Tip! **Convertible securities fall under the heading of compound instruments and therefore under HB3860. Both components should be measured and shown separately.**

Compensatory stock option plans

The main issue here is how to **measure** the costs associated with these plans. Since the compensation is nonmonetary, it is difficult to measure. Alternatives are discussed below.

STUDY STEPS

3. Becoming Proficient in Calculations and Journal Entries-Skills

Compensatory stock option plans

The issue is how to **measure** the costs associated with a compensatory stock option plan, since it should be accrued as part of payroll costs in order to be **matched** with revenues that the employee generates during the **service period**. The cost is determined on the date that certain details are known (i.e., how many shares the employee is entitled to. and the purchase price) usually at the **grant date**. It is calculated as follows:

[market price of shares—option price] x # of shares

It is booked by the following journal entry:

dr. deferred costs
    cr. contributed surplus

The amount should then be **amortized** over the period which it is expected to benefit. This is very difficult to determine and, in practice, many different amortization periods and methods are used. The deferred costs are often shown as contra accounts to the shareholders' equity section.

Tip! **The cost of compensatory stock option plans is measured at the grant date and is not subsequently remeasured.**

Stock appreciation rights carry with them different measurement problems. For stock option plans, the employee gets shares when they exercise the option (or a cash equivalent if they turn around and sell the shares). For SARs, the employee will get cash, not shares. Since it is difficult to determine the amount of this future cash payout (the value of the benefit) before the right is exercised by the employee, the cost is not measured until that time. However, all periods between the time that the right is granted and the exercise date benefit from the employee's service and, therefore, some attempt is made to **measure** the cost and **accrue** a bit in each period. During each period, the difference between the market price and the original share price times the notional number of shares is calculated and accrued. A portion is deferred to be amortized over the remaining service life of the employee, and the rest is expensed.

dr. deferred costs
dr. payroll / remuneration expense
    cr. accrued liabilities

This must be re-estimated every year until the employee exercises the right.

Options to acquire shares are required **disclosures** under Handbook Section 3240. SARs fall under the definition of a **financial liability** and, therefore, they must be disclosed in the notes. Options would be classified as **equity instruments** under CICA HB 3860 and are, therefore, bound by the disclosure requirements.

SARs create liabilities that must be re-estimated every year. Their final measurement is at the payout date. **Tip!**

This treatment is inconsistent with the measurement of compensatory stock option plans since the cost of the latter is measured at the option grant date, whereas the cost of SARs is measured at the exercise date. The exercise date is probably a better date at which to measure the transaction, since it is a better measure of what the company has given up. **Tip!**

Earnings Per Share

EPS is a calculation that lets shareholders know what their share of the company's residual value is. EPS is generally calculated as follows:

$$\text{EPS} = \frac{\text{net income} - \text{dividends on PS}}{\text{weighted average \# of CS outstanding}}$$

Earnings per share shows the residual (or the common) shareholders what their shares have earned during the year. It does not necessarily bear any relationship to the amount of dividends paid out. Rather, it shows the amount of net income available after preferred shareholders have been allocated a return on their capital. **Tip!**

The basic calculation is as follows:

(net income – preferred dividends)/# of common shares

Preferred dividends are deducted for cumulative preferred shares regardless of whether the dividends have been declared. However, a deduction is only made for non-cumulative preferred shares if a dividend has been declared. **Tip!**

The number of shares is a weighted-average calculation, weighted by the length of time that shares are outstanding. Stock dividends or splits are treated as though they have been outstanding since the beginning of the year, even if they are issued after year-end. **Tip!**

There are several other types of EPS calculations:

- Basic EPS (covered above)—actual scenario.
- Adjusted basic—"what if" scenario.

- Fully diluted EPS—"what if" scenario.
- Pro forma EPS—"what if" scenario.

Adjusted basic EPS

Adjusted basic EPS calculates EPS in the situation where there has been an actual conversion of senior shares or debt to common shares during the year.

Tip! **The calculation shows what the basic EPS would look like if the conversion had taken place at the beginning of the year.**

The numerator of the basic EPS calculation is adjusted for dividends or after-tax interest that would have been avoided had the shares/debt been converted at the beginning of the year. The denominator assumes that the conversion took place at the beginning of the year.

Fully diluted EPS

Fully diluted EPS shows what EPS would look like if all convertible debt or equity were converted and if all options to purchase common stock had been exercised. The numerator of the basic EPS is adjusted for dividends and after-tax interest that would have been avoided had the conversion taken place at the beginning of the year and the denominator assumes that the shares on conversion/option exercise were issued at the beginning of the year.

For warrants and options, if they are exercised, cash would generally be paid into the company since the holder of the option would buy a share. The incremental effect on the EPS calculation is, therefore, after-tax return that would be earned on this capital infusion.

Tip! **Only conversion rights and options effective within the next 10 years are considered in the "what if" fully dilutive calculation.**

Tip! **Only conversions and/or exercise of options that are dilutive (i.e., decrease basic EPS) would be included in the calculation. Conversions that increase EPS are known as anti-dilutive.**

Pro forma EPS

Pro forma EPS restates both basic EPS and fully diluted EPS. It would be calculated where one of the following occurs subsequent to the balance sheet date:

- Common shares issued for cash where proceeds used to retire debt or senior shares.
- Conversion of senior shares/debt.
- Reorganization.

Tip! **The calculations are based on the assumption that the transactions happened at the beginning of the current year.**

The above calculations are required for most companies although there are a few exceptions. The EPS should be shown either at the bottom of the income statement or in the notes for current and comparative years. Also, the calculations should be done for income before discontinued operations and extraordinary items and for net income. Multiple choice questions and problems are presented in this chapter to assist you in working through basic calculations.

4. Pulling It All Together—A Critical Look At Compensatory Share Plans

STUDY STEPS

There has been some criticism over the inconsistent treatment of costs associated with compensatory stock option plans and SARs. The stock option plans measure and accrue the cost on the day that the options are issued. Subsequent changes in share price up to the day that the options are exercised, are ignored completely. However, for SARs, the

cost is measured on the day that the SAR is exercised.

The question arises as to why these two plans should be measured differently given that in substance, they are both forms of compensation and the differences between the plans are really only a matter of legal form. This difference in measurement creates lack of comparability and could affect net income significantly if the plans were significant to the company. Suggestions have been made to value the options in both cases using options pricing models; however, at present, there is not yet any GAAP that stipulates how either plan should be measured. Current practice is a matter of convention with the differing treatments being a function of the difficulty in measuring the SARs.

MULTIPLE CHOICE QUESTIONS

1) Which of the following is not considered a factor in the determination of whether a stock option plan is compensatory or non-compensatory?

a) the discount from market price of the shares

b) time frame for exercising the warrant

c) participating parties

d) price of the options

2) A phantom stock option plan (stock appreciation rights plan) may be best described as which of the following:

a) a stock option plan whereby the employee is entitled to the increase in value of the company shares without having to actually hold the shares.

b) a stock option plan whereby the employee is entitled to the increase in value of the company shares where the employee must also hold the shares to benefit from them.

c) a stock option plan whereby the employer sets aside shares for employees and employees are allowed to buy the shares later at a fixed price.

d) a stock option plan where the employer sets aside shares in a separate trust for later issue to the employees upon exercise of options.

3) The cost of a compensatory stock option plan is accounted for as follows:

a) a capital transaction that is measured at the grant date.

b) an expense that is measured at the grant date.

c) an expense that is measured at the exercise date.

d) a capital transaction that is measured at the exercise date.

4) Which of the following are not considered to be dilutive securities?

a) debt that is convertible into preferred shares

b) convertible preferred shares

c) stock options

d) stock warrants

5) When should the cost of a compensatory stock option plan be expensed?

a) at the time of issue

b) at the time of exercise

c) over the period of service

d) never

6) When calculating basic EPS the numerator should be adjusted for:

   a) all dividends declared for the year.

   b) dividends declared during the year for preferred shares only.

   c) dividends declared during the year for the current year only.

   d) dividends declared during the year for all preferred shares and undeclared dividend for the year on cumulative preferred shares.

7) Which of the following does not require a retroactive adjustment when calculating weighted average number of shares for the basic EPS calculation?

   a) a stock split

   b) a reverse split

   c) a stock dividend

   d) a share conversion

8) End Company has 100,000 shares outstanding at the beginning of the year (January 1). On June 30, 30,000 shares were issued and on January 1 of the following year there was a 2 for 1 stock split. Calculate the weighted average number of common shares for the current year.

   a) 130,000

   b) 115,000

   c) 230,000

   d) 260,000

9) And Company has the following securities. Note which one would not be included in the fully diluted EPS calculation. Basic EPS is $2 based on 100,000 shares and earnings of $200,000 (after deducting taxes of $200,000). Assume an after-tax ROR on investment of 6%.

   a) $100,000—10% convertible bonds—each $1,000 bond is convertible into 10 shares.

   b) $200,000—5% convertible preferred shares—each of the 20,000 shares is convertible into 1 common share

   c) 10,000 warrants allowing holders to purchase 1 share each for $15

   d) 10,000 share options under a stock option plan offered to key executives. The executives do not have to pay anything when they exercise the option. Assume that any costs associated with the plan have already been expensed.

10) Fully diluted EPS would not be reported except in which of the following situations?

   a) the potential dilution is less than 3% of net income

   b) all dilutive securities result in an anti-dilutive impact on EPS

   c) the only dilutive securities are warrants that will not be exercisable until beyond 10 years after the balance sheet date

   d) convertibles share, currently convertible will result in a lower EPS number if converted

SOLUTIONS TO MULTIPLE CHOICE

1) d) The price of the options by itself is not a determining factor. The exercise price, as well as, the option price determines the cost to the employee of purchasing the share. This would be compared to the market price of the share to determine whether the discount is excessive.

2) a) The main feature of a phantom stock option plan is that it entitles the employees to participate in the increases in value of the shares without the employee actually having to buy the shares.

3) b) It is accounted for as an expense since it is determined to be part of compensation expense. The cost to the company is measured at the grant date.

4) a) The concept of dilutive pertains to the common shareholders and the act of diluting their respective interest in the company, as well as, their share of the earnings. As such warrants, options and convertible preferred shares are dilutive since, if issued or converted, this would result in more common shares and less earnings for each of the remaining groups of common shareholders.

5) c) The cost should be expensed over the period of service since this is the period that the employee is being motivated to work harder due to the plan.

6) d) Care should be taken to deduct undeclared dividends on cumulative preferred shares for the current year only, as well as ,any declared dividends for the year.

7) d) A share conversion would be accounted for prospectively since it would also affect earnings.

8) c) the weighted average common shares would be calculated as follows:

   [100,000 + (30,000 X 6/12)] X 2 = 230,000

9) a) The convertible bonds are anti-dilutive since they will result in 1000 new shares issued and result in \$5,000 saved interest—shares = 100,000 + 1,000; earnings = \$200,000 + (\$100,000 X 10% X .5) = \$205,000. The new EPS would be \$205,000/101,000 = \$2.03, which is higher than basic EPS. The preferred shares would be dilutive = \$10,000/20,000 = .5 as would the warrants = \$9,000/10,000 = .9 as well as the options which would result in more shares being issued but with no impact on net income.

10) d) The dilutive securities must reduce EPS by a material amount within a reasonable time frame.

SHORT PROBLEM

Purpose: To illustrate EPS calculations in a more complex environment.

EPS Limited (EL) has the following capital structure at December 31, 1998:

8% convertible bonds, convertible into 2 pre-split common shares for every $100 bond in 2001	$1,000,000
10% bonds, due in annual instalments of $500,000 on January 1 of each year, beginning January 1, 1998	$5,000,000
4% cumulative preferred shares, convertible into common shares December 31, 2009 2 preferred shares for 1 pre-split common (125,000 outstanding)	$3,000,000
Common shares-400,000 outstanding	$4,000,000

The following additional information is available:

- During the year, $1,000,000 6% convertible bonds were converted into 20,000 common shares on June 30, 1998. The 8% convertible bonds were issued at the same time.
- Under a stock appreciation plan, key executives are entitled to receive shares equal to the increase in market value of 30,000 pre-split common shares over $40 ($20 post-split).

The plan was initiated on January 1, 1998 and is in effect for five years, which is the average expected lifespan for key executives at EL. Executives have not exercised their rights to collect under the plan to date. At year-end, the shares were trading at $26, a $4 increase over the price at the beginning of the year, once the stock split is taken into account. Once executives exercise their rights under the plan, it is no longer in effect.

- On March 31, 1997, 25,000 warrants were issued for $2 each allowing the holder to purchase 1 pre-split common share per warrant for $50.
- Income tax rates are 40%.
- On September 30, 1998 there was a 2-for-1 stock split.
- Net income after taxes for the year ended December 31, 1998 was $1,100,000. Investment income on excess cash is 10% pre-tax.
- It is a company policy to update all agreements after a stock split, such that arrangements made prior to the split are adjusted to reflect the split. For instance, if a bond was convertible into 2 pre-split shares, the understanding after the split would be that the bond would be convertible into 4 post-split shares.

Required

(a) Calculate basic EPS for EL for the year ended December 31, 1998.

(b) Calculate adjusted basic EPS if required. Explain why or why not required.

(c) Calculate fully diluted EPS.

SOLUTION TO SHORT PROBLEM

(a) Earnings = \$1,100,000—(\$3,000,000 x .04) = \$980,000.
Weighted-average # of shares:

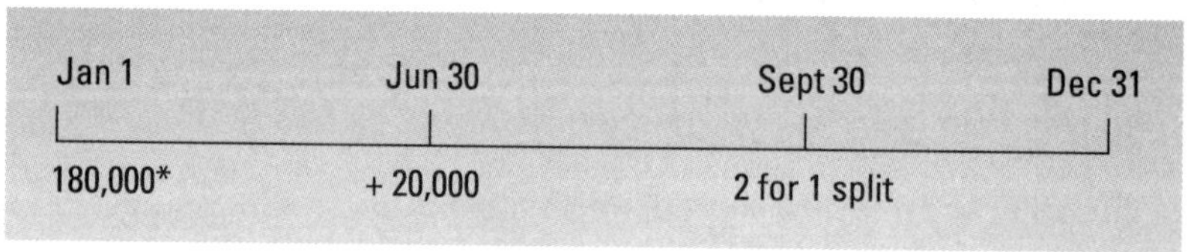

(+200,000)

180,000 shares ⟶ 200,000 ⟶ 400,000 ⟶

* 400,000/2—20,000 = 180,000
Closing balance adjusted for split — Bond conversion

180,000 x 2 x 6/12 = 180,000
200,000 x 2 x 6/12 = 200,000
380,000

or

180,000 x 6/12 = 90,000
200,000 x 3/12 = 50,000
40,000 x 2 = 280,000
400,000 x 3/12 = 100,000
380,000

or

180,000 x 12/12 = 180,000
20,000 x 6/12 = 10,000
190,000
x 2
380,000

Basic EPS = \$980,000/380,000 = \$2.58

(b) Adjusted basic EPS is required since the 6% bonds were converted during the year.

Earnings = \$980,000 + (\$1,000,000 x .06 x 6/12 x .6)
= \$998,000

If the bonds had been converted at the beginning of the year, EL would have avoided paying interest to June 30. **Tip!**

Weighted-average shares:
200,000 x 2 x 12/12 = 400,000

Adjusted basic EPS:
\$998,000/400,000 = \$2.50

(c) Fully diluted EPS should be calculated since there are dilutive securities and share options.

First, identify the securities and options.

- 8% bonds
- 6% convertible bonds
- 4% preferred shares
- warrants
- share issue commitment from the share appreciation plan

The latter is included although this is a judgement call. It makes sense on the basis that the *CICA Handbook* Section 3500 states that contingent issuances should also be included. **Tip!**

Second, calculate the incremental effect of conversion on the basic EPS.

8% BONDS:

Impact on earnings:

\$1,000,000 x .08 x .6 x 6/12 = \$24,000

Had the bonds been converted, \$24,000 in interest would have been avoided. This is an after-tax number since the basic EPS is based on net income after tax. Also, interest would have been avoided for only half a year because the bonds were only issued in June.

Impact on share calculations:

1,000,000/100 x 2 = 20,000 would have been issued. This must be weighted since the bonds were only issued June 30. If the bonds had been outstanding since the beginning of the year, there would have been no need to weight the shares. Further, the stock split would have to be taken into account. The conversion rate of 2 for 1 is stipulated in pre-split shares. These shares would be worth 2 new shares each.

20,000 x 6/12 x 2 = 20,000

Incremental impact:

$24,000/20,000 = $1.20

Since this is less than the basic EPS, the potential conversion is dilutive.

6% BONDS:

Impact on earnings:

$1,000,000 x .06 x .6 x 6/12 = $18,000

Tip!

We must consider these bonds even though they had been converted by year-end. Again, the objective is to show all actual and potential dilutive conversions as though they had happened at the beginning of the year (unless the convertible securities or options were issued later).

Impact on shares:

20,000 shares issued x 2 x 6/12 = 20,000

Again, we must account for the stock split. We must weight this calculation because the basic calculation already assumes conversion June 30.

Incremental impact:

$18,000/20,000 = .90

Since this is less than the basic EPS, this is considered dilutive.

4% PREFERRED SHARES:

Impact on earnings:

Tip!

This conversion will not take place until 2006, which is beyond the 10-year mark. Likely, this would not be considered in the calculations since the potential conversion is so far away.

WARRANTS:

Impact on earnings:

If the 25,000 warrants were exercised, the company would receive 25,000 x 50 = $1,250,000 which would likely be invested.

$1,250,000 x .10 x .6 x 9/12 = $56,250

The rate of return of 10% is adjusted for taxes and is 6% after taxes. Also, it is prorated since the warrants were not issued until March 31, 1997.

Impact on share calculation:

25,000 shares x 2 x 9/12 = 37,500

The share conversion must be adjusted for the split and since the warrants were only issued March 31, the calculation must be weighted.

Incremental impact:

$56,250/37,500 = $1.50

Since this is less than the basic EPS, it is considered to be dilutive.

SHARE APPRECIATION PLAN:

If the rights under the plan had been exercised at the beginning of the year, it would have been worth:

30,000 x 2 x ($22—$20) = $120,000

The above takes into account the stock split. Since the benefit is receivable in shares, this would have resulted in the following number of shares being issued:

$120,000/$22 = 5,455

It would also have resulted in a lower charge to income for accrual for the plan. At year-end, the shares were $26, $6 above the $20 benchmark. The $40 benchmark is adjusted for the stock split. This benefit was therefore worth $6 x 60,000 = $360,000. Again, since the agreement includes pre-split numbers, they must be adjusted. 30,000 old shares would be equivalent to 60,000 new shares. Assuming that the company chose to amortize this over the estimated service lives of the executives (5 years), this would have resulted in an after-tax charge/accrual of $360,000/5 years x .6 = $43,200. If the rights had been exercised, the $120,000 would have been amortized over the 5 years.

$120,000 / 5 years x .6 = $14,400

Therefore, the incremental impact on net income if the rights had been exercised on Jan 1 would have been $43,200—$14,400 = $28,800.

Incremental impact on EPS:

$28,800/5,455 = $5.28

This is clearly anti-dilutive since it is greater than basic EPS and would therefore increase it.

The third step is to rank the potential dilutions from most dilutive to least dilutive.

6% bonds ($.90), 8% bonds ($1.20), warrants ($1.50), and lastly, share appreciation plan ($5.13).

The fourth step is to actually calculate the fully dilutive EPS.

	Earnings	Wt.-av.shares	EPS
Basic	$980,000	380,000	$2.58
6% bonds	18,000	20,000	
	998,000	400,000	2.50
8% bonds	24,000	20,000	
	1,022,000	420,000	2.43
Warrants	56,250	37,500	
	1,078,250	457,500	2.36
Share apprec. rights	28,800	5,455	
	1,107,050	462,955	2.39

The EPS declines for all of the dilutive instruments; however, it starts to increase again with the share appreciation rights. This signals anti-dilution and, since we are trying to show a worst case scenario, we should ignore any instruments that cause the EPS to increase. The fully diluted EPS is therefore $2.36.

Tip!

The EPS information would be presented either in the notes or at the bottom of the income statement. Basic, adjusted, and fully diluted would be shown for the current year and the preceding year, if comparative statements are disclosed. Remember that the preceding year calculations would be adjusted to reflect the stock split.

CASE

UNION CARBIDE CORPORATION

Union Carbide Corporation (UC) is the world's largest producer and marketer of ethylene glycol. The product (or a derivative of the product) is used in the textile industry to create antifreeze and bottles. The shares trade primarily on the New York stock exchange. In September 1990, UC set up an employee stock option plan (ESOP) to be effective January 1991. Under the plan, UC issued 15.1 million preferred shares ($325 million) to a trust that was set up to administer the plan. The purchase of the shares by the trust was funded by a 15-year, 10% loan from a UC subsidiary.

Subsequently, the loan was assigned to UC and recorded as "Unearned employee compensation" ($300 million at December 31, 1991) along with the preferred shares (the ESOP shares-$324 million at December 31, 1991), between debt and equity on the balance sheet. The ESOP shares are convertible to common shares on a one-for-one basis and have voting rights equal to common shares. Annual stock dividends of $1.90 per ESOP share are paid. The dividends are paid annually in ESOP shares.

Unearned employee compensation is reduced as ESOP stock is allocated by the trustee to employee accounts. Substantially, all employees are eligible to participate and UC matches employee contributions under the plan. The cost of the plan is recognized as incurred and was $28 million in 1991. During 1991, the trust allocated 1,163,865 shares to employees' accounts. Also 40,754 ESOP shares were redeemed at $21.50 each.

In the 1991 annual financial statements, the net loss applicable to common shareholders was $28 million and the weighted-average number of common shares was 126,766,208. Dividends of $19 million after tax were paid on the ESOP shares. The only other potentially dilutive securities, as shown in the notes to the financial statements, were $345,000,000 of 7.5% convertible subordinated debentures due 2012, convertible to common stock at $35.50 per share. Basic EPS and fully diluted EPS of 22 cents per share loss were shown in a note to the financial statements. The note stated that the preferred shares and the convertible debt had been taken into account in the calculation of fully diluted EPS. The consolidated effective tax rate is 34%.

The financial statements were given a clean opinion by the company's auditors.

Required

a) Identify and discuss the substance of the arrangement. Discuss the accounting issues.

b Recalculate basic and fully diluted EPS. Explain why they are the same given that there are dilutive securities and the notes to the statements specify that they have been taken into account in the calculations.

SOLUTION TO CASE

UNION CARBIDE CORPORATION

Use the Study Steps in the TOOLKIT to help analyze this complex transaction. **Tip!**

Understanding the transaction and analyzing the financial reporting issues.

The **substance** of this arrangement is not easy to decipher from the information given in the financial statements. The **legal form** of the transaction is quite complex and does not readily divulge the real substance. It would appear that the following arrangement has been set up by the company:

- The company has set aside a special class of shares (ESOP shares) for purchase by employees in the plan. All employees are eligible to join the plan.
- Only 1,163,865 of the 15,200,000 total available shares have actually been issued to employees

Tip! **It is usually helpful to draw a diagram noting main parties and what the company is giving up and what it is getting.**

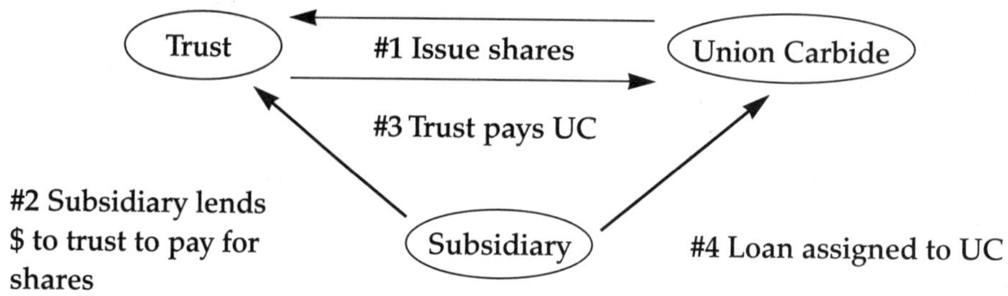

Tip! **Next, let's attempt to journalize the transaction on the books of UC.**

#1. Shares issued

dr. receivable from trust
  cr. preferred shares

#2. Subsidiary lends $ to trust (no JE on UC books)

#3. Trust pays UC

dr. cash
  cr. receivable from trust

#4. Loan assigned to UC

dr. receivable from trust
  cr. intercompany payable to subsidiary

Note that the intercompany account would be eliminated on consolidation of subsidiary. This leaves UC with the preferred shares issued and the receivable from the trust. Note that the receivable from the trust has been renamed "unearned employee compensation" and is classified as a contra account to the preferred shares. As the shares are issued to the employee (and compensation awarded), the unearned compensation account is decreased.

dr. compensation expense
  cr. unearned compensation

Now we understand the mechanics of the transaction, i.e., how it was journalized.

Tip! **Next let's look at the intent.**

The **intent** of the stock option plan is not clear. The shares are available to all employees, which would seem to signal that the intent of the plan was to raise funds. However, since the company is paying for half of the shares and the employee need only pay for the other half, it would appear to be compensatory (deeper discount). UC appears to be treating this as a compensatory plan and therefore, this signals its intent.

Remember that costs of issuing shares under non-compensatory plans are treated as capital transactions and under compensatory plans, costs are treated as expenses. Therefore, it is important to determine the type of plan up-front. **Tip!**

Recognition issue:

The accounting here is very interesting and, to a certain extent, is made more complex by the way the transaction was effected. For instance, the **economic substance** in part (a) above is quite simplistic and would normally require very straightforward accounting. Setting aside a special class of shares for an employee stock plan would normally require no more than note disclosure. Furthermore, the issuance of shares under the plan would normally generate the following entry, assuming that it was considered to be a compensatory plan:

dr. remuneration expense/deferred cost	$12.5 million	
dr. cash	12.5 million	
cr. preferred stock		25 million

(1,163,865 shares times $21.50 = approx 25 million
$21.50 = $325 million total/15.1 million shares in total)

The debit to expense would be for the amount funded by the company. It could be treated as a type of remuneration (as above) or the shares could just be issued at half the price with the following entry, assuming that it is considered to be a non-compensatory plan:

dr. cash
    cr. preferred stock

Compare the above to how it has actually been accounted for (see previous journal entries and diagrams above). Keep in mind that all details are not known and that we are merely trying to piece together the transaction from the information presented in the annual report. Also remember that the company follows U.S. GAAP, which may be different from Canadian GAAP.

When the plan was initiated, no shares had yet been issued to employees and, therefore, it would not make sense to book anything. In this case, however, the full amount of designated shares were in fact issued to a trustee, the intent being that the trustee would then allocate the shares to employees. This might have been done to save issue costs or to formalize the plan for the employees.

Remuneration costs were separately identified as $28 million for the year in the financial statements. These costs were **recognized** as the shares were issued to the employees and the compensation costs **incurred**. Another approach might be to **amortize** these costs over the period benefited by the existence of the plan. The former is less **conservative** as it recognizes the full cost at the end, when the employee actually gets the shares. Presumably, the company might benefit from the plan starting from when the plan is put in place to when the shares are issued (the **service period**).

Since preferred shares are shown net of the unearned employee compensation account on the balance sheet, this results in the same accounting as we identified initially. Net preferred stock has a balance of $325—$300 = $25 million and compensation expense is

$25 million ($28 million, in actual fact). It is unclear how the dividends have been accounted for. Retained earnings/net income have been debited for the full amount but it is not clear where the credit has been booked (perhaps contributed surplus). Also, the ending balance in the net preferred shares account is actually $24 million and this is presumably due to the redemption of some of the shares as noted in the statements (40,754 x $21.50 = $876,211 or $1 million rounded).

Measurement:

How should the compensation expense be **measured** since it is **nonmonetary**? The value would appear to be determined by the value initially assigned to the special preferred shares. Since there is no market for these shares, it would be difficult to value these shares. The higher the value assigned, the higher the compensation expense.

Presentation/classification:

The classification of the preferred shares outside the shareholders' equity section is interesting, especially since the shares carry voting rights and would appear to be equity from a legal perspective. According to the 1990 statements, this was done in order to conform with the Securities Exchange Commission requirements.

(b) Basic EPS = $(28,000,000)/126,776,208 = $(.22)

Fully diluted EPS should presumably take into account the convertible preferred shares and the convertible debt. However, it is the same as the basic EPS number. Why is this?

Whenever there is a situation where there is a loss per share for the basic EPS calculation, a fully diluted calculation does not make sense. Since we are looking only for dilutive securities, we would only include securities that increase the basic loss per share.

Interestingly, anytime the denominator or the weighted-average number of shares increases (which it always will with any fully diluted calculation since we are looking at what would happen if the instrument was converted and more shares issued), the loss per share will decrease. Therefore, any instrument will be anti-dilutive.

For example, if the debt was converted, it would result in $345 million/$35.50 = 9,718,310 additional shares being issued and $345 million x .075 x .66 = $17 million in interest being avoided. Even if we ignore the interest savings, the calculation would be:

$(28,000,000)/(126,776,208 + 9,718,310) = $(.21)

If we include the interest savings:

[$(28) million + $17 million]/136,494,518 = $(.08)

Both show EPS as being greater than the basic EPS. The same happens for the convertible preferred shares. Therefore, the fully diluted calculation is the same as the basic EPS since the convertible securities are anti-dilutive.

SELECTED SOLUTIONS FROM THE TEXTBOOK

EXERCISE 18-8

Quadeville Limited
JOURNAL ENTRY
September 1, 1998

Cash	4,220,000	
Unamortized Bond Issue Costs		30,000
Bonds Payable (4,000 x $1,000)		4,000,000
Premium on Bonds Payable—Schedule 1		136,000
Contributed Surplus Stock Warrants—Schedule 1		24,000
Bond Interest Expense—Schedule 2		90,000
(To record the issuance of the bonds)		

Schedule 1

Premium on Bonds Payable and Value of Stock Warrants	
Sales price (4,000 x $1,040)	$4,160,000
Face value of bonds	4,000,000
	160,000
Deduct value assigned to stock warrants (4,000 x 2 = 8,000; 8,000 x $3)	24,000
Premium on bonds payable	$136,000

Schedule 2

Accrued Bond Interest to Date of Sale		
Face value of bonds	$4,000,000	
Interest rate		9%
Annual interest		$360,000
Accrued interest for 3 months—($360,000 x 3/12)		$90,000

EXERCISE 18-10

(a) Computation of the value of the stock option using the date of the grant as the basis for valuation:

Market value of 30,000 shares at date of grant ($47 per share)	$1,410,000
Option price of 30,000 shares ($40)	1,200,000
Value of stock option and amount of executive compensation	$210,000

(b) January 2, 1997

Deferred Compensation Expense	210,000	
Contributed Surplus—Stock Options		210,000
(To record compensation expense for 2-year		

period based on difference between fair market value and option price at date of grant)

December 31, 1997		
Compensation Expense	105,000	
Deferred Compensation Expense		105,000
(To allocate expense under stock option plan to 1997 [1/2 x $210,000])		

December 31, 1998		
Compensation Expense	105,000	
Deferred Compensation Expense		105,000
(To allocate expense under stock option plan to 1998 [1/2 x $210,000])		

January 3, 1999		
Cash (20,000 x $40)	800,000	
Contributed Surplus—Stock Options ($210,000 x 2/3)	140,000	
Common Shares (20,000 x $48)		940,000
(To record issuance of 20,000 shares upon exercise of options at option price of $40 and a market price of $47 at date of grant)		

(Note: The market price of the shares has no relevance in this entry and the following one.)

May 1, 1999		
Cash (10,000 x $40)	400,000	
Contributed Surplus—Stock Options ($210,000 x 1/3)	70,000	
Common Shares		470,000
(To record issuance of 10,000 no-par value shares upon exercise of options at option price of $40 and a market price of $47 at date of grant)		

EXERCISE 18-23

1. (a) Number of shares for basic earnings per share:

Initial issue of shares	800,000
April 1, 1998, issue (3/4 x 400,000)	300,000
Total	1,100,000

(b) Number of shares for fully diluted earnings per share:

Initial issue of shares	800,000	
April 1, 1994, issue (3/4 x 400,000)	300,000	
Conversion of bonds (1/2 x 600 x 40)	12,000	
Total		1,112,000 shares

2. (a) Earnings for basic earnings per share:

After-tax net income		$1,435,000

(b) Earnings for fully diluted earnings per share:

After-tax net income		$1,435,000
Add back interest on convertible bonds net of income tax:		
Interest (600,000 x .08 x 1/2)	$24,000	
Less income taxes (40%)	9,600	14,400
Total		$1,449,400

(Note: In this problem, the earnings per share computed for basic earnings per share is $1.31 ($1,435,000 ÷ 1,100,000) and the fully diluted earnings per share is also 1.31.As a result, only one earnings per share number would be presented as the basic earnings per share is the same as a regular computation of earnings per share.)

SOLUTION TO PROBLEM

PROBLEM 18-9

(a)

Powassan Corporation
SCHEDULE COMPUTING NET INCOME
For the Year Ended September 30, 1998

	Income Before Extraordinary Item	Extraordinary Item	Net Income
As tentatively reported	$830,000		$830,000
Gain on expropriation		$270,000	270,000
Inventory write-off	(200,000)		(200,000)
Adjusted income	$630,000	$270,000	$900,000

Note: The gain on settlement of the lawsuit would be reported as a prior period adjustment and described in a note to the financial statements. The note would include the per share amount ($0.64).

Event Outstanding	Dates Outstanding	Shares ment	Restate- of Year	Fraction Shares	Weighted
Beginning balance	Oct. 1—Dec. 1	100,000	2	2/12	33,333
Issued shares	Dec. 1—March 1	620,000*		3/12	155,000
Reacquired shares	March 1—Apr. 1	560,000		1/12	46,667
Issued shares	Apr. 1—Sept. 30	620,000		6/12	310,000
Weighted average number of shares outstanding					545,000

*(100,000 x 2) + 420,000

OR

	Number of Shares			Share-Months	
Date	Increase (Decrease)	Outstanding	Months Outstanding	Original	Restated
10/1/97	100,000		2	200,000	
12/1/97	2 for 1 split	200,000		x 2	400,000
12/1/97	420,000	620,000	3		1,860,000
3/1/98	(60,000)	560,000	1		560,000
4/1/98	60,000	620,000	6		3,720,000
			12		6,540,000

Weighted average shares = 6,540,000 ÷ 12 = 545,000

Earnings per share

Basic earnings per share:

Income before extraordinary items ($630,000 ÷ 545,000)	$1.16
Extraordinary gain ($270,000 ÷ 545,000)	.50
Net income ($900,000 ÷ 545,000)	1.65

(b)

Schedule A
Computation of Earnings per Share

	Number of Shares	Income	Per Share Amount
Basic earnings per share	545,000	$4,125,000	$7.57
Dilutive securities:			
Convertible debentures (Exhibit 3)	90,000	151,200	1.68
Subtotal	635,000	4,276,200	6.73
Series A warrants (Exhibit 1)	80,000	480,000	6.00
Total	715,000	4,756,200	6.65

Fully diluted earnings per share (the lowest possible amount) is $6.65.

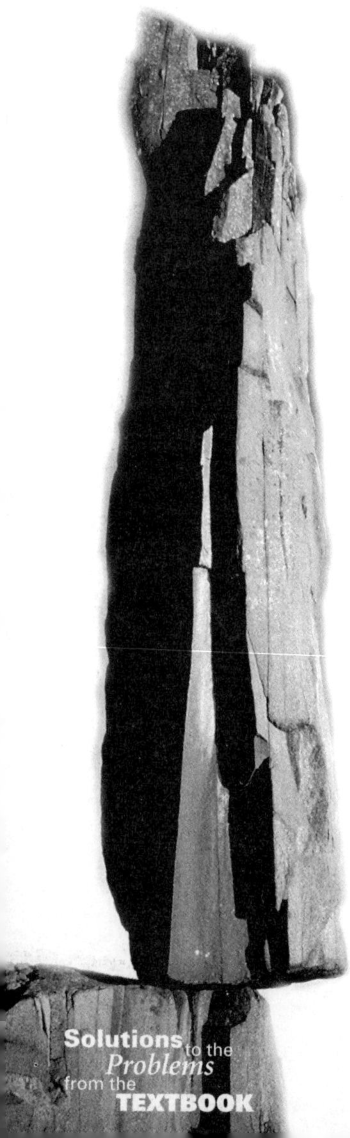

Exhibit 1
Stock Purchase Warrants—Series A

Income that would have been earned on the proceeds from exercise of the warrants from October 1, 1997 to September 30, 1998 (40,000 x 2 x $30 x .20)	$480,000
Issuable common shares (40,000 x 2)	80,000
Earnings per share effect of exercise of stock options ($480,000 ÷ 80,000)	$ 6.00

Exhibit 2
Stock Purchase Warrants—Series B

Income that would have been earned on the proceeds from exercise of the warrants from April 1, 1998 to September 30, 1998 (30,000 x $45 x 6/12 x .20)	$135,000
Issuable common shares (30,000 x 6/12)	15,000
Earnings per share effect of exercise of stock options ($135,000 ÷ 15,000)	$ 9.00

$9.00 per share is greater than $7.57 (basic EPS) therefore these securities are antidilutive.

Exhibit 3
7% Convertible Debentures

Interest expense reduction as a result of conversion ($3,600,000 x .07 x [1—.4])	$151,200
Number of common shares issuable upon conversion ([$3,600,000 ÷ 1,000] x 25)	90,000
Earnings per share effect of exercise of stock options ($151,200 ÷ 90,000)	$ 1.68

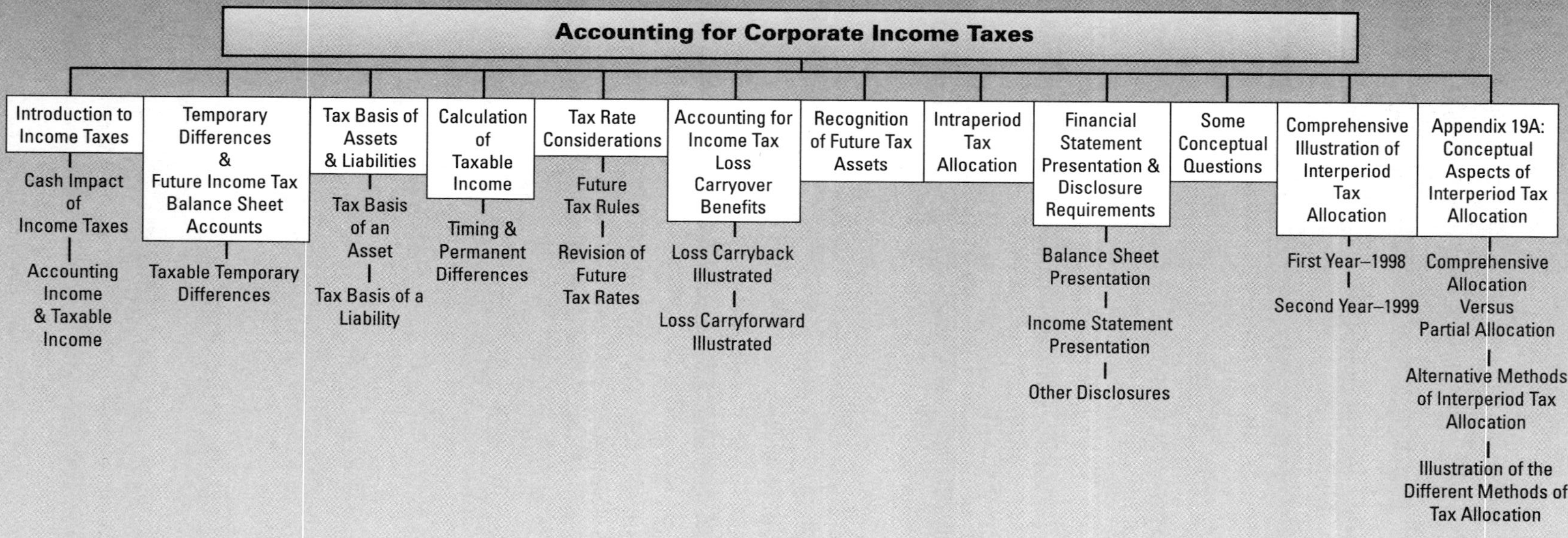

Accounting for Corporate Income Taxes
Introduction to Income Taxes
Cash Impact of Income Taxes
Accounting Income & Taxable Income
Temporary Differences & Future Income Tax Balance Sheet Accounts
Taxable Temporary Differences
Tax Basis of Assets & Liabilities
Tax Basis of an Asset
Tax Basis of a Liability
Calculation of Taxable Income
Timing & Permanent Differences
Tax Rate Considerations
Future Tax Rules
Revision of Future Tax Rates
Accounting for Income Tax Loss Carryover Benefits
Loss Carryback Illustrated
Loss Carryforward Illustrated
Recognition of Future Tax Assets
Intraperiod Tax Allocation
Financial Statement Presentation & Disclosure Requirements
Balance Sheet Presentation
Income Statement Presentation
Other Disclosures
Some Conceptual Questions
Comprehensive Illustration of Interperiod Tax Allocation
First Year–1998
Second Year–1999
Appendix 19A: Conceptual Aspects of Interperiod Tax Allocation
Comprehensive Allocation Versus Partial Allocation
Alternative Methods of Interperiod Tax Allocation
Illustration of the Different Methods of Tax Allocation

chapter 19

ACCOUNTING FOR CORPORATE INCOME TAXES

PERSPECTIVE

This area is similar to pensions and leases in that there is a theoretical component of reasonable complexity, as well as, a complex technical component. To add to the complexity is the fact that historically, accountants have not been able to agree on the accounting. In 1997, a new Handbook section was issued (Handbook 3465) which is effective for years ending on or after January 1, 2000. This new standard brings the accounting more in line with U.S. and international standards.

INSIGHTS

- *Even though the new standard does not take effect for some time, it will be the focus of this material since it is quite radically different from the old method and since the CICA encourages earlier adoption. Note that the Handbook requires retroactive application.*
- *A sound understanding of the theoretical underpinnings is required here, as well as a solid grasp of the calculations. Therefore, this chapter will cover both aspects.*

STUDY STEPS

1. Understanding the Nature of Income Taxes

STUDY STEPS

Net income versus taxable income

Income taxes are charged by the government and are calculated based on net income as defined by the Tax Act ("**taxable income**"). The area is complicated because **net income**, as defined by GAAP, is not the same as taxable income. Net income for GAAP purposes is **calculated according to accounting principles or rules (i.e., GAAP)**, with the objective being to provide information that is **useful for decision making**. This objective encompasses principles that deal with when and how to recognize revenues and costs, among others.

Taxable income is calculated **according to rules and regulations laid out in the Income Tax Act**. The objectives of the Tax Act are quite different from the objectives of GAAP. The Tax Act is more specific (i.e., to provide guidance in the calculation of taxable income). Furthermore, the rules encompassed by the Tax Act were set out for various reasons (e.g., to stimulate spending in certain areas by allowing the expenditures to be tax deductible immediately, to discourage certain expenditures by not allowing them to be deducted in arriving at taxable income [e.g., club dues], to maximize revenues collected by the government from taxes, etc.).

Tax **expense** per the income statement is based on **net income** for GAAP or accounting purposes, and taxes actually **paid** to the government per the tax return are based on **taxable income**, which must be calculated separately. Differences between the two give rise to **future tax assets** or **future tax liabilities**.

	Calculated According to . . .	Based on . . .
Tax expense per income statement	GAAP	Net income for accounting purposes
Taxes per tax return	Tax Act	Taxable income

Interperiod versus intraperiod tax allocation

Interperiod tax allocation deals with allocating taxes between different reporting periods, such as this year and future years. **Intraperiod tax allocation** deals with allocating taxes between different lines on the income statement (e.g., tax expenses may be allocated to net income from continuing earnings, discontinued earnings, and extraordinary items). In general, with respect to the latter, the tax expense should be matched with the net income that it relates to. The bulk of this chapter will be devoted to interperiod allocation since this is the more complex of the two.

Special tax rules relating to loss years

If a company suffers losses in a given year it does not have to pay taxes. Furthermore, a company may refile its past years' tax returns and deduct the losses from past years' taxable income. By doing this, they reduce past years' taxable income and therefore the taxes payable for past years. Often they are then able to recover the excess of the taxes that they actually paid for these past years over the new taxes payable calculated. The losses may also be carried forward to offset and reduce future taxable income, thereby reducing taxes payable in the future.

To the extent that the company can reduce the amount of taxes either from past or future years, this represents a benefit to the company. According to the Tax Act, a company may carry tax losses back three years and forward seven years.

To the extent that the company can usually recover taxes already paid if it uses the losses to offset past income, it is wise to carry the taxes back first. Any remaining tax loss may be carried forward to offset future income. **Tip!**

The company may also refile the tax return adjusting for discretionary deductions such as CCA. CCA need not be taken each year, unlike depreciation.

2. Understanding How Income Taxes Fit into the Financial Reporting Model and Conceptual Framework -Analysis and Critical Thinking

STUDY STEPS

Exhibit 19-1: Income Taxes
Relevant criteria, definitions and issues

	How it relates to taxes	Relevant criteria/definitions	Topic specific analysis- how it should be	What makes the analysis challenging–how it is
Recognition	• when should taxes be recognized in the f/s?	• general principle is to recognize FTL or FTA if recovery or settlement of asset or liability will result in future taxes payable or receivable • for FTA–realization must be **likely** • **definition of asset and liability** • **matching** supports comprehensive tax allocation	• basis for determination of FTL or FTA is whether there is a **difference between tax basis and carrying value of assets and liab on B/S (=temporary differences)** • DTD are TD that will result in future tax deductions (=FTA) • TTD are TD that will result in future taxable income (=FTL) • NB specific rules for determining tax basis • reassess likelihood of realization of FTA	• complexities of application • gross up provisions where tax base is less than cost • netting provisions where the tax base is greater than cost
Measurement	• how should they be measured if recognized? • which tax rates?	• since the tax amounts are future receivables or payables, must re-estimate every B/S date	• use enacted rates • must re-estimate at every balance sheet date–booked as future tax expense–FTE	• no discounting due to subjectivity
Presentation	• how to classify • disclosure	• current taxes payable/ receivable as current assets/liabilities • taxes receivable from LCB as current assets • segregate current portion of FTA/FTL (base on underlying A and L) •may offset CTL/FTL and CTA/FTA if same tax authority • disclosures		

Prepared by Irene Wiecek

It may be useful to review the definitions in #3 below prior to reviewing the exhibit. **Tip!**

3. Becoming Proficient in Related Calculations.

STUDY STEPS

Terminology

Before getting into the calculations, it is worthwhile to the accounting terminology used. These definitions come from *Handbook* 3465.

CICA HANDBOOK

Definitions:

Cost (benefit) of current income taxes = amount of income taxes payable/(recoverable) in respect of the period = **CTE** or current tax expense for expense portion

Cost (benefit) of future income taxes = change during the period in future income tax liabilities/future income tax assets = **FTE** or future tax expense for the expense portion

Future Tax Asset (FTA) = amounts of income tax benefits arising in respect of
- i) deductible temporary differences
- ii) carryforward of unused tax losses
- iii) carryforward of unused income tax reductions

Future Tax Liabilities (FTL) = amounts of income taxes arising from taxable temporary differences

Temporary differences (TD) = differences between the tax basis of an asset or liability and its carrying amount on the balance sheet. Temporary differences may be either:

Deductible temporary differences = **DTD**, which are TD that will result in tax deductions in future years when the carrying amount of the assets or liability is recovered or settled or, **Taxable temporary differences** = **TTD**, which are TD that will result in taxable amount in future years when the carrying amount of the asset or liability is recovered or settled

Method for calculating journal entries

The relationship between these items is examined below. Calculating the income taxes and journal entries is best achieved by the following three steps:

Income years

1) Calculate taxable income (TI) according to the Tax Act.

Tip! **Begin with net income per financial statements and add/deduct reconciling items. What you are doing here is converting net income from a GAAP basis to a Tax basis and using the Tax Act as a source of rules versus GAAP.**

2) Multiply TI by the current tax rate to give you CTE. Complete part 1 of the journal entry.

Tip! **The tax rate in this step is always the same—the current tax rate. This amount is the current amount of taxes that the company must pay to the government according to its tax return.**

Tip! **Begin putting together the journal entry. This first part is very straightforward: dr. CTE (the expense) and cr. TP (current liability).**

3) Prepare a tax balance sheet and compare to the financial statement balance sheet. Calculate the difference between the two on a line by line basis. Complete part 2 of the journal entry.

These differences = TD and are either deductible (DTD) or taxable (TTD) in future years. **Tip!**

DTD result in FTA and TTD result in FTL. **Tip!**

To assist in remembering the above relationship, remember that future tax deductions have benefit to the company and, therefore, result in assets or FTA. Future taxable amounts will result in the company paying out more taxes in the future and, hence, are recognized as a liability or FTL. **Tip!**

Multiply DTD/TTD by the future tax rate (if enacted) to give you FTE and FTA/FTL: dr. FTE and cr. FTL, or dr. FTA and cr. FTE. **Tip!**

Let's look at some examples.

EXAMPLE #1

Assume the following for Company A:

Company A
Balance sheet
December 31, 1999

	1999	1998
Cash	$120	$100
Inventory	20	20
Fixed assets	90	100
	$230	$220
Equity	230	220

Company A
Income Statement
Period ended December 31, 1999

Revenues	$50
Cost of Sales	(20)
Depreciation	(10)
	20

Other:

- CCA = $25

Tip! **CCA = capital cost allowance, which is, essentially tax depreciation.**

- Tax rate = 40% -no future rates enacted yet

Step #1—Calculate TI

Taxable income is calculated as follows:

Net income	$20
Add back depreciation	10
Deduct CCA	(25)
Taxable income	5

Step#2—Calculate current taxes payable

TI X tax rate = $5 X 40% = $2.

Therefore, the amount of taxes payable is $2. This is recorded as dr. CTE (expense) $2 and cr. TP (current liability) $2.

Step #3—Compare tax and book (financial statement) balance sheets and calculate FTA or FTL

	F/S	Tax	TD
Cash	$120	$120	—
Inventory	20	20	—
Fixed assets	90	75	15

Tip! **You need only look at assets and liabilities as equity will be merely a balancing figure.**

Tip! **The tax balance sheet is the opening tax balance sheet (= to the f/s opening balance sheet in this case) adjusted for items from the tax return or reconciling items from #1 above. Therefore, tax fixed assets are $100—CCA or $25 = $75. Note that inventory is the same for book and tax, since there were no reconciling items in step #1 relating to these items and there is otherwise no information given that would lead us to conclude that the tax basis is different from the book basis.**

Tip! **The TD of $15 relating to fixed assets is a TTD since we have already had the benefit of accelerated tax deductions in the current year. This means that the company will have to pay more taxes in future years—(hence a TTD and FTL).**

The TTD is multiplied by the current tax rate since there are no enacted future tax rates and, therefore, the current rate is the best estimate of the future rate. **Tip!**

The second part of the journal entry is as follows: $15 X 40% = $6: dr. FTE, cr. FTL. The total journal entry is as follows:

dr. CTE	$2	
dr. FTE	6	
cr. TP		2
cr. FTL		6

EXAMPLE #2

Let's assume that, in the year 2000, everything remains the same except the expected future tax rate increases to 45% and depreciation = CCA at $10.

Assume net income = $30 and there are no additional TD for simplicity's sake.

Step #1

Net income	$30
Add back depreciation	10
Deduct CCA	(10)
Taxable income	$30

Step #2

TP = $30 X 40% = $12

dr. CTE $12 cr. TP $12

Step #3

	F/S	Tax	TD		Tax rate		FTL
Cash	$120	$120	—		—		—
Inventory	20	20	—		—		—
Fixed assets	80	65	15	X	45%	=	$7

Note that the balance sheet keeps track of cumulative TD. The calculation above recalculates the cumulative TD and then re-estimates the tax impact by using the new tax rate. **Tip!**

The new tax rate is used because it is enacted and is the best estimate of the future amount that will be paid out. **Tip!**

It is still a tax liability since the tax basis is lower and therefore this will result in more taxes being paid out in future. **Tip!**

Tip! **At this point we must take the new estimate of $7 and deduct the amount already booked = $6 and just book the change. Changes to FTA and FTL are booked through FTE: dr. FTE $1, cr. FTL $1**

The total journal entry is as follows for year 2000:

dr. CTE	$12	
dr. FTE	1	
cr. TP		12
cr. FTL		1

TTDs and DTDs examined

At this point, it is worthwhile to review examples of TD, DDT and TDT. The following chart looks at some examples of each:

Examples of DDT and TDT:

Capital assets
- NBV> UCC = TTD = FTL since deductions already taken for tax earlier
- UCC> NBV = DTD = FTA since the higher UCC means higher CCA deductions in future = benefit

Revenues
- % of completion used for book purpose, and revenues recognized on completion for tax
  - related B/S account = CIP less Billings plus AR. The tax balance would be nil if no cash yet collected since no revenues yet recognized. Therefore, the book assets are greater (like NBV > UCC above) and this is a TTD and FTL. This one is intuitive since these are revenues already recognized for book that will be recognized in future for tax, resulting in future TI and future taxes payable

Development costs deferred for book and deducted for tax
- in this case, the book asset would again be greater than the tax asset (=0 since already deducted on tax return instead of being deferred). This means TTD and FTL since the deductions have already been taken up front for tax resulting in no tax shelter later.

Warranty costs deducted for book on an accrual basis but not for tax until actually paid out.
- in this case, the books would have a liability and the tax balance sheet would have nothing. This is a DDT or FTA since this is a future tax deduction that will decrease future TI.

These are a few common examples. There are additional examples in the text and in the Handbook.

Tip! **Although this list is not conclusive, it may be used as an aid in understanding the reasoning behind how to classify these items.**

Tax basis examined

Now that we understand the basic method and have a grasp of how to identify the types of TD, it is worthwhile to look more closely at the method for calculating the tax basis for the purposes of identifying TD.

As a general rule, when looking at the tax basis of an asset, begin with cost and deduct any amounts subsequently deducted on the tax return (e.g., capital assets). If the amounts are not deductible until the asset is sold, the tax basis would be the amount that is deductible according to the Tax Act when the asset is sold (e.g., portfolio investment).

When the cost of an asset is never deductible from taxable income but any proceeds on disposition are not taxable either, then the tax basis is equal to the carrying amount and there are no TDs (e.g., life insurance policy).

There are some exceptions to the above. Sometimes an asset is purchased where the tax base is lower than the book base. This asset would be worth less since it does not have the usual "tax breaks" associated with it. Conversely, if you had the opportunity to buy an asset whose full value you could deduct on your tax return to reduce TI versus an asset, where only some of the cost was deductible, which one would you pay more for? The latter one is worth less and, therefore, the amount that you paid would reflect this. The Handbook section attempts to adjust for this since it argues that the asset is now valued net of tax impact, whereas other assets and liabilities on the balance sheet are not booked net of tax. In this case, the asset would be grossed up and a FTL recorded.

The gross-up is calculated as follows:

$$\frac{(\text{Cost of asset—tax basis}) \text{ X tax rate}}{(1\text{—tax rate})}$$

EXAMPLE #3

If an asset was purchased for $5,000 and the tax base was $3000, the gross-up would be calculated as follows, (assuming a tax rate of 40%):

$$\frac{(\$5000\text{—}\$3000) \text{ X } 40\%}{60\%} = \$1333$$

The asset would be recorded as follows dr. asset $6,333, cr. cash 5,000, cr. FTL 1,333. This may be verified by looking at the new TD, which would be calculated as follows:

$6,333—3,000 = 3,333

The FTL would be $3,333 X .4 = 1, 333, or the amount recorded above.

If the tax basis was higher, the asset would be recorded at a lower value and a FTA recorded.

The "gross-down" would be calculated in the same manner . **Tip!**

Loss years

Accounting for income taxes in loss years is different than accounting for income taxes where there is taxable income. As previously noted, no taxes would be payable and there might even be some benefit to the extent that the loss may be used to shelter past or future taxable income.

Loss years

1) Calculate Taxable Loss according to the Tax Act.

Tip! **Begin with net loss per financial statements and add/deduct reconciling items. As with the income year, what you are doing here is converting net income from a GAAP basis to a tax basis and using the Tax Act as a source of rules as opposed to GAAP.**

Tip! **Things like depreciation will always be added back since they are not deductible for tax purposes. CCA, however, is a discretionary deduction that may not be taken in a loss year.**

2) Take the loss from 1 and carry it back up to 3 years to reduce TI in any of those three previous years.

Tip! **Normally, companies carry the loss back to the earliest year, since as they move forward in time, they eventually lose the option of recovering taxes from the earlier years.**

3) Multiply the loss by the historic tax rate to give you CTE. Complete part 1 of the journal entry.

Tip! **The benefit is measured at the rate that the company previously paid taxes at i.e., the historic rate.**

Tip! **Begin putting together the journal entry. Since this is a benefit, the entry is reversed from the norm: dr. taxes receivable/TP, and cr. CTE.**

4) If there is still some loss left over, it may be carried forward and used to shelter future TI. Note that this would only be booked if realization of the benefit is likely.

Tip! **Take the remaining loss and multiply it by the future tax rate if enacted and if realization of the benefit is likely. The journal entry would be: dr. FTA, cr. FTE.**

5) Prepare a tax balance sheet and compare to the financial statement balance sheet. Calculate the difference between the two on a line by line basis. Complete part 2 of the journal entry. This is the same as for income years.

Note that analysis must be done where losses are carried forward and used to shelter future income. This is because there is less certainty of realizing the benefit than if the loss is carried back. On a loss carryback, all the company has to do to get their hands on the benefit, is to refile the return. On a going forward basis, there has to be TI for the benefit to be realized and there is no way the company can predict this.

The basic test is that realization must be likely. **Tip!**

Details to include in the analysis include both positive and negative evidence. These are summarized in the text and in the Handbook and are the subject of the case.

EXAMPLE #4

Assume Company A began operations in 1997 and had a TI of 100 on which it paid taxes of $50 at 50%. Assume there were no TD.

The following year, they suffer a tax loss of $150. Assume again that there are no TD. The tax rate in 1998 is 45% but, beyond that, no future tax rates have been enacted.

Step # 1—Calculate Taxable Loss according to the Tax Act.

Tax loss given—$150

Step #2—Take the loss from 1 and carry it back up to 3 years to reduce TI in any of those three previous years.

In this case, carry back to 1997 as follows:

Loss	$150
LCB	(100)
Remaining loss	50

Step #3—Multiply the loss by the historic tax rate to give you CTE. Complete part 1 of the journal entry.

Loss	$150
LCB	(100) X 50% = $50
Remaining loss	50

So far the journal entry would be as follows:

dr. taxes receivable	$50	
cr. CTE		$50

Step #4—If there is still some loss left over, it may be carried forward and used to shelter future TI. Note that this would only be booked if realization of the benefit is likely.

Loss	$150
LCB	(100) X 50% = $50
Remaining loss	50 X 45% = $22.5

Tip! **Assume that realization is likely in order to simplify the situation although, in real life, in this case, that would be a difficult point to argue.**

Tip! **Use the future rate since that is the best estimate of what the benefit will be realized at.**

dr. FTA	$22.5	
cr. FTE		$22.5

Tip! **Note that this gets booked as a FTA although it may be classified as a current FTA if it is likely to be realized in the following year.**

Step #5—Prepare a tax balance sheet and compare to the financial statement balance sheet. Calculate the difference between the two on a line by line basis. Complete part 2 of the journal entry. This is the same as for income years.

Not applicable for this example.

MULTIPLE CHOICE QUESTIONS

1) P Company Limited recognizes revenues for tax purposes earlier than it recognizes revenues for book or financial statement purposes. This would result in which of the following:

   a) TTD and therefore FTA
   b) TTD and therefore FTL
   c) DTD and therefore FTA
   d) DTD and therefore FTL

2) An enterprise owns a life insurance policy with a cash surrender value of $400,000. Proceeds received from the policy will not be taxable and premiums paid are not deductible. This results in which of the following:

   a) TTD and FTL
   b) DTD and FTA
   c) DTD and FTL
   d) None of the above

3) Assume that F Company Limited has accrued a fine in its financial statements for polluting the environment. Fines are never deductible for tax purposes. This would result in which of the following:

a) TTD and FTL

b) DTD and FTA

c) No TD

d) TTD and FTA

4) H Company Limited earned income in 1999 and suffered a loss for tax purposes in 2000. H Company decided to carry the loss back to 1999 in order to realize a benefit of the loss. The journal entry would be booked as which of the following?

a) dr. CTE cr. TP

b) dr. TP cr. CTE

c) dr. FTE cr. FTA

d) dr. FTA cr. FTE

5) M Company Limited earned income in 1999 and suffered a loss in 2000. Assume that even after carrying the loss back and recovering taxes previously paid, there was still some loss remaining for carry forward. The partial journal entry related to the recognition of any benefit from the carry forward would be recognized as follows (assume realization is likely):

a) dr. FTE cr. FTA

b) dr. FTA cr. FTE

c) dr. FTA cr. CTE

d) dr. TP cr. CTE

6) I Company Limited purchased an asset for $10,000 cash; however, $12,000 was deductible for tax purposes (40% tax rate). The journal entry to book the asset purchase would be as follows:

a) dr. asset	$10,000	cr. cash $10,000	
b) dr. asset	$12,000	cr. FTL $2,000	cr. cash $10,000
c) dr. asset	$ 8,667	dr. FTA $1,333	cr. cash $10,000
d) dr. asset	$8,000	dr. FTA $2,000	cr. cash $10,000

7) In 1998, G Company has TTD, which will reverse in 2000 and 2001 when the estimated tax rates are 45% and 46%. Current enacted rates are 43%. Historic rate is 40%. The TD should be recognized at which of the following rates:

a) 40%

b) 43%

c) 45% and 46%

d) 45%

8) Assume the same information as 7 above except assume it is one year later and the current enacted rate is now 44%. The FTL account would be adjusted using the following journal entry:

   a) no entry required since the future rates are still not enacted
   b) dr. FTE cr. FTL
   c) dr. CTE cr. FTL
   d) dr. CTE cr. TP

9) FTA relating to unused tax losses would only be recognized where it is more likely than not that the benefit would be realized. Some evidence is unfavourable and would support no recognition of the FTA. Which of the following would not be seen as unfavourable evidence?

   a) history of tax losses
   b) losses expected in early future years
   c) unsettled circumstances that, if unfavourably resolved, would adversely affect future operations and profit levels on a continuing basis
   d) the limitation imposed by the 3 year carryback and 7 year carryforward period

10) Examples of favourable evidence that would support recognition of an FTA relating to a loss include all but which of the following:

   a) existing sufficient DTD relating to the same taxable entity and the same taxation authority which would result in taxable amounts against which the unused tax losses could be utilized
   b) existing contracts or firm sales backlogs
   c) excess of fair value over tax basis of the entreprise's net assets in an amount sufficient to realize the future income tax asset
   d) strong earnings history

SOLUTIONS TO MULTIPLE CHOICE QUESTIONS

1) c) Since the revenues have already been recognized for tax purposes, this will not result in future taxable amounts, or a FTL.

2) d) According to Handbook 3465.12 c, when the cost of an asset is not deductible for tax purposes and any proceeds on settlement or recovery would not be taxable, the tax basis is equal to the carrying amount and, therefore, there is no TD at all.

3) c) According to Handbook 3465.13, the tax basis of the accrual would be equal to its carrying value, resulting in no TD.

4) b) The loss carry back would result in a credit being recognized on the income statement and a receivable being booked as a current asset (or a dr. to current taxes payable).

5) b) The carryforward would result in an asset and a credit to the income statement. However, it would be booked as FTA and FTE.

6) c) Since the tax basis is higher, there is an additional tax benefit implicit in the price paid. This should be separated out and recorded separately as FTA as follows:

(10,000—12,000) 40% / 60% = $1,333

This can be proved as follows: carrying value $8,667—tax basis $12,000 multiplied by tax rate 40% = $1,333

7) b) The future rates are only estimated rates and are not yet enacted. Therefore, the current enacted rate would be used as the best estimate of the future rates.

8) b) The FTL would be adjusted to reflect a more current estimate of the eventual payout. Any adjustments due to rate changes are booked as FTE (3465.64).

9) d) This is a normal time frame for loss recognition and would not unduly influence the decision to recognize or not recognize the FTA. It would only be an issue if the normal time frame were restricted such that realization of the benefit would be unlikely.

10) a) Existing TTD would be an example of favourable evidence to support recognition of an FTA relating to a loss (NOT existing DTD).

SHORT PROBLEMS

1) Purpose: To illustrate the three step method in calculating and preparing income tax journal entries.

The following information has been provided for Tax Allocation Inc. (TAI) for the year ended December 31, 2000.

Net income before taxes for f/s purposes	500,000
Included as expenses on f/s:	
• Nondeductible club dues accrued	10,000
• Provision for warranties (expense)	25,000
• Depreciation	100,000

Other information:

- Capital cost allowance (CCA) 200,000
- Tax rate 50%
- Actual costs incurred during 2000 for fixing products under warranty - 0
- The opening FTL account consists of the following as at January 1, 2000:

	Timing Diffs.	FTA/ (FTL) dr./(cr.)	Rate
NBV<UCC	$300,000	$135,000	45%
Warranty provision>costs	75,000	33,750	45%
Opening balance 1/1/00	$375,000	$168,750	45%

Assume no fixed asset purchases or disposals during the year. Fixed assets were $4,700,000 at the beginning of the year. Warranty accruals are booked as current liabilities.

Required

Using the three step method, calculate tax balances and prepare the journal entry required to book income taxes for the year ended December 31, 2000.

2) Purpose: To illustrate the financial statement balance sheet presentation for future taxes.

Required

Assume the same information as 1 and show how the FTA would be classified on the balance sheet.

3) Purpose: To illustrate accounting for tax losses carried back.

Tax Loss Inc. (TLI) is a manufacturing company that has been in business since 1997 and has always shown reasonably healthy profits. In 2000, however, TLI suffered unexpected losses due to a rampant recession. Selected financial information for the company for the past four years is as follows:

	1997	1998	1999	2000
Net income per f/s	$100,000	$120,000	$150,000	$(200,000)
Depreciation expense	25,000	25,000	25,000	25,000
CCA taken	50,000	50,000	50,000	0
Tax rates	40%	45%	50%	50%

Assume that there is sufficient information given above to calculate all TD. Assets were purchased for $1,000,000 at the beginning of 1997. There have been no other acquisitions or disposals since then. Assume that tax rates are enacted in the current year, i.e., the company would only know the current year tax rate and not future tax rates.

Required

Prepare the journal entries using the 3 or 5 step method for each of the four years. Assume that the company does not adjust previously taken CCA.

4) Purpose: To illustrate accounting for a loss carryforward.

TLCF suffered losses in 2000 of $1,200,000. The following tax information is available:

Tax rate	45%
Depreciation	$200,000
CCA taken	0

Required

Prepare the journal entry for 2000. Assume that it is more likely than not that any benefits will be realized and that the losses will not be carried back to offset past taxable income, if any. Also, assume that the opening Taxable Temporary Differences from prior years (booked at a historical rate of accumulation of 48%) is equal to Temporary Differences arising during 2000 such that, at year-end, there are no Temporary Differences remaining.

5) Purpose: To illustrate the accounting for a loss carryforward in the absence of likelihood of realization of the benefit.

Assume the same information as in 4; however, assume that it is not likely that the benefit will be realized.

Required

Prepare the journal entry and/or required note disclosures.

SOLUTIONS TO SHORT PROBLEMS

1)

Step #1—calculate TI
Taxable income is calculated as follows:

Net income	$500,000
Add back provision	25,000
Add back club dues	10,000

Add back depreciation	100,000
Deduct CCA	(200,000)
Taxable income	$435,000

Step #2—calculate current taxes payable

TI X tax rate = $435,000 X 50% = $217,500.

Therefore, the amount of taxes payable is $217,500. This is recorded as:

dr. CTE (expense) $217,500, cr. TP (current liability) $217,500

Step #3—compare tax and book (financial statement) balance sheets and calculate FTA or FTL

Since there is insufficient information to do a full balance sheet, a partial one will be re-created here. TD will be identified from step #1 and from other information in the question.

	F/S B/S	Tax B/S - "Tax Basis"	Difference	Rate	FTA
	←	(000's)			→
NBV / UCC	$4,600 (1)	$4,800 (2)	$200	50%	$100
Warranty accrual	100 (3)	—	100	50%	50
Club dues accrual	10	10 (4)			
TD			$300		150
X current rate(5)			50%		
FTA			$150		
Less already booked			168.75		
Adjustment required			18.75		

1) opening balance $4,700—depreciation $100
2) opening balance = $300 more than opening balance for NBV = $4,700 + 300 — CCA 200
3) opening balance $75 + current accrual 25. NB, the tax balance would be NIL since nothing has been accrued per tax return and no cash has been spent to fix assets under warranty
4) tax basis of club dues would be equal to carrying value (Handbook 3465.13)

use current enacted rate as best estimate of future rate

dr. FTE	$18,750	
cr. FTA		$18,750

Tip!

The cumulative TD must be identified each period and then the FTA/FTL account adjusted from the opening balance to the new balance. Any adjustments are booked through FTE.

2)

Balance Sheet
December 31, 2000

Assets:	
Current:	
FTA	$50,000
Non-current:	
FTA	$100,000

N.B. The TP would be shown as current liabilities

Tip! **Classification of the FTA is a function of how the underlying asset or liability is classified on the balance sheet. For instance, the NBV is classified as a non-current asset and, therefore, any related FTA are also classified as non-current. The warranty accrual is classified as a current liability and, therefore, any related FTA are also classified as current.**

3) First complete the income years

Step #1—calculate TI and Step #2—calculate current taxes payable

Taxable income is calculated as follows:

	1997	1998	1999
Net income	$100	$120	$150
Add back depreciation	25	25	25
Deduct CCA	(50)	(50)	(50)
Taxable income	$75	$95	$125
Tax rate	40%	45%	50%
	$30	$43	$62.5
dr. CTE (expense)	$30	$43	$62.5
cr. TP (current liability)	$30	$43	$62.5

Step #3—compare tax and book (financial statement) balance sheets and calculate FTA or FTL

Since there is insufficient information to do a full balance sheet, a partial one will be re-created here. TD will be identified from step #1 and from other information in the question.

	F/S B/S	Tax B/S - "Tax Basis"	Difference	Rate	FTL	Difference
NBV / UCC						
1997	$975	$950	25	40%	10	$10
1998	950	900	50	45%	23	13
1999	925	850	75	50%	38	15

Journal entries	1997	1998	1999
dr. FTE	$10	$13	$15
cr. FTL	$10	$13	$15

Tip!

The cumulative TD must be identified each period and then the FTA/FTL account adjusted from the opening balance to the new balance. Any adjustments are booked through FTE.

Tip!

For income statement purposes, the FTE should be broken down into two amounts: 1) the adjustment to the opening FTL balance to bring it to current rates and; 2) the Current TD

Loss year—2000

Step #1—Calculate Taxable Loss according to the Tax Act.

Net income/(loss)	$(200)
Add back depreciation	25
Tax loss	(175)

Step #2—Take the loss from 1 and carry it back up to 3 years to reduce TI in any of those three previous years.

Step #3—Multiply the loss by the historic tax rate to give you CTE. Complete part 1 of the journal entry.

In this case, carry back to 1997, 1998 and part to 1999 as follows:

Loss	$175		
1997	(75) X 40%	=	$30
1998	(95) X 45%	=	43
subtotal	5		
1999	(5) X 50%	=	2.5
remaining loss	—		$75.5

So far the journal entry would be as follows:

dr. taxes receivable	$75.5	
cr. CTE		$75.5

Step #4—If there is still some loss left over, it may be carried forward and used to shelter future TI. Note that this would only be booked if realization of the benefit is likely.

Not applicable for this example

Step #5—Prepare a tax balance sheet and compare to the financial statement balance sheet. Calculate the difference between the two on a line by line basis. Complete part

2 of the journal entry. This is the same as for income years.

	F/S B/S	Tax B/S - "Tax Basis"	Difference	Rate	FTL	Difference
NBV / UCC						
1997	$975	$950	25	40%	10	$10
1998	950	900	50	45%	23	13
1999	925	850	75	50%	38	15
2000	900	850	50	50%	25	(13)

The final part of the journal entry for the loss year would be as follows:

dr. FTL	$13	
cr. FTE		$13

Don't forget to split the FTE into the two components (adjustment to opening balance for rate change and current TD). **Tip!**

4)

Net loss	$(1,200,000)
Add back depreciation	200,000
Tax loss	1,000,000
X current Rate 45%	45%
	$450,000

The journal entry to recognize the benefit assuming no carryback and more likely than not, that the benefit will be realized is as follows:

dr. FTA	$450,000	
cr. FTE		$450,000

The benefit would be recognized as FTA and FTE, not as TP and CTE. **Tip!**

To adjust for changes in TD, the opening balance must be determined as follows:

Opening balance is equal to current TD except that they are TTD and, therefore, result in FTL of:

$200,000 X 48% = $96,000

At year-end, these have been reversed such that closing TD = 0 and, therefore, the FTL must be reversed at the old rate.

dr.FTL	$96,000	
cr. FTE		$96,000

Assuming that these taxes are all payable to the same taxation authority and are in the same jurisdiction, the taxes may be offset and the journal entries combined.

5) There would not be any benefit recognized; however, the amount of unused loss would be recorded in the notes to the financial statements (Handbook 3465.91).

The journal entry to adjust the TD would still be booked:

dr. FTL	$96,000	
cr. FTE		$96,000

CASE

BAKER COMPANY LIMITED

Baker Company Limited (BCL) was founded in 1997. 1997 had been a good year, as start-up years go, and the company broke even, showing a very small profit. Just as the company was getting established in the market, a full-fledged recession hit in 1998 with devastating effects. Demand for BCL's products in retail markets declined as consumers tightened their purse strings. Through tight cost controls, BCL managed to hold their own and recorded a small profit for 1998.

The recession finally petered out by the end of 1999; however, BCL was unable to remain profitable and suffered large operating losses. The losses were significantly greater than the profits reported in the previous two years. BCL management was not overly alarmed by the losses and had the following comments to make:

> The losses were expected given the widespread recession. Since the bulk of our sales are in retail markets and given the record unemployment levels, it is not surprising that consumer demand has fallen off. If BCL is compared with the industry, you will see that we fared much better than our competitors, some of whom went bankrupt.
>
> Keep in mind that we are a relatively new company and managed to record a profit in two out of our first three years. We attribute this to our strong management team and our ability as a streamlined company to react to the recession with cost control measures and an aggressive, yet flexible sales staff.
>
> We see ourselves positioned for a new growth spurt given that the economy seems to have recovered and a lot of "dead wood" (i.e., competition) has been cleared out. As a matter of fact, in that regard, the recession will have a positive impact on our short—to mid-term growth potential.

> BCL is on the verge of introducing two new products that will revolutionize the industry and assure us a solid earnings base for the future. These products will be introduced in 2000 and we have already lined up sufficient buyers that we predict we will at least break even in terms of net income in 2000. This is a very conservative forecast.

Although the effects of the recession were lessening, unemployment was still high in early 2000 and consumer spending had not increased significantly. Some economists were predicting that it would take two or three years for consumer confidence and spending to pick up to pre-recession levels.

Required

Adopt the role of the company's auditor and determine whether BCL should recognize the benefits of the losses suffered in the 1999 financial statements.

SOLUTION TO CASE

Overview

Assume that **GAAP** is a constraint since the financial statements are being audited. The **role** is that of company **auditor** and, therefore, the auditor would lean towards a more **conservative** interpretation of GAAP. **Management** seems to have high expectations of the company's ability to turn around and continue to grow.

The issue is whether the benefit from the 1999 losses should be recognized in the 1999 financial statements.

Loss carryback

To the extent that taxes were paid in previous years, the losses would first be carried back to recover these taxes and a partial benefit could be recognized.

Loss carryforwards

The real issue is whether there is sufficient certainty to recognize the benefits that might be realized if the losses are carried forward. Handbook 3465.24 states the benefits may be recognized if it is **more likely than not** that the benefits will be **realized**. The Handbook goes further to state that that this ultimately depends on the existence of sufficient taxable income in the carryforward period to be able to utilize the loss and shelter future taxable income.

Analysis and Recommendations

On the one hand, the Handbook notes that forming a conclusion that the benefits are likely to be realized is difficult when certain **unfavourable evidence** exists. In this case, unfavourable evidence would include the fact that there is a history of marginal profits only (and, of course, the loss) and the fact that this company is still in its formative years. It is not unusual for companies to sustain losses in the start-up period.

Furthermore, it might be argued that the current state of the economy is unsettled. Unemployment is still high and consumer spending has still not increased significantly. The fact that economists are predicting that it might take two to three more years for consumer spending to recover results in more uncertainty.

On the other hand, management has big plans to expand into new markets with new products. As a matter of fact, two new products are scheduled to be introduced and there are sufficient customers lined up to purchase the products, such that the company is predicting at least a break even situation using conservative estimates.

The fact that the company did not suffer pre-recession losses in its first two years is a signal that they must be doing something right. With respect to the economists, it might be argued that no-one can really predict the future. Management has better insight into its own company and customers and, therefore, might be in a better position to predict the future.

The fact that numerous competitors have gone under will hopefully open up new markets and help increase market share.

In conclusion, although management might be able to make a strong case for profitability, it is still a projection at best and, given that the economy still appears to be slow, it might be more conservative not to recognize the benefit. This is in keeping with the role of auditor. The unrecognized benefits and expiry dates would be note disclosed.

SELECTED SOLUTIONS FROM THE TEXTBOOK

EXERCISE 19-3

(a) Income taxes payable, 1998

Taxable income of $400,000 (given) x .40 = $160,000

(b)

	Future Years		
	1999	2000	Total
Future taxable (deductible) amounts	$175,000	$175,000	$350,000
Tax rate	40%	40%	
Future tax liability (asset)	$70,000	$70,000	$140,000
Future tax liability at the end of 1998			$140,000
Future tax liability at the beginning of 1998		90,000	
Future tax expense for 1998 (increase required in future tax liability)		$ 50,000	

Current Income Tax Expense	160,000	
Income Tax Payable		160,000
Future Income Tax Expense	50,000	
Future Income Tax Liability		50,000

(c)

Income before income taxes		$525,000
Less income tax expense		
Current tax expense	$160,000	
Future tax expense	50,000	210,000
Net income		$315,000

Note to instructor: Because of the flat tax rate for all years, the amount of the temporary difference existing at the beginning of the year can be calculated by dividing $90,000 by 40%, which equals $225,000. The difference between the $225,000 temporary difference at the beginning of 1998 and the $350,000 temporary difference at the end of 1998 represents the net timing difference originating during 1998 (which is $125,000). With this information, we can reconcile accounting income with taxable income as follows:

Net income	$315,000
Accounting income	$525,000
Timing difference originating giving rise to net future taxable amounts	(125,000)
Taxable income	$400,000

EXERCISE 19-10

(a) 1994

Income Tax Refund Receivable	39,400	
Current Income Tax Benefit (due to loss carryback)		39,400
($40,000 x .3) + ($17,000 x .2) + ($48,000 x .5)		

Loss remaining to be carried forward:
$150,000—($40,000 + $17,000 + $48,000) = $45,000

Future Income Tax Asset	18,000	
Future Income Tax benefit (due to loss carryforward)		18,000
$45,000 x .4		

(b) 1994

Loss before income taxes		$(150,000)
Income tax benefit:		
Current benefit due to loss carryback	$39,400	
Future benefit due to loss carryforward	18,000	57,400
Net loss		$ (92,600)

(c) 1995

Taxes are currently payable on $60,000—$45,000 = $15,000

Current Income Tax Expense	6,000	
Income Taxes Payable($15,000 x .4)		6,000
Future Income Tax Expense	18,000	
Future Income Tax Asset		18,000
To record reduction in tax benefit of tax loss carryforward.		

(d) 1995

Income before income taxes		$60,000
Less income tax expense:		
Current tax expense	$ 6,000	
Future tax expense	18,000	24,000
Net income		$36,000

(e) 1998

Income Tax Refund Receivable	24,000	
Current Income Tax Benefit (due to loss carryback)		24,000

Carried back to 1995:	$60,000—45,000 = 15,000 x .4 =	$ 6,000
Carried back to 1996:	$30,000 x .4 =	12,000
Carried back to 1997:	$60,000—$15,000—$30,000 =	
	$15,000 x .4 =	6,000
		$24,000

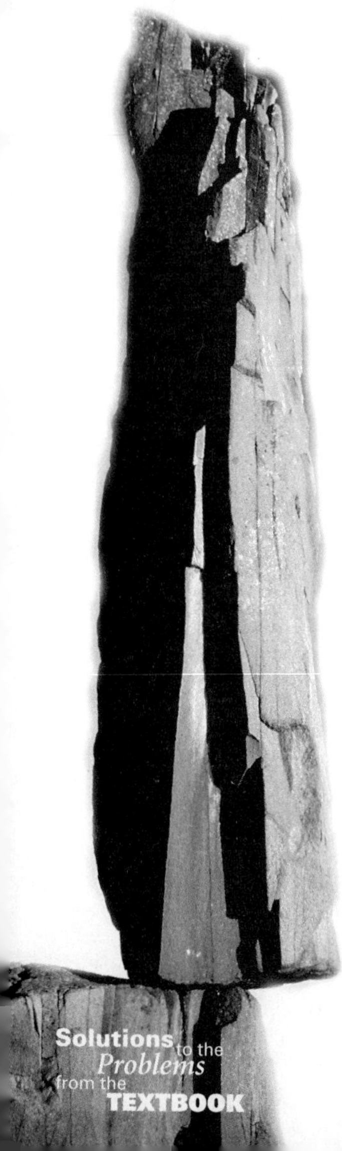

(f) 1998

(Loss) before income taxes	$(60,000)
Current income tax benefit of loss carryback	24,000
Net loss	$(36,000)

EXERCISE 19-18

(a)

	Future Years					
	1998	1999	2000	2001	2002	Total
Future taxable (deductible amounts)						
Litigation			$(5,000)	$(23,000)	$(2,000)	$(30,000)
Depreciation	$16,000	$16,000	16,000	16,000	16,000	$80,000
Enacted tax rate	50%	40%	40%	30%	30%	
Future tax (asset)			$(2,000)	$(6,900)	$(600)	$(9,500)
Future tax liability	$8,000	$6,400	$6,400	$4,800	$4,800	$30,400
Net future tax liability						$20,900

Future tax liability at the end of 1997	$30,400
Future tax liability at beginning of 1997	0
Future tax expense for 1997 (increase required in future tax liability	$30,400
Future tax asset at the end of 1997	$9,500
Future tax asset at the beginning of 1997	0
Future tax benefit for 1997	(9,500)
Future tax expense for 1997	30,400
Net future tax expense for 1997	$20,900

Current Income Tax Expense	40,000	
Income Tax Payable ($80,000 x .5)		40,000
Future Income Tax Expense	20,900	
Future Income Tax Liability ($20,900—$0)		20,900

(b)

Income before income taxes*		$130,000
Income tax expense		
Current tax expense	$40,000	
Future tax expense	20,900	60,900
Net income		$69,100

*Accounting income + $30,000—$80,000 = Taxable income of $80,000
Accounting income, therefore, is $130,000

b) An income tax refund receivable account totalling $61,500 will be reported under current assets on the balance sheet at December 31,1997. This type of receivable is usually listed immediately above inventory in the current asset section. This receivable is normally collectivle within two months of filling the amended tax returns reflacting the carryvack. A future tax asset of $14,000 should also be classified as a current asset because the benefits of the loss carryforward are expected to be realized in the year that immediately follows the loss year which means the benefits are expected to be realized in 1998. A current future tax asset is listed at or near the end of the list of current assets on the balance sheet. Also, retained earnings is increased by $75,500 ($61,500 + $14,000) as a result of the entries to record the benefits of the loss carryback and the loss carryforward.

c)

Loss before income tax		$(200,000)
Add: Income tax benefit		
Current tax benefit due to loss carryback	$61,500	
Future tax benefit due to loss carryforward	14,000	75,500
Net loss		$(124,500)

d)

Income before income tax		$60,000
Income tax expense:		
Current tax expense	$10,000	
Future tax expense	14,000	24,000
Net income		$36,000

SOLUTION TO PROBLEM

PROBLEM 19-6

The future taxable (deductible) amounts are scheduled as follows:

	Future Years				
	1998	1999	2000	2003	Total
Future taxable (deductible) amounts:					
Instalment sale	$ 30,000				$30,000
Depreciation	(90,000)	60,000	40,000		10,000
Accrued expenses				$(20,000)	(20,000)

(a)

Temporary Difference	Future Taxable (Deductible) Amounts	Tax Rate	Future Tax (Assets)	Future Tax Liability
Instalment sale	$30,000	30%a		$9,000
Depreciation	(90,000)	30%a	$(27,000)	
Depreciation	60,000	30%b		18,000

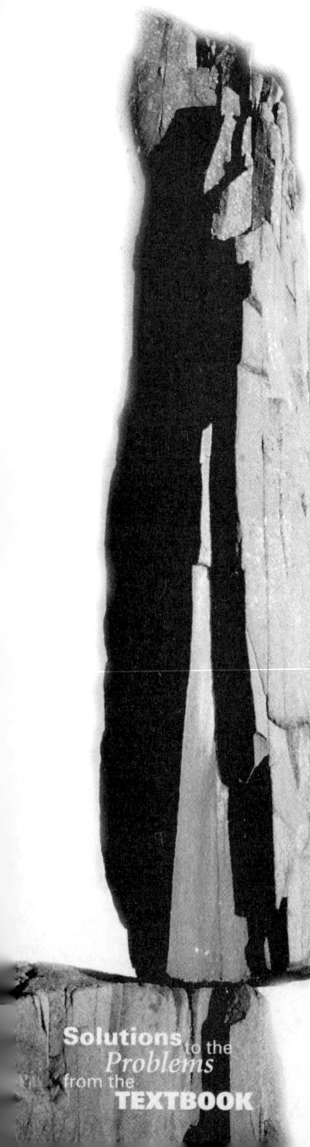

Depreciation	40,000	25%c		10,000
Accrued expenses	(20,000)	25%d	(5,000)	
Totals	$20,000		$(32,000)	$37,000

Net future income tax liability = $37,000—$32,000 = $5,000
a Tax rate for 1998 b Tax rate for 2000
b Tax rate for 1999 d Tax rate for 2003

Temporary Difference	Resulting Future Tax (Asset)	Liability	Related Balance Sheet Account	Classication
Instalment sales		$ 9,000	Instalment rec.	Current
Depreciation		1,000 [e]	Plant assets	Noncurrent
Accrued expenses	$(5,000)		Accrued liability	Noncurrent
Totals	$(5,000)	$10,000		

[e] $(27,000) + $18,000 + $10,000 = $1,000 net future tax liability related to the depreciation temporary difference.

Other assets (noncurrent)

Future tax asset $4,000 [f]

[f] $(5,000) + $1,000 = $(4,000)

Current liabilities

Future tax liability $9,000

(b) Current income tax expense, 1997

$60,000 (taxable income) x .35 =	$21,000
Future income tax expense ($5,000—0) =	5,000
Total income tax expense, 1997	$26,000

(c)

Current Income Tax Expense	21,000	
Income Tax Payable ($60,000 x .35)		21,000
Future Income Tax Expense	5,000	
Future Income Tax Liability ($5,000—0)		5,000

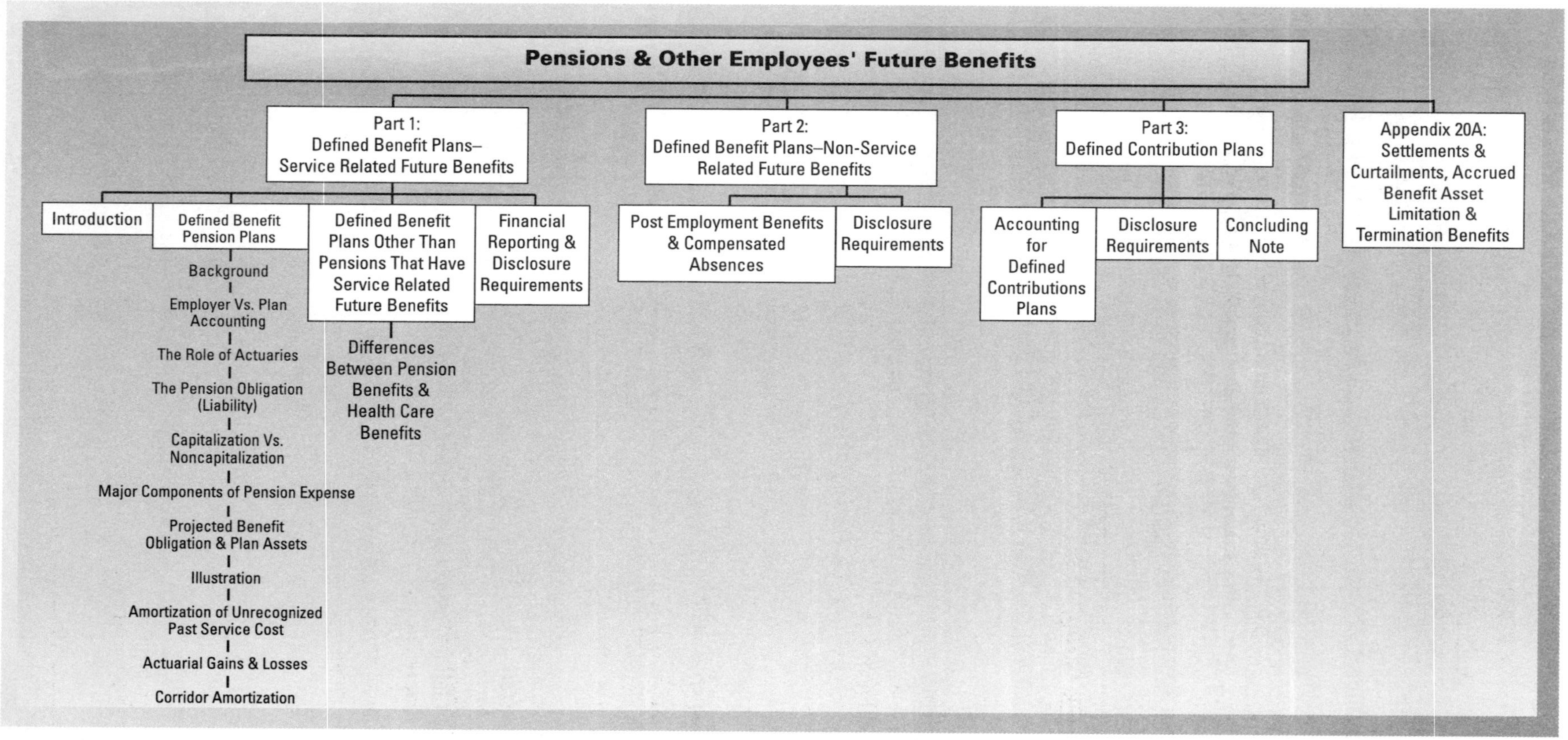

Pensions & Other Employees' Future Benefits
Part 1: Defined Benefit Plans–Service Related Future Benefits
Introduction
Defined Benefit Pension Plans
Background
Employer Vs. Plan Accounting
The Role of Actuaries
The Pension Obligation (Liability)
Capitalization Vs. Noncapitalization
Major Components of Pension Expense
Projected Benefit Obligation & Plan Assets
Illustration
Amortization of Unrecognized Past Service Cost
Actuarial Gains & Losses
Corridor Amortization
Defined Benefit Plans Other Than Pensions That Have Service Related Future Benefits
Differences Between Pension Benefits & Health Care Benefits
Financial Reporting & Disclosure Requirements
Part 2: Defined Benefit Plans–Non-Service Related Future Benefits
Post Employment Benefits & Compensated Absences
Disclosure Requirements
Part 3: Defined Contribution Plans
Accounting for Defined Contributions Plans
Disclosure Requirements
Concluding Note
Appendix 20A: Settlements & Curtailments, Accrued Benefit Asset Limitation & Termination Benefits

chapter 20

PENSIONS AND OTHER EMPLOYEE'S FUTURE BENEFITS

PERSPECTIVE

This topic is challenging since it exposes the student to (i) a new type of business transaction with significant measurement uncertainty and new terminology, (ii) a ***new spreadsheet model*** *for calculating pension expense and the related journal entries, and (iii) a CICA Handbook Section that has recommendations that are viewed by some to be a "political compromise."*

It is further complicated by the fact that an Exposure Draft was issued by the CICA in June 1997 (has not yet formally been accepted into the HB as of November 1997). The Exposure Draft basically improves required disclosures and reduces choice of items such as amortization periods and asset valuation methods. Finally, it proposes to incorporate post-retirement benefits other than pension within the same HB section.

INSIGHTS

- *This is an excellent example of the problems involved in estimating where there is* ***significant measurement uncertainty****.*
- *This is also a good example of* ***discounting*** *in practice.*
- *The Exposure Draft proposes to apply the same accounting standards to post- retirement benefits other than pension plans. This is a very good example of* ***economic substance over legal form****.*

STUDY STEPS

1. Understanding the Transaction/Pension Arrangement—Business Content

STUDY STEPS

What is a pension plan?

CICA HANDBOOK

> A pension plan is an arrangement (contractual or otherwise) whereby the employer promises to provide benefits to employees after retirement, for services provided by the employees while they were employed. The arrangement need not be documented in writing.

The employer contributes funds to the plan each year based on the agreement, and eventually, the plan will pay out the funds to the employees when they retire. The plan also earns investment income as the funds are invested.

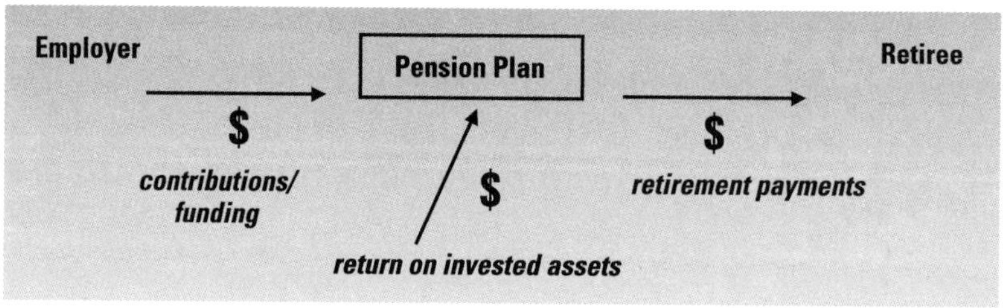

The employee **earns** the pension during the **service period** and gets paid **benefits** during the **retirement period**. The employer **contributes** to the plan during the **service period** and the **plan pays the employee** after retirement.

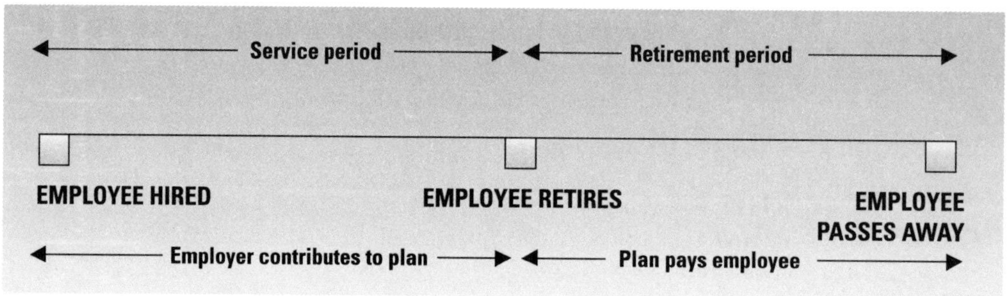

The employer/sponsor financial statements versus the pension plan financial statements

Accounting and financial reporting for the plan may be viewed from different perspectives:

1. From the perspective of the **employer or sponsor company** as a separate reporting entity or,
2. From the perspective of the **pension plan** itself as a separate reporting entity.

The **sponsor company** will record some sort of **expense** and **liability** on its books in order to recognize the cost of providing the pension benefit. The **pension plan**, however, will record the **pension assets ("PA")** and an estimate of the **total pension benefit obligation ("PBO")** owed to the employee group based on the pension benefit earned by each employee up to the reporting date. The assets are accumulated from the contributions made by the employer and are held in a pension fund under the plan. They are usually invested in securities, bonds, or other investments and will be used in settlement of the pension.

The CICA Handbook discusses "pension plan financial statements" in Section 4100 and "pension plan accounting as it relates to employer or sponsor financial statements" in Section 3460. This chapter deals with the latter, although it will be seen that changes in the financial statements of the pension plan affect the accounting for the plan on the sponsor financial statements.

This chapter deals with pension accounting from the employer's perspective. **Tip!**

The players in the transaction

A **trustee** (e.g., any trust company) often administers the plan, keeps the books and holds the assets. Therefore, the trustee would keep the bank account and the securities / assets that the plan holds as investments. Decisions about which assets to buy, sell, or hold may also be made by the trustee or by an **asset manager**. An **actuary** is used to calculate the pension expense, the pension obligation, and the cash funding required to meet the obligation. Initially, as the employee earns the benefits, they are not **vested. Vesting** is the legal entitlement by the employee to the benefits. The benefits become vested once an employee has worked for the company for a certain prespecified period of time (dictated by company policy and law). If the employee leaves the company prior to the point where the benefits vest, he forfeits the right to the benefits. As long as he waits until the benefits are vested before leaving, he is entitled to receive the full accumulated amount of benefits.

Defined benefit versus defined contribution plans

There are two distinct types of plans. One is a **Defined Benefit plan**, whereby the employer promises to pay $x to the employee on retirement, and the other is a **Defined Contribution plan**, whereby the employer promises only to contribute $x to the plan each year that the employee is employed. The former is preferable to the employee in most cases since the pension payout is agreed to up-front, whereas with the latter, the employer is not agreeing to the payout, only the annual contribution to the plan. This chapter focuses mainly on accounting for Defined Benefit plans since accounting for Defined Contribution plans is relatively straightforward.

Pension accounting for defined contribution plans is fairly straightforward. **Tip!**

Most of the issues arise with accounting for defined benefit plans and revolve around measurement of the estimated cost of the plan to the employer. **Tip!**

Defined benefit plans—details

An example of a defined benefit plan is as follows. The employer promises to pay 2% of an employee's highest paid salary (during the time that the employee works for the company) times the number of years worked. Therefore, if the highest salary is estimated as $40,000 and the employee has worked 10 years to date, she will be entitled to a payout on retirement of:

$40,000 x .02 x 10 = $8,000 per annum

The actuary would then estimate how long the employee would collect the benefit (x years) and discount the stream of payments to determine what the obligation is worth today (= $B) as follows:

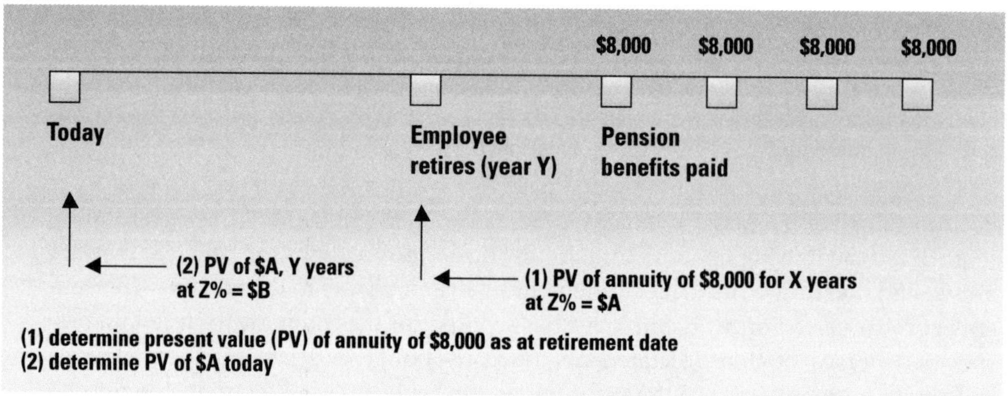

This PV calculation represents the pension obligation as of today.

Post-retirement benefit plans

These are similar to pension plans except that instead of offering a pension to retired employees, it offers things such as health and legal coverage. The major differences here are that these benefits are generally not funded up-front and the benefits and use of the program are more difficult to predict.

STUDY STEPS

2. Understanding How the Transaction Fits into the Financial Reporting Model and Conceptual Framework—Analysis and Critical Thinking

The most important issues are recognition and measurement, with presentation and disclosure being important because of the way the first two issues are handled.

Exhibit 20-1: Pensions
Relevant criteria, definitions and issues

Business transaction: what makes this topic more difficult to study, is the long term nature of the arrangement and the fact that employees perform the services now but get paid later, when they retire. In estimating the value today, of the obligation, discounting is applied which further adds to the softness of the number. The chart below summarizes the issues for defined benefit plans.

	How it relates to pensions	Relevant criteria/definitions	Topic specific analysis-how it should be	What makes the analysis challenging–how it is
Recognition	• when to recognize expense and liability	***liability*** • **obligation** to pay • **can't avoid** paying • **event** obligating entity has occurred • **probable** payout	• required to pay pension according to plan and since employee provided service (contractual obligation) • although not all will be paid out, large portion will be	• company **bias** towards not fully recognizing liability since affects debt/equity ratio and net income • CICA HB see as a **political compromise**–since often, increases in changes in **obligation not recorded when incurred, changes in assets/ liability smoothed** • under current CICA HB section, may end up with credit (income) vs. expense which is counterintuitive • in this case, may end up with **pension asset**–caution –may not be able to recognize asset (see EIC #1– Pension surplus recognition and discussed in ED).
		expense • transaction **occurred in period** • **matching**	• is equal to a remuneration cost even though payments will not be made until retirement, must accrue now to match with revenue	
Measurement	• $ value of liability, asset or cost	• at **transactions cost** • **measurable?**	• transaction cost difficult to determine–need best estimate • use actuary (specialist) to assist in estimate using **management best estimate** assumptions • discounting used–rate? • *should* disclose **more** due to uncertainty and complexity of business transaction	• management best estimate assumptions may be biased • CICA formula for measuring pension expense allows amortization of many items such that full effect of changes in obligation/asset not immediately reflected • discount rates vary from company to company
Presentation/ Disclosure	• how to present in f/s and note disclosure required	• **full disclosure**		•CICA HB only requires **minimal disclosure**–plan assets at market related value and plan obligation • full disclosure principle met?

Prepared by Irene Wiecek

3. Becoming Proficient in Pension Calculations—Skills

STUDY STEPS

The worksheet/spreadsheet

The worksheet approach taught in the text is an excellent tool / skill to help you in calculating the numbers that are needed to prepare the journal entry. Therefore, you should familiarize yourself with it as soon as possible.

Remember that you are trying to record the cost associated with the pension plan in order to accrue it while the employee is providing services to the company and thus match the costs (which are essentially compensatory costs) with revenues generated by the employee. **Tip!**

Remember also that the pension plan creates a liability to the company that should be recognized. **Tip!**

Tip! **The worksheet is only used to calculate the pension expense for defined benefit plans, not defined contribution plans.**

I have modified the worksheet slightly from the text. Use whichever worksheet makes more sense to you.

The plan creates a **liability** and should therefore be **accrued** on the **employer financial statements** as an expense and a liability. Therefore, assuming that the plan is new, as the employees work and **earn** their pension benefits, the liability should theoretically be accrued (**dr. expense, cr. liability**). As the plan is **funded**, i.e., as the employer contributes funds, it may be appropriate to record the contribution to the plan as a settlement of the liability (**dr. liability, cr. cash**). To recap, as the employees provide services and earn their pension, the cost gets recorded, as does a liability. As the employer sets aside funds for this liability, the liability reduces.

Liability

debit	credit
money paid into plan to meet obligation	liability increases as employees work

Even though the above liability account would be zero if the benefit was funded, the full PBO would be recorded on the **pension plan financial statements**, as would the PA.

Incorporating CICA HB 3460 into the worksheet

It is useful to begin to bring in the **CICA HB requirements** at this point. As previously mentioned in exhibit 1, the CICA Handbook does not require that the full liability be recorded nor subsequent changes to the liability. The reasoning will be discussed later. The CICA approach in HB 3460 **defers and amortizes many changes to the liability account**. The deferred amounts get deferred in a **memo account**. That is, they do not get booked on the employer financial statements when they occur. In subsequent years, a portion of the deferred amount (memo account) will get accrued/amortized on the employer financial statements as **dr. (cr.) pension expense and cr. (dr.) liability** such that, eventually, the full amount will get recorded. The worksheet helps us track the changes in the pension benefit obligation, (showing those booked by the employer and those not booked), the pension asset account, and the memo account.

CICA HB also gives a formula for calculating pension expense, defining it to include the following components:

- **current service cost** ("CSC")—which increases PBO, interest on the PBO, expected return on PA
- **amortization** of changes to PA due to **amendments/initiation**
- **amortization** of changes to PBO due to **changes in assumptions**
- **amortization** of changes to PBO/PA for **experience gains or losses**
- **gains/losses on settlements/curtailments**

- **amortization** of **transition** amount

Note that all of the above items affect PA or PBO on the pension plan financial statements. In essence, the idea is that **any changes in PA or PBO should be reflected in pension expense in the employer financial statement** (except for funding and benefit payments to retirees). Having said that, note that some adjustments to PBO and PA are booked straight to pension expense and that some are booked to the memo account, to be amortized to pension expense at a later date.

The components of pension expense will be discussed in the context of the example below.

An example

Assume that the company starts up a defined benefit plan that pays its employees the following benefit:

2% of their retirement year salary times the number of years worked

This means that the **more that the employees work**, the **higher their pension and the higher their retirement year salary**, the higher their pension. Assume further that the actuary advises us that the current service cost earned by the employees at the end of the first year is $100,000 and that we should set aside $80,000 cash in a separate pension plan to fund this benefit. The actual funding will take place at year-end. That is, a cheque will be issued to the pension plan by the employer.

Here is an example of a worksheet:

	EMPLOYER F/S			PENSION PLAN F/S		MEMO
description	pension expense (I/S)	change in cash	prepaid/ accrued pension (B/S)	pension benefit obligation PBO	pension plan asset PA	memo account

The worksheet has a minimum of seven columns. The first is a description column and should include all items defined by the CICA HB as part of pension expense plus a line for funding and benefits payments. The next three relate to accounts that are on the employer financial statements. Columns five and six relate to accounts that are on the pension plan statements. The last is the memo account that is not on any set of statements.

The prepaid/accrued pension account is the balance sheet account on the employer financial statements and **may either be a liability or in some cases an asset**. Let's post the two transactions to the worksheet.

	EMPLOYER F/S			PENSION PLAN F/S		MEMO
description	pension expense (I/S)	change in cash	prepaid/ accrue pension	pension plan obligation (B/S)	pension plan asset	memo account
CSC funding	$100,000	 (80,000)			$(100,000) 80,000	
subtotal	$100,000	(80,000)	(20,000)(1)			
			(20,000)	(100,000)	80,000	

(20,000)(2)

The CSC increases the PBO and also the pension expense (dr. expense, cr. PBO). The funding reduces the employer's cash account and increases the pension plan's PA (dr. cash, cr. PA). Note that at this point, no journal entry has been booked on the employer's financial statements. One of the main reasons for the worksheet is to do this.

1) The amount that is recorded on the employer financial statements as the prepaid/accrued pension (B/S) is the difference between what is accrued as expense and what is funded. Therefore, always add up the first two columns and the difference is the amount that gets booked to the balance sheet account on the employer financial statements. This line forms the journal entry as follows:

dr. pension expense	$100,000	
cr. cash		80,000
cr. ppd/accrued pension		20,000

2) The difference between the pension obligation and the pension asset on the pension plan financial statements is $20,000 in this case. Note that this is the same amount that is on the employer financial statements in the prepaid/accrued pension account. This should always be true except when there is an amount in the memo account, in which case this should be netted with the pension plan financial statement amounts first and then compared with the prepaid/accrued amount on the employer balance sheet. The prepaid/accrued pension account on the employer financial statements mirrors the net change in the PBO account, PA account, and the memo account.

Tip! **Each line on the worksheet should net to zero i.e., there should be debits and credits on each line.**

Tip! **Make sure that the worksheet balances at the end i.e., the PBO column total and PA column total (in the pension plan financial statements) and the total in the memo account column should net to an amount that equals the amount in the prepaid/accrued pension account column (on the employer financial statements).**

The journal entry is always taken from columns two, three and four. **Tip!**

So far, the worksheet model is consistent with the earlier comments on how the expense and liability should be calculated and recognized. Note that the PBO will also increase by an interest factor each year (dr. expense, cr. PBO), as PBO is a discounted number. The PA will likewise increase by an **expected** rate of return (i.e., interest, dividends, appreciation in value) each year (dr. PA, cr. expense).

The differences from our simplistic model arise when the PA or the PBO change for other reasons, such as the following:

- plan **initiation or amendment** (i.e., retroactive increases in the pension benefits—otherwise known as **past service costs**)
- **changes in assumptions** (mortality rates, discount rates, etc.)
- changes in the PA / PBO known as **experience gains/losses** (i.e., to reflect market or current estimates of PBO)

Where the PBO or PA changes as a result of these things, the adjustment is booked on the worksheet first, then to the memo account (dr./cr. PBO or PA, dr./cr. memo account), and then amortized to pension expense on the employer financial statements **over time** (dr./cr. expense, dr./cr. memo account—to reduce it). The **amortization period** for the amounts that are amortized is called the **"expected average remaining service life" or EARSL**. Amortization may begin the year of the change or the year following according to the CICA HB.

Settlements or curtailments also affect PBO and PA. For example, if an employee leaves and his benefits are vested, the plan must settle with him and actually pay him the value of the benefits. This results in the PBO decreasing since the obligation is settled, PA decreasing as there is a cash payout, and there may be a gain or loss which goes straight to pension expense (dr./cr. expense, dr. PBO, cr. PA). The **gain or loss does not get deferred and amortized s**ince the employee is no longer with the plan.

When the plan actually pays out the retirement benefits to retirees, the PBO is reduced, as is the PA (dr. PBO, cr. PA).

Finally, the pension expense includes a component for the "transition" amount. This is the amortization of the surplus or deficit in the plan at the date the current CICA HB section was implemented (for years beginning on or after December 31, 1986). If the plan did not exist at that time, there would be no transition amount. The calculation of the transition amount was a one-time calculation and was deferred in the memo account and amortized to pension expense over EARSL. Therefore, at present, it would be in the memo account and would be reducing over time as it was amortized to pension expense.

4. Pulling it All Together —A Critical Analysis of CICA HB 3460

STUDY STEPS

The unrecognized pension obligation/asset

To the extent that the employees have earned more benefits than the employer has funded at any point in time, PBO>PA on the pension plan financial statements, there exists a deficit in the pension plan (assets less obligation). That is, if the employer suddenly liquidated the plan, there would not be enough assets to cover the liability. Should this full deficit be recorded as a liability on the books of the employer? At present, it is not always recorded as some of it is in the memo account.

The **unfunded obligation** or deficit would appear to meet the definition of a liability according to Section 1000 in the Handbook in that:

- The obligation embodies a **duty** to others (i.e., to pay the pension).
- There is **no discretion to avoid** the responsibility in that the arrangement is a legal, binding contract.
- The **event** obligating the employer has already occurred (i.e., the employees have earned the pension).

However, as noted previously, all changes in the asset and obligation accounts (and the net amount or deficit/surplus) are eventually booked through the pension expense and hence the employer's balance sheet. Despite this, the CICA has adopted the approach of not recognizing these amounts immediately. Instead, the practice is to recognize them over time by amortizing them. This is a compromise position of sorts, which was likely influenced by politics.

A similar problem exists when assets exceed obligations, PA>PBO, resulting in a surplus. The issue then becomes whether the asset should be recognized on the balance sheet of the employer.

As mentioned previously, these amounts are booked in a memo account, off-balance sheet and the process of amortization also leads to criticisms of smoothing.

N.B.: The Exposure Draft does not really address the off-balance-sheet issue.

The disclosure issue

Exactly how much should an employer disclose in the notes to the financial statements regarding the plan? Assuming that the aim of financial reporting is to provide useful information, anything that might affect a decision that a financial statement user might make should be disclosed. The **suggested disclosures** as identified in the CICA Handbook Section 3460.61 are a good starting point. At present, only the **pension asset** and the **pension benefit obligation** are **required disclosures**. Since the amount recorded by the employer as an accrued pension (liability) or prepaid pension (asset) is not required to be disclosed separately on the balance sheet, it is often impossible for users to determine just how much of an unfunded/overfunded obligation/asset is unrecognized or unrecorded.

N.B.: The Exposure Draft enhances required disclosures significantly, although not as much as the required disclosures in the United States.

The use of management estimates

When the actuary calculates the pension obligation, the current service cost, and the amount that the employer should contribute to the plan, he must determine which underlying **assumptions** to use (i.e., discount rates, rates of return on assets, mortality rates, etc.). The actuary actually does two separate calculations of the estimated pension obligation:

- to determine the amount of funding or the contribution that the employer should make each year to the plan.
- to determine the best estimate of pension costs and obligation that the employer should book on his financial statements in order to match costs with revenues.

For the calculations, often different assumptions are used. For the latter calculation, management provides what it feels are the best or most realistic assumptions (**management best estimate assumptions**). For funding purposes, the actuary uses more conservative assumptions since the calculations will determine the amount of cash that the employer contributes. It is better to advise the employer to contribute a bit more to the plan than too little, since the employer is ultimately responsible for providing an agreed upon pension and since he relies on the actuary to advise him how much to contribute each year in order to meet that promise.

The issue really revolves around the management best estimate assumptions. Assumptions with respect to the expected rate of return on the assets and the discount rate are very **subjective**. Furthermore, there is the issue of whether to use long-term or short-term rates. The CICA Handbook gives some guidance in Section 3460.16, noting that assumptions should take into account the past, recognize the long-term nature of the plan, and not give undue weight to short-term or current experience. However, this is vague and leaves room for interpretation.

The choice of discount rate can result in PV calculations of the pension obligation that are very different, with a higher rate resulting in a lower PV. In practice, the actual rates used vary widely.

Because of the impact that the assumptions have on the calculations that are used to determine pension expense and obligations, it would make sense to at least require disclosure of the key assumptions, although presently, in Canada, this is not required.

N.B.: The Exposure Draft narrows the choice for assumptions. Specifically, the interest rate should be the current interest rate or current settlement rate (i.e., if the pension obligations were to be settled through buying annuities today, what rate would be available).

Valuation of plan assets

Another area where management estimates are used is in the **valuation of the plan assets**. The value affects the pension expense calculation and is a required note disclosure. The CICA Handbook states that **market-related values** be used (Section 3460.34). This again leaves much room for judgement since it may be actual market or a moving average market, which adjusts the PA to market over time—again, a smoothing element.

N.B.: The Exposure Draft calls for use of **fair values**, which would normally be market values.

MULTIPLE CHOICE QUESTIONS

1) When valuing pension plan assets for purposes of note disclosure in the employer financial statements, assets should be valued based on which of the following bases:

   a) historical cost
   b) lower of cost and market
   c) market values
   d) market related values

2) According to the CICA HB, the following actuarial valuation method should be used to determine the cost of providing pension plan benefits:

   a) projected benefit method pro-rated on services
   b) projected benefit method pro-rated on salaries
   c) level contribution method
   d) accumulated contribution method

3) Assumptions used in calculating the pension expense should reflect management's best estimate of the effect of future events on the actuarial present value of accrued pension benefits provided in exchange for services rendered. These assumptions should take into account the following:

   a) in recognition of the past history of the plan, actual experience.
   b) in recognition of the long-term nature of the plan, expected long-term future events.
   c) in recognition of the fact that the estimate is made as of a point in time, recent experience.
   d) all of the above.

4) Which of the following would not be considered a defined benefit plan?

   a) Benefit is fixed and based on years of services rendered
   b) Benefit is based on years of service rendered and the investment earnings earned to date of retirement.
   c) Benefit is based on years of service and compensation earned by employee over entire period of service.
   d) Benefit is based on years of service and compensation over a specified number of years.

5) The following information is available for the defined benefit pension plan for ABC company for the year ended December 31, 1998:

Benefit obligation based on current salary levels:	$478,000
Benefit obligation based on future salary levels:	$560,000

Vested projected benefit obligation:	$257,000
Pension assets at market values:	$343,000
Pension assets at market related values:	$360,000

Which of the following is the required note disclosure for the pension plan for ABC for the year ended December 31, 1998?

	Pension Benefit Obligation	Pension Assets
a)	$478,000	$343,000
b)	$478,000	$343,000
c)	$560,000	$360,000
d)	$257,000	$360,000

The following scenario relates to 6 and 7.

At the beginning of the year, Lee Inc. had an actuarial valuation done. The results of the valuation were as follows:

Accrued benefits	$5,000,000
Pension fund assets	3,000,000
Salary escalation	2%
Rate of return	8.5%
Expected annual expense of services rendered (assume incurred at the beginning of the year)	$500,000
Benefit payments (mid-year)	$350,000
Funding contribution required	$750,000

6) Which of the following amounts represents the interest on accrued benefits?

a) $425,000

b) $437,750

c) $452,625

d) $467,500

(CICA September 1996)

7) Which one of the following would not be included in the calculation of the expected year-end value of the accrued benefits?

a) benefit payments

b) funding contribution

c) interest on accrued benefits

d) rendering of services

(CICA September 1996)

8) According to generally accepted accounting principles, experience gains and losses for defined pension plans should be:

a) treated as prior period adjustments.

b) taken into income in the year the gains and losses are known.

c) amortized over a short period of time, such as five years.

d) amortized over the expected remaining service life of the employee group covered in the plan.

(CMA June 1994)

9)The following information relates to STV Ltd's defined benefit pension plan:

Service costs for 1994	$62,500
Pension benefits paid in 1994	$38,250
Estimated projected benefit obligation	
On Jan. 1, 1994	$522,800
Assumed discount rate	9%

STV Ltd.'s projected benefit obligation on December 31, 1994, assuming no change in actuarial estimates, is

a) $594,102

b) $547,050

c) $545,602

d) $623,550

(CMA June 1995)

10) Required disclosures under the new Exposure Draft relating to pension plans are

a) very similar to the current HB Section 3460.

b) greater than the current HB Section 3460, but less than the required disclosures in the United States.

c) less than the current HB Section.

d) greater than the current HB Section 3460 and greater than the required disclosures in the United States.

SOLUTIONS TO MULTIPLE CHOICE QUESTIONS

1) d) Although the historical cost principle generally prevails for asset valuation, market value provides more relevant information. A problem with using any market values is subjectivity. However, with pensions, often a large portion of the portfolio is made up of marketable securities or other publicly traded shares or debt and, therefore, market values are available and objective. Furthermore, many pension plans have the assets revalued by outside parties and both employer management and the pension committee, which includes employees/retirees, review the values. Therefore, this would presumably reduce reporting bias. The use of market related values is acceptable by the CICA HB; however, this introduces bias and allows smoothing. "Market related values" includes market value. The Exposure Draft proposes "Fair values", which would normally be market values.

2) a) The cost of providing the pension plan benefits should be estimated using the projected benefit method pro-rated on services since i) cost is a function of services provided/accrued to date, and this allows for better matching with revenues, ii) cost is based on future salary levels and therefore should incorporate projected salary levels, and iii) years of services rendered should be used to allocate the cost since it is the years of services rendered that gives rise to the pension.

3) d) The assumptions are a matter of professional judgement and should take into account all of the factors mentioned.

4) b) Under a defined benefit plan, the benefit is fixed. B) is the only option that would result in a variable pension payout since it varies with investment rate of return.

5) c) The required note disclosures include an estimate of the full pension obligation (vested and unvested) calculated using projected salary levels, and plan assets at market related values which may be equal to market values.

6) c)

Accrued benefits	$5,000,000
Expected annual expense of services rendered	500,000
Benefit payments ($350,000 X 50%)	(175,000)
	$5,325,000 X 8.5% = $452,625

7) b) Funding is not included.

8) d) Experience gains and losses should be amortized over EARSL.

9) a) $522,800 X 1.09 + $62,500—$38,250 = $594,102.

10) b) They are significantly greater than the present requirements, yet not as onerous as the required disclosures in the united States.

SHORT PROBLEMS

1) Purpose: To illustrate the use of the worksheet approach in calculating pension expense according to CICA Handbook Section 3460.

The following information has been provided for Pension Ltd. (PL), a Canadian manufacturing company for the year ended December 31, 1998:

Current Service Cost:		$ 12,000,000
Pension Obligation	-12/31/97	150,000,000
	-12/31/98	175,000,000
Pension benefits paid during the year (assume paid at end of year)		2,000,000
Expected rate of return on assets and interest on obligations		10%
Pension assets at market		
	-12/31/97	140,000,000
	-12/31/98	160,000,000
Funding-01/01/98		10,000,000
Transition amount at 01/01/92		22,000,000
EARSL at 01/01/92		11 yrs
EARSL at 12/31/98		15 yrs

Required

Using a pension worksheet, calculate pension expense for the year ended December 31, 1998 and prepare the journal entry.

2) Purpose: To illustrate the worksheet approach in a year where there are carryforward unamortized costs/losses.

The information for PL (see question 1 above) from 1 for 1999 is as noted below:

Current Service Cost:		$ 15,000,000
Pension Obligation	-12/31/98	175,000,000
	-12/31/99	205,500,000
Pension benefits paid during the year (assume paid at end of year)		2,000,000
Expected rate of return on assets		10%
Pension assets at market		
	-12/31/98	160,000,000

	-12/31/99	186,000,000
Funding	-01/01/99	13,000,000
Transition amount at 01/01/92		22,000,000
EARSL at 01/01/92		11 yrs
EARSL at 12/31/99		16 yrs

Required

3) Purpose: To focus on how the pension would be presented in the financial statements.

Required

Given 2, note what amounts would appear (and where) on the income statement, the balance sheet, and relevant note disclosures. Assume that the amounts are material.

SOLUTIONS TO PROBLEMS

1)

	EMPLOYER F/S			PENSION PLAN F/S		MEMO ACCT
Items	Pension expense	Cash	Ppd/ defer pension	Pension Oblig PBO	Assets PA	Unam costs/ trans amt.
12/31/97			-0-	$(150,000)	$140,000	$10,000*
CSC	$12,000			(12,000)		
Interest	15,000 (1)			(15,000)		
ROR exp	(15,000) (2)				15,000	
Contrib		(10,000)			10,000	
Benefits				2,000	(2,000)	
Trans	2,000 (3)					(2,000)
Subtotal				$(175,000)	$163,000	
Asset loss					(3,000)(5)	3,000
Subtotal	$14,000	$(10,000)	(4,000) (4)			
			$4,000	$(175,000)	$160,000	$11,000

Proof: amount in ppd/defer pension = PBO minus PA minus unam costs/trans amt = $(175,000)-160,000-11,000 = $(4,000).

* Five years left on transition amount. This assumes that there have been no other unamortized costs since inception.

(1) $150,000,000 x .10 = 15,000,000. There is a simplifying assumption here that the CSC, which increases the obligation, was incurred on the last day of the year. More realistically,

the CSC was earned/incurred evenly throughout the year, which would affect the obligation. Therefore, a more accurate interest calculation, based on the weighted-average outstanding balance of the obligation, would be:
[$150,000,000 + (12,000,000 x 6/12)] x .10 = $15,600,000
The benefit payment was made at the end of the year and therefore does not affect the calculation.

(2) [$140,000,000 + 10,000,000] x .10 = $15,000,000
The benefit payment was made at the end of the year and therefore does not affect the calculation. The funding payment was made at the beginning of the year and therefore gets full weighting.

(3) Transition amortization $22,000,000 / 11 yrs = $2,000,000

(4) Amount in the ppd pension/deferred pension balance sheet account is equal to the difference between the amount funded and the pension expense or $14,000-$10,000 = $4,000.

(5) The asset loss, also called experience loss, is calculated by comparing the expected asset value based on expected rate of return, contributions, and benefits paid, to the actual amount based on an asset valuation at year-end.

$163,000,000—$160,000,000 = $3,000,000 loss

There are two reasons why there might be a gain or loss. One reason is that the actual return on the assets might exceed or be less than the expected return. The other is that the market value of the assets may be different than their book values. This entry is essentially a plug to ensure that the ending balance is equal to the market value of the assets at year-end. The same would be done for the liabilities.

There is no amortization taken on this in the year that the loss arises. Amortization would begin next year, although it would be acceptable to begin amortization in the current year.

The journal entry is:

dr. pension expense	14,000	
cr. deferred pension (B/S)		4,000
cr. cash		10,000

The memo accounts do not get booked anywhere. However, the ending balances in the PBO and PA accounts are required disclosures in the pension note to the financial statements.

2)

	EMPLOYER F/S			PENSION PLAN F/S		MEMO ACCT
Items	Pension expense	Cash	Ppd/ defer pension	Pension Oblig PBO	Assets PA	Unam costs/ trans amt.
12/31/97			$(4,000)	$(175,000)	$160,000	$11,000
CSC	$15,000			(15,000)		
Interest	17,500 (1)			(17,500)		
ROR exp	(17,300) (2)				17,300	
Contrib		$(13,000)			13,000	
Benefits				2,000	(2,000)	
Amort	200 (6)					(200)
Trans	2,000 (3)					(2,000)
Subtotal				$(205,500)	$188,300	
Asset loss					(2,300)(5)	2,300
Subtotal	$17,400	$(13,000)	(4,400)(4)			
			$(8,400)	$(205,500)	$186,000	$11,100

Proof: amount in ppd/defer pension = PBO minus PA minus unam costs/trans amt = $(205,500) -186,000 -11,100 = $(8,400).

(1) $175,000,000 x .10 = $17,500,000. There is a simplifying assumption here that the CSC, which increases the obligation, was incurred on the last day of the year. More realistically, the CSC was earned/incurred evenly throughout the year, which would affect the obligation. Therefore, a more accurate interest calculation, calculated based on the weighted-average outstanding balance of the obligation, would be:

[$175,000,000 + (15,000,000 x 6/12)] x .10 = $18,250,000

The benefit payment was made at the end of the year and therefore does not affect the calculation.

(2) [$160,000,000 + 13,000,000] x .10 = $17,300,000
The benefit payment was made at the end of the year and therefore does not affect the calculation.

(3) Transition amortization $22,000,000 / 11 yrs = $2,000,000
The transition amortization does not change.

(4) Amount in the ppd pension/deferred pension balance sheet account is equal to the difference between the amount funded and the pension expense, or $17,400-$13,000 = $4,400.

(5) The asset loss, also called experience loss, is calculated by comparing the expected asset value based on expected rate of return, contributions, and benefits paid, to the actual amount based on an asset valuation at year-end.

$188,300,000-$186,000,000 = $2,300,000 loss

There are two reasons why there might be a gain or loss. One reason is that the actual return on the assets might exceed or be less than the expected return. The other is that the market value of the assets may be different than their book values. This entry is essentially a plug to ensure that the ending balance is equal to the market value of the assets at year-end. The same would be done for the liabilities.

There is no amortization taken on this in the year that the loss arises. Amortization would begin next year although it is acceptable to begin amortization in the current year.

(6) Amortization of the experience loss on the assets from last year: $3,000 / 15 yrs = $200. It makes more sense to amortize it over the EARSL for the employee group existing in 1998 when the loss arose.

The journal entry is:

dr. pension expense	17,400	
cr. deferred pension(b/s)		4,400
cr. cash		13,000

The memo accounts do not get booked anywhere. However, the ending balances in the PBO and PA accounts are required disclosures in the pension note to the financial statements.

3)
There are no requirements under CICA Handbook Section 3460 to disclose either the pension expense or the prepaid/deferred pension credit separately. Therefore, the pension expense might be grouped with payroll costs on the income statement and the deferred pension credit would probably be grouped with other liabilities or other deferred credits (other assets if a debit). Other deferred credits would be part of long-term liabilities due to their nature.

However, given that both amounts are material, and therefore useful to users of financial statements in making decisions, a case could be made for disclosing both items separately as line items on the income statement and the balance sheet. Alternatively, the detail could be shown in the notes to the financial statements.

Required disclosures include the value of the obligation and the market value of the assets as at December 31, 1999. These would normally be shown in the notes to the financial statement in a pension note. Although there are no requirements to show any other details, the full disclosure principle might dictate disclosing at least the type of plan and the major assumptions made, so that users could assess the impact of the plan and the assumptions.

CASES

1) Pablo Ltd.

Pablo Ltd. (PL) reproduces fine works of art on to posters. The company was started 10 years ago with used equipment. Demand for the posters has increased recently, since PL began to glue the posters onto a wood backing and laminate them. The old equipment has become very expensive to maintain and keeps breaking down, disrupting production. Pietro Pablo, the owner, has decided to go to the bank for a loan to buy new equipment. In preliminary talks with the bank, the manager indicated that financial statements are needed from PL for the year ended December 31, 1998.
The statements have been drafted; however, Pietro is not happy with the net income figure, which is lower than he had expected. Pietro calls you, his accounting manager, and asks if the net income has been correctly calculated. He points to the large payroll expense, which has increased over last year.

You note that the main reason for the increase is that pension expense has increased due to two reasons:

1. The pension plan with the employees was renegotiated at the beginning of the year and a key change was to increase the amount of pension benefits for each employee for each hour worked. The plan is a defined benefit plan and the amendment provided for retroactive application, so that the bulk of the employees, who were older, would benefit from the plan. The increase in the pension obligation arising from this amendment is being amortized to net income over 14 years beginning with 1998.

2. The actuary has recently prepared a new actuarial valuation of the pension obligation. In doing so, she suggested that the interest rate used for discounting be changed to reflect recent reductions in interest rates. Although short-term interest rates have declined, many economists predict that the mid- to long-term rates will remain more stable. The reduction in the interest rate for discounting has resulted in an increase in the pension obligation. The increase is also being amortized to net income over 14 years beginning with 1998.
Pietro asks you to go back and read the Handbook and determine whether there is any flexibility in applying the rules.

Required

Discuss the issues.

2) Eaton's 1997 Restructuring

In February 1997, Eaton's filed for protection under the Companies' Creditors Arrangement Act due to liquidity problems. The Act allows troubled companies time to restructure their debt and to hopefully avoid bankruptcy. As part of the restructuring process, Eaton's approached its employees and pensioners to split the surplus in the pension plan and allow Eaton's to withdraw a portion of the surplus in cash to help alleviate the liquidity problems.

In note 9 to the unaudited financial statements of The T. Eaton Company Limited, the following was disclosed with respect to the company's pension plan for the year ended December 31, 1996 (in thousands of dollars):

Plan assets at market	$735,501
Plan assets—four-year moving average market basis	$600,662
Projected Benefit Obligations	$327,101
Pension Surplus	$273,561
Unrecognized actuarial experience adjustment	$119,181
Pension surplus per financial statements	$154,380

The company further notes that, effective January 1, 1995, the interest rate assumption has been changed from 9% to 8% to reflect more conservative long-term interest rate expectations.

Required:

a) Explain the information contained in the note as excerpted above. In your explanation, include a discussion of where the surplus is likely booked in the financial statements (if at all) and whether there is theoretical justification for carrying it or part of it on the balance sheet.

b) Comment on the total amount that might possibly be available to the company under a pension surplus-splitting arrangement under the Ontario Pension Benefits Act. Explain how the change in interest rate assumptions affects the surplus.

c) In your opinion, what possible motivations might there be for overvaluing/undervaluing the surplus, from the perspectives of both the employer (Eaton's) and the employee (pensioners and future pensioners)

SOLUTION TO CASES

1) Pablo Ltd.

Overview

It would appear that the financial statements are being prepared for the **bank** for purposes of obtaining a loan or financing. The bank will want **conservatively prepared** statements with **full disclosures** so that they can make their decision. Pietro, on the other hand, is biased in that he wants the financial statements to look as good as possible to induce the bank to give him the financing. **GAAP** would appear to be a constraint since the bank will want **reliable** information.

You will likely advise Pietro to account for the pension such that the financial position of the company is presented in a favourable manner while still abiding by GAAP.

Analysis and Recommendations

The main issues are how to account for the amendment to the plan and whether the increase in the obligation due to the change in assumptions is valid and has been accounted for properly.

1. Amendment to the plan:

   The amendment to the plan results in the creation of a **past service cost**. According to Section 3460 in the *CICA Handbook*, the increase in the pension obligation resulting from the creation of past service costs should not be charged to pension expense all at once, but rather charged to pension expense over the **expected remaining service lives** of the employees (14 years in this case). There is an option to delay recognition, however, in the year in which the past service cost arose.

   CICA Handbook Section 3460.41 allows for **amortization** to commence in the following year. This would defer recognition of this charge and decrease pension expense and, therefore, is the recommended course of action.

2. Changes in the assumptions:

   The change in the assumption regarding the discount rate has caused the pension obligation to increase. This is undesirable since an increase in the pension obligation results in a higher pension expense. The lower rate is more **conservative** from the actuary's perspective since it will result in a higher required contribution from PL to the plan. This is desirable to the actuary since she wants to ensure that there will be enough money in the plan to pay off the retired employees.

   The choice of interest rate appears to reflect short-term interest rates, however. This is not necessarily appropriate since the pension plan obligation is of a long-term nature. *CICA Handbook* Section 3460.16, while unclear on whether short-term or long-term rates should be used, implies that the long-term nature of the plan should be considered without giving undue weight to short-term experience.

In addition to the above, there is also the issue as to whether the increase in the obligation should be charged to pension expense in the current year. Again, GAAP allows for the amount to be charged to pension expense over EARSL (14 years). The amortization need not begin until the year following the year in which the increase in obligation due to the change in assumption, occurred (Section 3460.45).

Therefore, pension expense should not be increased this year for this amount, but rather the increase in the obligation should be amortized beginning next year. However, it probably makes more sense to leave the discount rate at the old rate for accounting purposes, thereby creating no change in the obligation. The actuary may use a different rate for calculating the required funding.

The only required disclosures are the present value of the pension obligation and the market value of the assets at year-end.

2) Eaton's 1997 Restructuring

a) Eaton's has several plans by which it provides pension and other benefits to its employees. Of relevance here are the defined benefit plans and the surplus related therein. The Ontario Pension Benefits Act does not generally allow employers to access and "strip" pension surpluses from pension plans; however, it does allow for "surplus-splitting". "Surplus-splitting" allows the employer or sponsor of the plan and the employees to negotiate a sharing of the surplus. In this case, Eaton's is looking for some extra funds to help with its cash flow deficiency during and after the restructuring period allowed under the Companies' Creditors Arrangement Act. The surplus funds would also potentially be used to ease the burden on employees let go during the inevitable restructuring and downsizing. The **measurement** of the surplus is therefore very important within the context of this environment.

In the note, using plan assets valued at **market related values** (four-year moving average market basis) the surplus is valued at \$273,561. Note that only \$154,380 is recorded as an asset on the consolidated financial statements, as HB 3460 allows a **deferral** of **unrecognized actuarial experience adjustments**. Interestingly, the surplus would be significantly higher if straight market values were used. At \$735,501, the surplus would increase to \$408,400.

The surplus gets reported as a deferred pension cost (asset) on the consolidated balance sheet and comprises over 10% of the company's assets. Since it is reported as an asset, the company must justify that it meets the **definition of an asset**. EIC #1 allows for asset recognition even though the company has no **access** to the asset legally today, on the basis that there is a **future benefit** to the company via reduced future contributions. Note that future benefit will also be obtained through increased interest and other investment income on the excess assets. This will also reduce future contributions and ease future cash outflow requirements for the company to fund future service costs.

b) Depending on how the assets are valued, the amount available to be shared or split could be between $408,400 and $273,561. Use of market value increases the surplus. Note also that the interest rate assumptions have been changed to 8% from 9%. This causes the obligation to increase and thereby reduces the surplus. The change in interest rate does not affect the pension expense since changes in assumptions would be deferred and amortized over future periods.

c) It may be of benefit to the employees/future pensioners to want to have the surplus understated so that the "hidden" surplus was retained in the plan. Employees who were to be "downsized" might want to have a higher surplus if they were to share in the "surplus splitting" up-front. Eaton's, on the one hand, may wish to show a higher surplus in order to have access to much needed cash in the surplus-splitting. On the other hand, Eaton's might wish to show a lower surplus to protect the employees and possibly to save the excess to reduce future cash funding requirements. Regardless of any intended or unintended bias, the **measurement uncertainty** is very high and, in this case, measurement is doubly important since it will result in an actual cash outflow from the plan.

SELECTED SOLUTIONS FROM THE TEXTBOOK

EXERCISE 20-5

Browning Limited
Pension Work Sheet—1998

	General Journal Entries			Memo Record Entries		
	Annual Pension Expense	Cash	Prepaid/ Accrued Cost	Projected Benefit Obligation	Plan Assets	Unrecognized Actuarial Gain
Balance January 1, 1998				490,000 Cr.	490,000 Dr.	
Service cost	40,000 Dr.			40,000 Cr.		
Interest cost	41,650 Dr.			41,650 Cr.		
Proj. return on assets	41,650 Dr.				41,650 Dr.	
Asset gain					6,955 Dr.	6,955 Cr.
Funding		30,000 Cr.			30,000 Dr.	
Benefits				23,400 Dr.	23,400 Cr.	
Expense entry	40,000 Dr.		40,000 Cr.			
Contribution entry		30,000 Cr.	30,000 Dr.			
Balance December 31, 1998			10,000 Cr.	548,250 Cr.	545,205 Dr.	6,955 Cr.

$490,000 x .085 = $41,650

EXERCISE 20-9

Year	Corridor Amount (10% of greater of opening PBO or plan assets = (a)	Unamortized Net Actuarial Gain/ Loss at First of Year = (b)	Excess of (b) over (a)	Minimum Amortization
1996	$200,000	$0	$0	$0
1997	250,000	280,000 loss	30,000	(30,000/10) = $3,000
1998	290,000	347,000 loss*	57,000	(57,000/12) = $4,750
1999	360,000	352,250 loss**	0	0

* $280,000 + $70,000 - $3,000 = $347,000

** $347,000 + $10,000 - $4,750 = $352,250

PROBLEM 20-1

Bob Blunden Company
Pension Worksheet—1998 and 1999

	General Journal Entries			Memo Record Entries			
	Annual Pension Expense	Cash	Prepaid/ Accrued Cost	Projected Benefit Obligation	Plan Assets	Past Service Cost	Unrecognized Net Actuarial Gain/Loss
Balance January 1, 1998				4,200,000 Cr.	4,200,000 Dr.		
(a) Service cost - 1998	140,000 Dr.			140,000 Cr			
(b) Interest cost	252,000 Dr.			252,000 Cr.			
(c) Expected return	252,000 Cr.				252,000 Dr.		
(d) Funding		140,000 Cr.			140,000 Dr.		
(e) Benefits paid				200,000 Dr.	200,000 Cr.		
Expense entry, 1998	140,000 Dr.		140,000 Cr.				
Contribution entry, 1998		140,000 Cr	140,000 Dr.				
Balance December 31, 1998			0	4,392,000 Cr.	4,392,000 Dr.		
(f) Past service cost January 1, 1999				500,000 Cr.		500,000 Dr.	
(g) Service cost	180,000 Dr.			180,000 Cr.			
(h) Interest cost	293,520 Dr.			293,520 Cr.			
(I) Expected return	351,360 Cr.				351,360 Dr.		
(j) Asset loss					91,360 Cr.		91,360 Dr.
(k) Amortization PSC	90,000 Dr.					90,000 Cr.	
(l) Funding		184,658 Cr.			184,658 Dr.		
(m) Benefits paid				280,000 Dr.	280,000 Cr.		
Expense entry, 1999	212,160 Dr.		212,160 Cr.				
Contribution entry, 1999		184,658 Cr.	184,658 Dr.				
Balance Dec. 31, 1999			27,502 Cr.	5,085,520 Cr.	4,556,658 Dr.	410,000 Dr.	91,360 Dr.

(b) $2,542,000 = $4,200,000 x 6%
(c) $252,000 = $4,200,000 x 6%

(h) \$293,520 = (\$4,392,000 + \$500,000) x 6%
(i) \$351,360 = \$4,392,000 x 8%
(j) \$91,360 = \$351,360 -\$260,000

Reconciliation Schedule, 12/31/99

(b)	Projected benefit obligation	\$5,085,520 Cr.
	Fair value of plan assets	4,556,658 Dr.
	Funded status, underfunded	528,862 Cr.
	Unrecognized past service cost	410,000 Dr.
	Unrecognized net actuarial loss	91,360 Dr.
	Accrued pension cost liability	\$27,502 Cr.

CASE 20-2

1. Deferred pension cost is the cumulative contributions in excess of cumulative accrued pension expense. This item is reported in the asset section of the balance sheet and is reduced whenever the pension expense in a period is greater than the contribution made to the fund during the period.

2. Accrued pension cost is the cumulative pension expense accrued in excess of the employer's cumulative contributions. This item is reported in the liability section of the balance sheet and is increased whenever pension expense in a period is greater than the contribution made to the fund.

3. Pension expense is the amount recognized in an employer's financial statements as the expense for a pension plan for the period. Components of pension expense are service cost, interest cost, expected return on plan assets, amortization of the net actuarial gain or loss, amortization of past service cost, and amortization of the transaction amount.

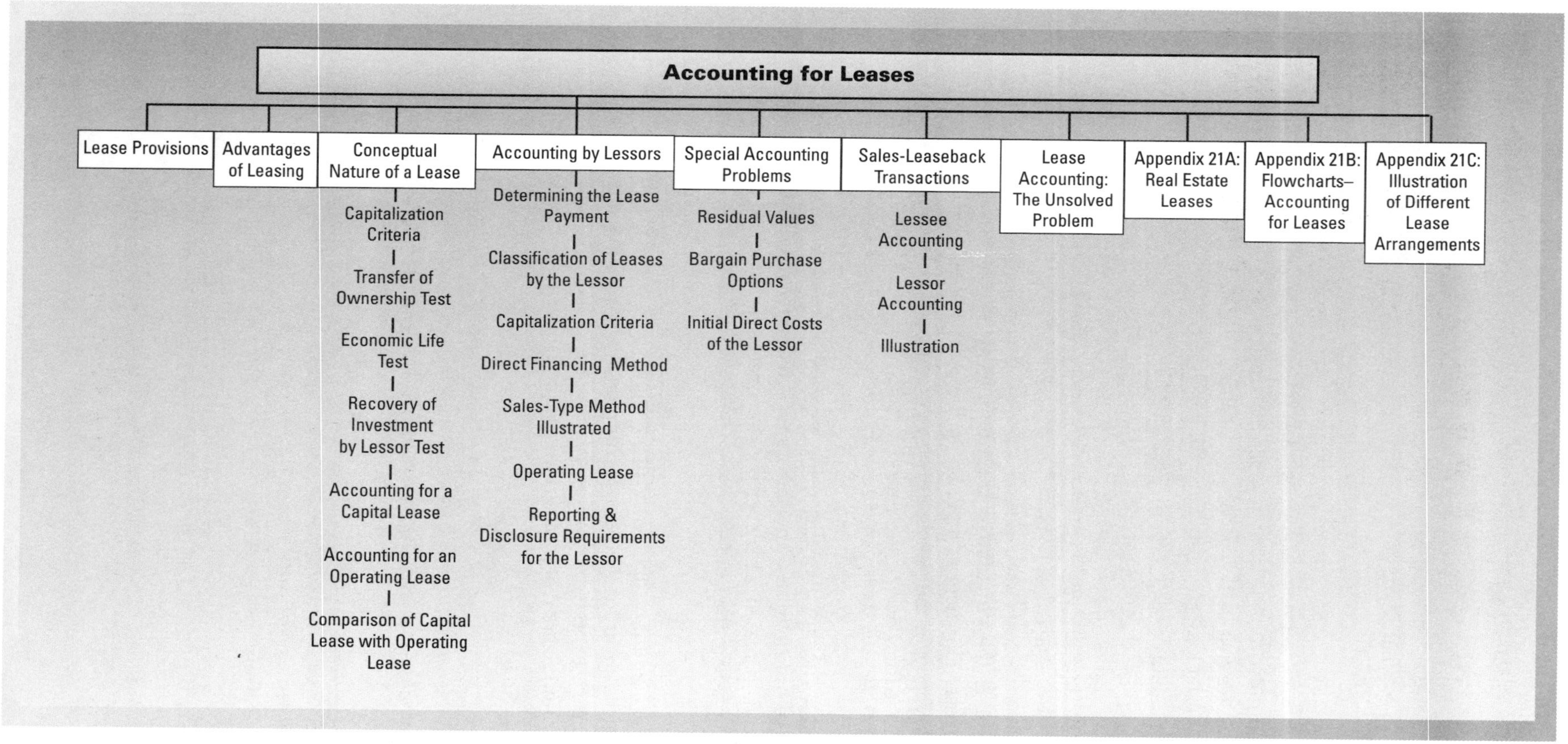

Accounting for Leases
Lease Provisions
Advantages of Leasing
Conceptual Nature of a Lease
Capitalization Criteria
Transfer of Ownership Test
Economic Life Test
Recovery of Investment by Lessor Test
Accounting for a Capital Lease
Accounting for an Operating Lease
Comparison of Capital Lease with Operating Lease
Accounting by Lessors
Determining the Lease Payment
Classification of Leases by the Lessor
Capitalization Criteria
Direct Financing Method
Sales-Type Method Illustrated
Operating Lease
Reporting & Disclosure Requirements for the Lessor
Special Accounting Problems
Residual Values
Bargain Purchase Options
Initial Direct Costs of the Lessor
Sales-Leaseback Transactions
Lessee Accounting
Lessor Accounting
Illustration
Lease Accounting: The Unsolved Problem
Appendix 21A: Real Estate Leases
Appendix 21B: Flowcharts– Accounting for Leases
Appendix 21C: Illustration of Different Lease Arrangements

chapter 21

ACCOUNTING FOR LEASES

Perspective

Students often find the study of leases difficult since it is (i) a new type of business transaction with new terminology, and, (ii) the journal entries are complex depending on the type of lease.

Insight

This is an excellent example where accounting follows the economic substance of the transaction instead of its legal form.

Study Steps

1. Understanding the Business Arrangement

What is a lease arrangement—the legal form versus the economic substance

> A lease is a contractual arrangement whereby one party (the lessor) agrees to the use of an asset (which is owned by him) by another party (the lessee).

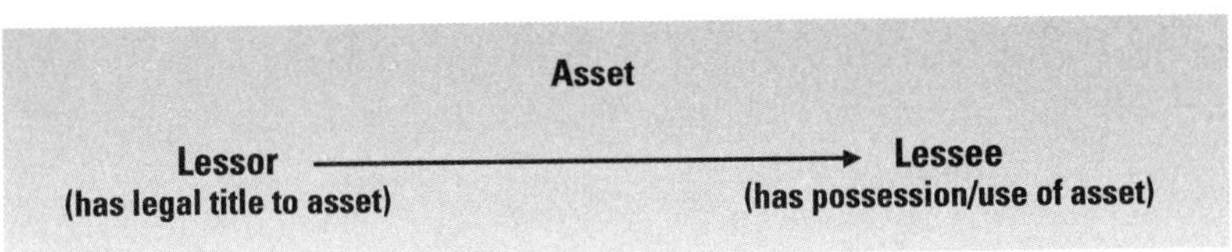

The lessor gives up **use** of the asset for a constant income stream (rent), while the lessee gives up cash over the lease term and has use of the asset.

While the **legal form** is such that the lessor has **legal title** to the asset and, therefore, owns it, the **economic substance** of the arrangement may be different. On the one hand, the lease may represent a pure rental arrangement (e.g., when a tenant signs a lease to rent a one-bedroom apartment in a large building for one year). However, the lease may be such that the economic substance indicates a **change in ownership** (e.g., when a lessee enters into a "lease to buy" arrangement for a new car).

In the latter case, the lessor is effectively **selling the asset** and the lessee is effectively **buying the asset**, even though, legally, the transaction may take the form of a lease contract, where legal title remains (at least initially) with the lessor.

The issue that must be dealt with here is as follows:

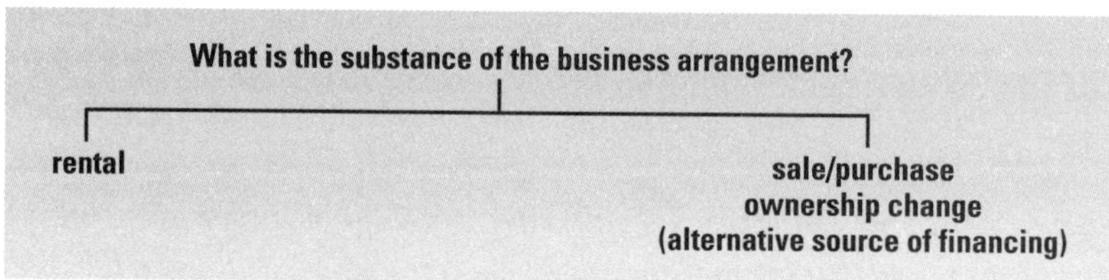

Many leases fall somewhere in between. Since accounting should ideally follow the substance of the transaction, as opposed to its legal form, the second type of lease where there is an ownership change in substance must be dealt with differently than the first type. It should be accounted for as though the lessor were selling the asset and the lessee purchasing the asset.

Leases often have an option to purchase the asset at the end of the lease term. If this option is at a price that is significantly less than the estimated FMV at the end of the lease (the **residual value**), then the option is termed to be a bargain—hence the phrase **bargain purchase option** (BPO). Some leases require that the lessee guarantee the value of the asset when it is returned. If it is not returned in good condition, the lessee must pay an additional amount to make up the amount guaranteed. This is called the **guaranteed residual value (GRV)**.

The **lease term** is the fixed non-cancelable term and may be extended under a **renewal option**. The option would again be a bargain if the terms of renewal are more favourable than arm's-length market terms (**bargain renewal option**).

Finally, there might be **penalties** for non-renewal.

2. Understanding How the Transaction Fits into the Financial Reporting Model and the Conceptual Framework—Analysis and Critical Thinking

The big issue is appropriate recognition of lease arrangements that transfer the risks and rewards of ownership. More minor issues are discussed in 3 below.

Exhibit 21-1: Leases
Relevant criteria, definitions, and issues

Business transaction: The legal form of this type of transaction is that it is a rental type arrangement. However, the economic substance of certain types of leases is the they transfer the risks and rewards of ownership. Therefore, the accounting challenge is whether these should be accounted for as purchases and/or sales.

	How it relates to leases	**Relevant criteria/definitions**	**Topic specific analysis-how it should be**	**What makes the analysis challenging–how it is**
Recognition	**lessee**–recognize effective purchase and financing of asset? **lessor**–recognize sale or disposition of asset?	**lessee**–BPO/title transfer • terms>75% ec life • PVMLP>90% FMV **lessor**–same as above plus: normal credit risk and costs estimable	• the intent of the section is to see if **R & R are transferred** from lessee • if the lessee has **use** of the asset for most of its life and effectively **pays approximately FMV** through the lease payments, then this is like a purchase • if the lessor has given up **possession** and the transaction is measurable and **$ collectible** then this is like a sale • consider intent–EIC #30	• bias towards accounting for transaction as a rental arrangement as lessee since does not show obligation • as lessor, bias to show as a sale, since may get to record profit and remove asset from books–no depreciation • NB for tax, would want to take CCA, therefore, conflicting motivation
Measurement	• $ value of asset and lease obligation–lessee • profit on sale and treatment of unguaranteed residual value	• at **transactions cost** • **measurable?**	• transaction cost difficult to determine due to long-term nature of arrangement • need to discount • same as above for lessor • exclude URV from sales and COS–since asset will return to lessor after lease • cash flow emphasis • show MLP for lessee and reconcile to PVMLP • for lessor, gross and net investment in lease	• pre-defined formula promotes consistency • choice of discount rate limited to promote consistency
Presentation/ Disclosure	• how to present in f/s and note disclosure required	• **full disclosure**		• disclosures adequate

Prepared by Irene Wiecek

3. Becoming Proficient in Lease Calculations and Journal Entries—Skills

This topic will be covered first from the lessee's perspective, and then from the lessor's perspective. See the TOOLKIT for a decision tree on the different types of leases and how they are classified for accounting purposes. The following covers only capital, sales-type, and direct financing leases as these are the most difficult.

Lessee—capital leases

From the lessee's perspective, if the substance is such that there is an ownership change (sale/purchase), the lease is called a **capital lease**. Therefore, the lessee accounts for the lease just the same as if he had purchased the asset as follows:

Recognition—journal entries

1. Record the asset and the obligation for financing the asset:

    dr. leased assets

        cr. obligation under lease

This is almost the same as if it had been purchased outright, in which case the journal entry would have been:

dr. fixed assets
    cr. loan payable to bank

Keep in mind that although the substance is the same, the legal rights may be quite different, in which case disclosure is critical.

Tip! **The accounting for leases should follow the economic substance of the transaction.**

2. Depreciate or amortize the asset.

There is a choice as to whether to depreciate it over the **lease term** or the **expected useful economic life**. If the asset had been purchased outright, it would be depreciated over its useful life. However, under a lease arrangement, the asset may not contribute to revenues over the full useful life (i.e., if the lease term is for a period that is less than the useful life and the lessee intends to return the asset to the lessor at the end of the term). In this case, the choice hinges on whether the asset will be used by the lessee over the economic life of the asset or just over the lease term.

One way to determine this is to look at the terms of the lease. If there is an **option to purchase** the asset from the lessor at the end of the lease at a price that is less than the fair market value (FMV) of the asset, it is likely that the lessee will exercise this **bargain purchase option** (BPO) and, therefore, use the asset for its full **economic life**.

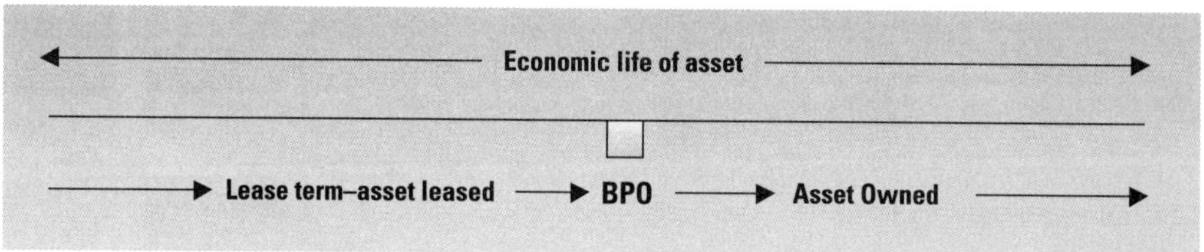

In this case, the depreciation period would be the economic life. If the lease agreement includes a clause that provides for the **legal title of the asset to pass** to the lessee at the end of the lease term without any payment, again the lessee will use the asset for the economic life and the asset will, therefore, be depreciated over the **economic life** in order to match costs with revenues.

Tip! **Depreciate over the lease term unless there is a BPO or title transfer in the lease contract.**

3. Accrue interest on the obligation

Interest expense will be booked on the outstanding obligation as though it were a loan payable to the bank. As payments are made, the outstanding obligation will reduce, just as a loan would. The lease payment contains an interest component and a principal component. An amortization table will be used to determine the breakdown between interest and principal.

Use an amortization table to determine how much of the lease payment is interest and how much reduces the recorded obligation. **Tip!**

Measurement—calculating the PVMLP

When the lessee records a capital lease, the value is determined by a formula (i.e., the present value of the minimum lease payments [PVMLP]).

dr. leased assets	$PVMLP	
cr. obligation under lease		$PVMLP

PVMLP is defined in the text, however, an attempt should be made to understand what is included in this formula and why. As an overview, the calculation is meant to **measure** the lease transaction. Purchased assets are normally recorded at historical cost, which is usually determined by an invoice. In the case of a lease, there is no invoice, only the lease contract which does not include a purchase or sales price. The measurement problem is compounded by the fact that the asset will be "purchased" over time by the lessee and that there is an interest factor included in the monthly payment.

The PVMLP attempts to measure the present value of what the lessee will pay for the asset. In other words, it attempts to approximate the cash exchange price. **Tip!**

This calculation would include the actual lease payments, but what about purchase options or guarantees of residual values (GRV)? One way of looking at it is to determine what the **intent** is on the part of the lessee. Does she plan to keep the asset at the end of the lease, or give it back? These options are mutually exclusive and therefore should be treated as an either/or situation (i.e., the lessee cannot keep the asset and give it back at the same time). The likelihood of the lessee keeping the asset may be determined by the lease itself (e.g., if the lease contains an option to purchase the asset at the end of the lease at less than FMV, the lessee will likely exercise the option and keep the asset). The intentions of the lessee must also be considered.

PVMLP is the PV of the most likely $ amounts that will be paid out under the lease. **Tip!**

In deciding what to include, consider management intent and terms in lease contract that are inducements to act one way or another. **Tip!**

If the lease arrangement includes both BPO and GRV, the intent of the lessee must be reviewed again. Will she keep the asset or give it back? Normally the presence of a BPO would indicate the former. Therefore, it would not make sense to include both the BPO and the GRV in the PVMLP since the situations in which the costs would be incurred are mutually exclusive. Whether the purchase option is a bargain is a question of judgement. If the option price is close to FMV, the lessee might not be induced to keep the asset, in which case,she would likely return it and the option price will not be paid.

Inclusion of BPO or GRV/Penalty in PVMLP

Lessee

- **incentive/intent to keep asset at end of lease***
  - **include any BPO in PVMLP since will likely incur when exercised**
- **no incentive/intent to keep asset at end of lease**
  - **include GRV/penalty in PVMLP since will likely incur when asset returned**

* this would be evidenced by the following things:
- BPO in lease agreement
- legal title transfer at end of lese in lease agreement
- significant penalty or unreasonable GRV in lease agreement
- asset specially built for lessee/no other users for asset if returned to lessor etc. or clear indication by management that they intend to keep it (EIC#30)

Tip! **Whether a purchase option is a bargain or not is a question of professional judgement. In general, it would be a bargain if it were less than the FMV of the estimated residual value at the end of the lease.**

When calculating the PVMLP, the payments must be **discounted**. The question arises as to which rate to use. Since the **implicit rate** (i.e., the rate of return required by the lessor) is often not known to the lessee, the lessee must find a substitute discount rate. Therefore, the lessee's **incremental borrowing rate** is often used. If the lessee happens to know the implicit rate, then the **lower of the two rates** should be used. It is not eminently clear as to why the implicit rate is not used; however, the lower the discount rate, the higher the obligation under lease. Thus, use of a lower rate would be more conservative as far as recording the obligation is concerned.

Tip! **When discounting (lessee), use the lower of the IR and the IBR.**

Lessor—sales-types and direct financing leases

From the lessor's perspective, if the substance is such that there is an ownership change (purchase / sale) then the lease will be accounted for as a **direct financing lease** or a **sales-type lease**. A sales type lease occurs when the lessor makes a profit or loss on the transaction (excluding interest from the financing). The lease arrangement is accounted for as though a sale has taken place and therefore the following entries are booked:

Recognition—journal entries

1. Record the sale of the asset (sales-type lease):

    dr. lease payment receivable (LPR)
    dr. cost of goods sold
        cr. revenues

cr. equipment inventory
cr. unearned interest

If the journal entry is rearranged, it is the same as the standard journal entry that would be booked upon the sale of other goods in a standard sale:

dr. accounts receivable (LPR)
cr. revenues
cr. unearned interest

dr. cost of goods sold
cr. inventory

The only difference is that some of the account names are different and that the lease transaction produces some revenues that are not yet earned (i.e., interest revenues). The interest will be earned over time, being a function of the length of time that the LPR is outstanding.

For a direct financing lease, omit the sales and cost of goods sold entry, since there is no profit on the deal.

dr. accounts receivable (LPR)
cr. inventory
cr. unearned interest

2. Since the asset has, in effect, been sold, depreciation is not necessary.

3. Interest revenues will be earned over time based on the **outstanding principal** balance in the lease payment receivable account. The amount of interest earned each year may be calculated by the amortization table. The LPR includes the full amount of the lease payments including interest.

Measurement

The measurement of the transaction is difficult for the lessor for the same reasons as for the lessee. There are, however, two components to measure for the lessor:

1. The **cost** of the asset sold.
2. The **sales price**.

The cost

As a general rule, the cost of the asset sold is the laid down cost that the lessor paid for the asset when it was purchased. Inventory is credited with the cost of the asset in order to remove it from the balance sheet. The cost of sales is usually debited for the same amount (unless there is an unguaranteed residual value, which will be dealt with later).

The sales price

As a general rule, the sales price will be the FMV of the asset since the lessor will want to ensure that he recovers the FMV in a lease transaction, just as he would if it were an outright sale. This amount, however, does depend on how much the lease payments are and if there is any residual value. Just how the lessor determines what the lease payment will be is discussed later.

The amount booked as the LPR is a good starting point and the sales price may be derived from there. The LPR is the sum of all the lease payments (excluding executory costs), including any BPO if there is one. If there is a BPO, the lessee will likely exercise the option to purchase as discussed above. Therefore, this is an additional amount that will be paid by the lessee for the asset and, therefore, it should be included in LPR.

As discussed above, if there is no BPO and the title to the asset does not pass as part of the terms of the lease, it is likely that the asset will return to the lessor and, therefore, the residual value is important. In this case, the residual value should be included in the LPR.

Tip! **When determining whether to include BPO/GRV/penalty in LPR, use the same principles as for the lessee and the chart shown under lessee that deals with the same issue.**

Tip! **If the asset will return to the lessor at the end of the lease, then include the residual value in lease payments receivable whether it is guaranteed or not. This is different from the lessee where you would only include the GRV.**

If the asset is returned to the lessor, the lessor will reclassify the residual value from the LPR account to a fixed asset account, since the substance is now that he owns the asset again (dr. fixed asset, cr. LPR). The amounts are not discounted in the LPR calculation. The amount recorded as a sale is simply the discounted value of whatever has been included in the LPR account and the difference between the sales account and the LPR account is the unearned interest.

The only exception is if there is an unguaranteed residual value. The present value of this amount should not be included in the sales amount and for that matter, should also be deducted from the cost of goods sold amount.

Tip! **The unguaranteed residual value should not be included in the sales price or the cost of sales, although it will be included in the lease payment receivable.**

Tip! **The amortization table will be the same for either a guaranteed residual value or an unguaranteed residual value, i.e., the residual value would be included in the table.**

Tip! **The lessor would always discount at the rate implicit in the lease, which is their desired rate of return.**

Calculating the lease payment

How does the lessor calculate the lease payment? Basically, he wants to recover the FMV of the asset that he is selling or, for that matter, he would like to recover whatever he can. This is usually capped at FMV, as this is all that the lessee is willing to pay.

The lessor, therefore, starts with whatever he thinks that the lessee will pay (usually FMV). From this, he deducts any special payments that will be made by the lessee -BPO or the residual value. Again, the deduction will depend on whether the lessee will likely purchase the asset at the end of the lease or return the asset. If she plans to purchase the asset, then the BPO is relevant. If she plans to give the asset back, then the residual value, guaranteed or not, is relevant. The remainder is divided by an annuity factor to determine the payments.

The lessor's implicit rate in the lease is the rate of interest that the lessor charges the lessee for providing financing. The lessor not only sells the assets to the lessee but also provides financing. The rate is usually higher than the lessor's own borrowing rate so that the lessor makes a profit on the interest spread. The rate is also adjusted for the risk associated with the particular lessee (i.e., the risk that the lessee will not pay).

The annuity table used depends solely on when the lease payment is made. If the payment is made at the beginning of the year, an annuity due table is used. If the payment is made at the end of the year, an ordinary annuity table is used.

Initial direct costs

The basic principle that dictates how the initial direct costs should be accounted for is the matching principle (i.e., costs should be matched with the revenues to which they relate). First determine the type of type of lease and then the type of revenue earned under the lease, e.g., under an operating lease, rental income is earned over the term of the ease and therefore any up-front costs should be deferred and recognized over the term of the lease to match the revenues. Direct financing leases yield interest income and, therefore, any up-front costs should be deferred and amortized to match the costs and revenues. Sales-type leases yield both profit and interest income and the costs could be deferred or recognized when incurred. The latter approach is taken since it is more conservative and since most up-front costs are seen as costs of sales.

Executory costs

All of the lease calculations should be made without making reference to executory costs. The executory costs are not payments for the actual use of the asset. Rather, they are payments made for other expenses that are related to the asset.

MULTIPLE CHOICE QUESTIONS

1) Assuming that the lessee intended to return the asset at the end of the lease to the lessor, which of the following would not be included in the PVMLP from the lessee's perspective?

   a) a partial guarantee of the residual value by a third party related to the lessee
   b) a guarantee of the full residual value by a third party related to the lessee
   c) a residual value guaranteed by a party related to the lessor
   d) a residual value that is guaranteed by a parent company of the lessee

2) Which of the following would not be considered part of the lease term:

   a) a period that represents a potential extension of the lease at the lessor's option
   b) a period covered by a renewal option
   c) all periods for which failure to renew would impose on the lessee a penalty sufficiently large that renewal appears reasonably assured
   d) all periods covered by ordinary renewal options during which the lessee has undertaken to guarantee the lessor's debt related to the leased property

3) The economic life of leased property may be best described as which one of the following:

   a) estimated remaining period during which the property is expected to be economically usable with all repairs and maintenance, for the purpose for which it was intended at the inception of the lease and without limitation of the lease term.
   b) estimated remaining period during which the property is expected to be economically usable without major repairs and maintenance, for the purpose for which it was intended at the inception of the lease, and without limitation of the lease term.
   c) estimated remaining period during which the property is expected to be economically usable with normal repairs and maintenance, for any purpose, and without limitation of the lease term.
   d) estimated remaining period during which the property is expected to be economically usable with all repairs and maintenance, for the purpose for which it was intended at the inception of the lease and no greater than the lease term

4) For purposes of statement presentation, the lessor's net investment in the lease would not include:

   a) minimum rental payments called for by the lease over the lease term (net of any executory costs).
   b) unguaranteed residual value of the leased property accruing to the lessor.
   c) unearned finance income remaining to be allocated to income over the lease term.
   d) any guaranteed residual value (by a third party unrelated to the lessee or the lessor).

The following scenario applies to questions 5 and 6:

On January 1, 1996, Plumco sold its office building and then leased it from the buyer. The building had a net book value of $20 million and was sold for $60 million, the fair market value at the time of the transaction.

The terms of the lease are as follows:

- The lease is for ten years.
- Annual lease payments of $7.5 million are to be made at the beginning of the year.
- Plumco has the option to purchase the building at fair market value at the end of the lease.
- If Plumco does not buy the building at the end of the lease, it is required to make a penalty payment of 20% of the fair market value at that time.

Plumco's incremental borrowing rate is 10%. The estimated remaining economic life of the building is 20 years.

5) Which one of the following classifications best describes this transaction for accounting purposes in Plumco's financial statements?
   a) Capital lease.
   b) Direct financing lease.
   c) Operating lease.
   d) Sales–type lease.

(CICA September 1996)

6) Assuming that Plumco has the option of acquiring the building at the end of the lease for $20 million (a bargain purchase price), which one of the following amounts would be recorded as a liability on January 1, 1996 excluding any deferred gain?
   a) $46,050,000
   b) $50,700,000
   c) $53,850,000
   d) $58,500,000

(CICA September 1996)

7) Cato Company, leased an asset from Nina Limited under a ten-year lease. There is a purchase option in the lease, which allows Cato to purchase the asset at the end of the lease for less than fair value. Cato uses the straight-line method to depreciate its assets. Cato should depreciate the asset:
   a) over the term of the lease.
   b) over the life of the asset, after deducting any residual value at the end of the lease term.
   c) over the term of the lease, after deducting the BPO.
   d) over the life of the asset, after deducting the residual value at the end of the asset's economic life.

8) Dectin Limited is planning to lease an asset worth $100,000 to another company under a non-operating 5-year lease. Dectin expects a 12% return with payments due at the end of the year. The residual value of the asset at the end of the lease is $5000. What should be the rental payment that Dectin charges under the lease?

   a) $26,953

   b) $27,739

   c) $24,770

   d) $24,069

9) In its 1997 balance sheet Karen Company reported a capital lease obligation of $85,150, which was net of a current portion of $1,350. A payment of $10,000 was made on the first day of the following year. Karen Company's incremental borrowing rate on the date of the lease was 11% and the lessor's implicit rate, which was known to the lessee, was 10%. In its 1998 balance sheet, what amount should Karen Company report as a capital lease obligation, net of the current portion?

   a) $83,665

   b) $86,500

   c) $84,517

   d) $85,015

10) Company B leases equipment from Company C. The lease is a capital lease. Other information about the lease is as follows:

Fair value of the equipment at the inception of the lease	$178,000
Carrying value of the equipment in the books of Company C at the date of the lease	$145,000
Present value of all future minimum lease payments	$175,000
Original cost of equipment paid by Company C	$170,000

   Company B will record the asset and obligation at the inception of the lease in:

   a) $178,000

   b) $145,000

   c) $175,000

   d) $170,000

(CMA June 1995)

SOLUTIONS TO MULTIPLE CHOICE QUESTIONS

1) c) Otherwise, any residual value that is guaranteed by the lessee or a related third party, which would include the parent company, would be included in the PVMLP.

2) b) An ordinary renewal option would not be included (only renewal options where there was an inducement to renew would be included).

3) b) Major repairs would not be expected.

4) c) The net investment is the discounted stream and therefore does not include interest.

5) a) The fact that the lessee has the option to purchase the asset at fair value and there is a significant penalty for non-renewal will induce the lessee to obtain ownership at the end of the lease (EIC #30).

6) d) PVMLP $7.5 million x 5.76 + $7.5 million	=	$50,700,000
$20 million x .39	=	$7,8000,000
		$58,500,000

7) d) Since the HB requires that the asset be depreciated over the life of the asset where there is a BPO. Since the PO is for less than the FMV, this would be assumed to be a bargain. When using the straight-line method, the residual value at the end of the asset life would be deducted.

8) a) $100,000—2,835* = $97165 / 3.605** = $26,953

*present value of the residual value using a factor of .567

** factor for 5 years, ordinary annuity since due at end of year

9) a) $85,150 x 10% = 8,515 INTEREST; $10,000—8,515 = 1,485. The balance is therefore reduced by the $1,485 (the current portion), leaving $83,665. Note that the 10% would be used since it is the lower of the two rates and that both rates are known to the lessee.

10) c) Since the lease will be recorded at the PVMLP.

PROBLEMS

1) Purpose: To illustrate the judgement involved in determining whether there is a bargain purchase option or not, and to show the impact on the lease payment.

Lessor Inc. (LI) signed a contract with Lessee Limited (LL) to lease a machine to LL under a three-year lease. The equipment was manufactured by LI at a cost of $18,000. At the end of the lease, the equipment will have a value of $2,000; however, at present, the fair market value of the equipment is $25,000. LL has negotiated an option to purchase the equipment for $1,900 since they want to use the asset for the remainder of its life (1 year). Although LI expects that LL will be able to make the payments, LI has determined that the interest rate implicit in the lease will be 2% above LI's own borrowing rate of 10%. The lessee plans to cover all other costs related to the ownership of the asset.

Payment is to be made at the end of each year. The lease was signed on January 1, year 1, which is the effective date of the lease.

Required

Calculate the lease payment.

2) Purpose: To illustrate the preparation of an amortization table and the relationship between the amortization table and the journal entries for the lessor.

Assume the same facts as in 1) above.

Required

Prepare the amortization table and the journal entries for the first year from the lessor's perspective.

3) Purpose:

To illustrate the preparation of the amortization table and the relationship between the amortization table and the journal entries for the lessee.

Assume the same information as in 1) and calculate the amortization table for the lessee. Assume that there is no BPO and that the lease payment is $9,815. Assume further that the lessee does not know the rate implicit in the lease and that the incremental borrowing rate is 11%.

Required

Prepare the lease amortization table and the related journal entries.

SOLUTIONS TO SHORT PROBLEMS

1) First, the lessor will want to recover FMV. Since there is nothing in the question to indicate that the lessee will not pay, we will assume that the FMV will be recovered. The next issue is to determine whether there is a bargain purchase option. The purchase option is for $1900 and the FMV of the asset at the end of the lease or the residual value is $2,000. Since the BPO is almost equal to the FMV of the asset at the end of the lease, it is unclear if there is a bargain.

We must determine whether it is a BPO, since if it is, the lessee will likely exercise the option and, therefore, we will deduct the present value (PV) of the BPO from the FMV in calculating the payment. Otherwise, we will deduct the PV of the residual value. The determining factor with respect to which of these numbers is relevant in the calculation is whether the lessee will keep the asset or give it back. Since we cannot determine whether the purchase option will induce LL to keep the asset, we must look for other clues. In the question, it states that LL specifically negotiated a purchase option because it wanted to use the asset after the lease. Therefore, we might conclude that there is intent to keep the asset and the option will be exercised.

FMV	$25,000	
PV of BPO	(1,352)	(1,900 @ .71178)
	$23,648	
divided by	2.40183	
Payment	$9,846	

The discount rate is taken from the ordinary annuity table since the payment is made at the end of the year. For the BPO, the table used is not an annuity table but rather the table for the PV of $1, since the BPO will only be paid once.

If we conclude that the option is not really a BPO and that LL might change its mind at the end of the lease and not keep the asset, the residual value is relevant and the payment is [$25,000—(PV of $2000)] / 2.402 = $9,815.

Either solution would be acceptable.

2)

Amortization table:

	Payment	Interest	Principal	Balance
				$25,000
Year 1	$9,846	$3,000	$6,846	18,154
Year 2	9,846	2,178	7,668	10,486
Year 3	9,846	1,260	8,586	1,900
	1,900	-0-	1,900	-0-
Total	$31,438	$6,438	$25,000	-0-

Because the payment is made at the end of the year, the first payment includes interest on the principal balance. Also, the BPO is included in the payment column. If we had decided that the residual value was relevant, it would be included in this column instead (regardless of whether or not it was guaranteed). The balance of the last column should always end up at zero.

Journal entries:

Before we book the lease, we must determine which type of lease we have. Since (1) the lease term is equal to 75% of the economic life of the asset (3/4 =75%), (2) collectibility is reasonably assured, and (3) the lessee plans to cover all other costs (therefore no unreimbursable costs), it appears that the risks and rewards of ownership have been transferred and that is an ownership change lease.

It is a sales-type lease since the lease payments and the BPO will result in the lessee making a profit on the sale.

Jan 1	dr. lease payment receivable	31,438	
	dr. cost of goods sold	18,000	
	cr. sales		25,000
	cr. inventory		18,000
	cr. unrealized interest rev		6,438

The profit is $7,000 ($25,000-$18,000) and the interest income has been deferred until earned. The numbers for the LPR, sale, and interest come from the table. Further, the relationship between the LPR and the sale (i.e, the sale includes the same things as the LPR except that the sales number has been discounted)

Dec 31	dr. cash	9,846	
	cr. LPR		9,846

The LPR account is reduced for the full amount of the payment because the full amount of the payment was initially included as part of the LPR (i.e., [3 x $9,846] + $1,900).

Dec 31	dr. unrealized interest	3,000	
	cr. interest income		3,000

The number comes from the amortization table. It is 12% times the principal balance outstanding for the year. Since the first payment was not made until the end of the year, the $25,000 was outstanding for the full year, therefore $25,000 x 12% = $3,000.
If there had been an unguaranteed residual value (URV) instead of a BPO, the sales and cost of goods sold numbers would be reduced by the present value of the URV, but the interest and LPR would stay the same. The calculations would be as follows:

Lease payment:

FMV	$25,000	
PV of URV	(1,424)	(2,000 x .71178)
	$23,576	
	divided by 2.402	
	=	
Payment	$9,815	

Amortization schedule:

	Payment	Interest	Principal	Balance
				$25,000
Year 1	$9,815	$3,000	$6,815	18,185
Year 2	9,815	2,182	7,633	10,552
Year 3	9,815	1,263	8,552	2,000
	2,000	-0-	2,000	-0-
Total	$31,445	$6,445	$25,000	-0-

The residual value, guaranteed or not, is always included in the schedule for calculation of the interest since the residual value is part of the LPR.

Journal entries:

Jan 1	dr. lease payment receivable	31,445	
	dr. cost of goods sold	16,576	
	cr. sales		23,576
	cr. inventory		18,000
	cr. unearned interest		6,445

The present value of the URV has been deducted from the sales and cost of goods sold numbers.

Dec 31	dr. cash	9,815	
	cr. lease payment receivable		9,815
	dr. unearned interest	3,000	
	cr. interest income		3,000

3) The lessee would treat this as a capital lease or a purchase since the lease term is 75% of the economic life (i.e., 3/4 = 75%).
The PVMLP is calculated as follows:

$$\$9{,}815 \times 2.44371 = \$23{,}985$$

Since the PVMLP is less than the FMV, the lease will be recorded at $23,985. If the present value of the lease payments is greater than FMV, the lease is booked at FMV. The discount rate used is the incremental borrowing rate of the lessee since the implicit rate is not known.

Amortization table:

	Payment	Interest	Principal	Balance
				$23,985
Year 1	$9,815	$2,638	$7,177	16,808
Year 2	9,815	1,849	7,966	8,842
Year 3	9,815	973	8,842	-0-
Total	$29,445	$5,460	$23,985	-0-

The table is different from the lessor's table. It does not have to be the same. In this case, it is different because the discount rate is different and because the residual value is not included. The residual value is not included because it is not guaranteed by the lessee and, therefore, it is not part of what the lessee has to pay for. The rate is different because the lessee does not know the implicit rate and therefore must use the next best thing,— the incremental borrowing rate of the lessee. If the residual value were guaranteed, this would have to be stipulated in the lease. If the lease does not state whether a residual value is guaranteed, it is safe to assume that it is not.

Journal entries:

Jan 1	dr. leased asset	23,985	
	cr. obligation under lease		23,985
Dec 31	dr. obligation under lease	7,177	
	dr. interest expense	2,638	
	cr. cash		9,815

The interest calculation comes from the table and is essentially 11% times the obligation balance outstanding over the year.

Dec 31	dr. amortization expense	7,995	
	cr. accumulated amortization		7,995

Since there is no BPO and the title to the asset does not pass at the end of the lease, the lease is amortized over the lease term.

CASES

1) Crown Inc.

Crown Inc. (CI) is a public company that manufactures a special type of cap that fits on a bottle. At present, it is the only manufacturer of this cap and therefore enjoys market security. The machinery used in production of this cap has been in use for 20 years and is due for replacement. CI has the option of buying the machine or leasing it. Currently, CI is leaning towards leasing the machine since it is expensive and funds would otherwise have to be borrowed from the bank. At present, the debt-to-equity ratio is marginal and if the funds were borrowed, the debt-to-equity ratio would surely worsen. CI's top management is anxious to maintain the ratio at its present level.

The dilemma for CI is that if the machine is leased, it may have to set up a long-term obligation under the lease and this would also affect the debt-to-equity ratio. Since this is clearly unacceptable, CI decided to see if the leasing company, Anchor Limited (AL), could do anything for it. After much negotiation, the following terms were agreed upon and written into the lease agreement:

- AL would manufacture and lease to CI a unique machine for making caps.
- The lease would be for a period of 12 years.
- The lease payments of $150,000 would be paid at the end of each year.
- CI would have the option to purchase the machine for $850,000 at the end of the lease term, which was equal to the FMV at that time; otherwise, the machine would return to the lessor.
- CI also had the option to lease the machine for another eight years at $150,000 per year.
- The rate implicit in the lease is 9%.

The machine was expected to last 20 years. Since it was a unique machine, AL had no other use for it if CI did not purchase it at the end of the lease or renew the lease. If CI had purchased the asset, it would cost $1.9 million. Although it was purposefully omitted from the written lease agreement, there was a tacit understanding that CI would either renew or exercise the option.

Required

Assume the role of CI's auditors and discuss the nature of the lease, noting how it should be accounted for. The controller of the company has confided in you that the machine will likely be purchased. Assume that you are aware of top management's position on adding debt to the balance sheet.

2) Eaton's—www.eatons.com

Many of the Eaton's stores are anchor tenants in medium to large sized retail shopping malls. This space would be primarily leased under real estate leases as disclosed in note 16 to the consolidated financial statements. As can be seen from the note, aggregate commitments under both capital and operating leases amount to over $1.3 million.

As part of Eaton's restructuring and downsizing plans, Eaton's announced in early 1997 that it planned to close down 31 of its 85 stores by June 30. Subsequently, it announced that it might keep certain stores open until February 1998 if the landlords were prepared to provide an appropriate level of financial support. Eaton's also announced that landlords who allowed the stores to close June 30 (the earlier date) would be given a bonus of three months free rent.

Required

For the January 25, 1997 financial statements, discuss how Eaton's might account for the rent free "bonus", the "appropriate level of financial support," and the fact that some of the stores that would be closed would be covered by leases that were non-cancelable.

For purposes of the discussion, assume that Eaton's had made the decision to close the stores involved prior to the financial statement date, but was still negotiating with the landlords as to incentives to cancel the lease and the date that Eaton's would close the stores.

SOLUTION TO CASES

1) Crown Inc.

Overview

CI's management obviously has a financial reporting **bias**; that is, they do not want to increase the debt that is presently on the balance sheet. **GAAP** is a constraint since CI is public. Since the company appears to have other debt, the **creditors** will be key users. They will want objective information and will be concerned with the debt-to-equity ratio to assess how leveraged the company is, and thereby assess the company's ability to repay debt.

Analysis

The issue is whether the lease is a **capital lease** or an **operating lease**. Analysis of the lease within a GAAP framework shows the following:

1) There is no evidence that **legal title** passes to CI at the end of the lease.
2) There is no **BPO** since the purchase option allows CI to purchase at the FMV.
3) The **term** of the lease is only 12 years, which is less than 75% of the **economic life** of 20 years.

4) The PVMLP is as follows:

$150,000 x 7.16073 = $1,074,109

$1,074,109/$1,900,000 = 56.5% which is less than 90%

Therefore, it would appear, on the surface, that the lease was an operating lease. On the other hand, given that the asset is manufactured specifically for CI, there is no other possible use for the machine, and AL likely does not want the machine back, it would appear to be common sense that the lease is indeed a capital lease that represents a purchase **in substance** by CI. The written agreement should not be reviewed in isolation but rather within the context of the reporting environment (management bias) and the additional unwritten agreement to purchase.

This is an excellent example of the inappropriateness of using specific rules in the Handbook. While they provide specific guidance, there is always a way to work around them (like the proverbial loophole in the Income Tax Act). Note that these are only guidelines. The principle hinges on the transfer of the risk and rewards of ownership. In this case, both the auditor and the client know that the substance is such that the lease has been used as alternative financing in order to obtain off-balance-sheet financing; however, the client will argue that it is not a capital lease since it does not meet the criteria.

As an auditor, there is an overriding concern that the financial statements are fairly presented, the implication being that the substance of all transactions is appropriately reflected in the financial statements. In this case, the evidence is too strong that this is a capital lease and, therefore, the auditor should argue to capitalize the lease, especially if the amounts are **material**.

2) Eaton's

The business environment:

The larger issue here is that Eaton's likely has numerous non-cancelable lease contracts. It is now in the position that it must attempt to extricate itself from these commitments. The landlords would ideally like these leases to run their full course; however, since Eaton's is not able to continue to operate all of these stores, this is not possible. Therefore, a new arrangement must be made. The landlords would rather keep Eaton's in as long as possible in order to give them time to find another tenant.

While on the one hand, Eaton's may have to pay some sort of cancellation fee to cancel the lease, the landlords might be willing to offer some assistance to Eaton's (through reduced rent perhaps) to keep the stores open as long as possible. The question arises as to how to account for any cancellation fee or inducements. It is likely that each contract with each landlord would have to be negotiated separately.

Assuming that Eaton's knew that it would be downsizing at year-end, there is a **recognition** issue and a **measurement** issue. Should the costs (or inducements offered by landlords) be accrued in the January 1997 financial statements? If so, at what amount? In general, this would fall under **contingency** accounting. If it is **likely** that these costs will be incurred and it is **measurable**, then they should be accrued. In this case, the leases are presumed to be non-cancelable and therefore, it is likely that there are some costs involved with cancelling them. On the other hand, it would appear that the negotiations are at a very preliminary stage and that the landlords might be willing to offer some inducements/concessions to Eaton's to stay longer. Therefore, the outcome of the uncertainty is **not yet determinable** and recognition is not recommended. This would be further supported since, even if it is argued that the costs are **likely**, it is difficult to **measure** the cost. At the one end of the spectrum, the landlords could require the full commitment to the end of the lease be honoured. At the other end, the landlord might agree to a lesser amount, i.e., Eaton's would pay rent until a new tenant is found.

SELECTED SOLUTIONS FROM THE TEXTBOOK

EXERCISE 21-3

Capitalized amount of the lease:

Yearly paymen	$70,000.00
Executory costs	470.51
Minimum annual lease payment	$69,529.49

Present value of minimum lease payments (i=12%, n=10)

$69,529.49 x 6.32825 = $440,000.00

	Debit	Credit
January 1, 1998		
Leased Building Under Capital Leases	440,000.00	
Obligations Under Capital Leases		440,000.00
January 1, 1998		
Executory Costs-Property Taxes	470.51	
Obligations Under Capital Leases	69,529.49	
Cash		70,000.00
December 31, 1998		
Depreciation Expense ($440,000.00 ÷ 10)	44,000.00	
Accumulated Depreciation—Capital Lessee		44,000.00
December 31, 1998		
Interest Expense	44,456.46	
Interest Payable		44,456.46
January 1, 1999		
Executory Costs-Property Taxes	470.51	
Interest Payable	44,456.46	
Obligations Under Capital Leases	25,073.03	
Cash		70,000.00
December 31, 1999		
Depreciation Expense	44,000.00	
Accumulated Depreciation—Capital Leases		44,000.00

	December 31, 1999		
Interest Expense		41,447.70	
Interest Payable			41,447.70

Lease Amortization Schedule (Lessee)

Date	Annual Payment Less Executory Costs	Interest (12%) on Unpaid Obligation	Reduction of Lease Obligation	Balance of Lease Obligation
Jan. 1, 1998				$440,000.00
Jan. 1, 1998	$69,529.49	$ 0.00	$69,529.49	370,470.51
Jan. 1, 1999	69,529.49	44,456.46	25,073.03	345,397.48
Jan. 1, 2000	69,529.49	41,447.70	28,081.79	317,315.69

EXERCISE 21-4

Computation of annual payments:

Cost (fair market value)	$160,000.00
Less: Present value of salvage value (residual value in this case) $8,000 x .82645 (Present value of 1 at 10% for 2 periods)	(6,611.60)
Amount to be recovered through lease payments	$153,388.40
Two periodic lease payments $153,388.40 ~ 1.73554*	$88,380.79

*Present value of an ordinary annuity of 1 for 2 periods at 10%.

Computation of lease payments receivable

Annual payments ($88,380.79 x 2)	$176,761.58
Salvage value (residual value)	8,000.00
Lease payments receivable	$184,761.58

Computation of unearned interest revenue

Gross investment by lessee	$184,761.58
Asset cost (fair value)	160,000.00
Unearned interest revenue	$24,761.58

Castle Leasing Company (Lessor)
Lease Amortization Schedule

Date	Annual Payment Less Executor Costs	Interest On Net Investment	Net Investment Recovery	Net Investment
Jan. 1, /98				$160,000.00
Dec. 31, /98	$88,380.79	$16,000.00	$72,380.79	87,619.21
Dec. 31, /99	88,380.79	8,761.58*	79,619.21	8,000.00
		$24,761.58		

*Adjusted due to rounding.

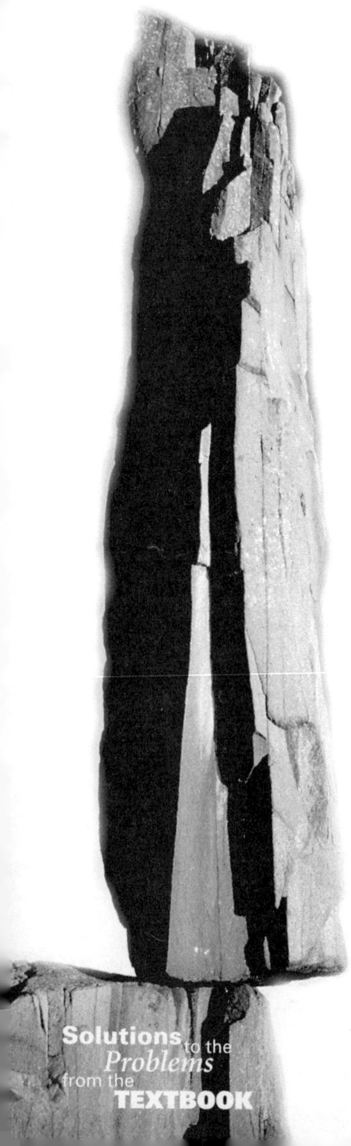

(a)

January 1, 1998		
Lease Payments Receivable	184,761.58	
Equipment		160,000.00
Unearned Interest Revenue—Leases		24,761.58
December 31, 1998		
Cash ($88,380.79 + $5,000)	93,380.79	
Executory Costs Payable (or Executory Expense)		5,000.00
Lease Payments Receivable		88,380.79
Unearned Interest Revenue—Leases	16,000.00	
Interest Revenue—Leases		16,000.00
December 31, 1999		
Cash	93,380.79	
Executory Costs Payable (or Executory Expense)		5,000.00
Lease Payments Receivable		88,380.79
Unearned Interest Revenue—Leases	8,761.58	
Interest Revenue—Leases		8,761.58

(b)

Cash	8,000.00	
Lease Payments Receivable		8,000.00

EXERCISE 21-11

(a) Entries for Trake Co. are as follows:

January 1, 1998		
Building		4,200,000
Cash		4,200,000
December 31, 1998		
Cash	200,000	
Rental Revenue		200,000
Depreciation Expense ($4,200,000 / 50)	84,000	
Accumulated Depreciation - Building		84,000
Property Tax Expense	45,000	
Insurance Expense	10,000	
Cash	55,000	

(b) Entries for Suffolk Inc. are as follows:

December 31, 1998		
Rental Expense	200,000	
Cash		200,000

(c) The real estate broker's fee should be amortized equally over the 10-year period. As a result, real estate fee expense of $3,000 ($30,000/10) should be reported in each period.

EXERCISE 21-14 (20-30 MINUTES)

The lease should be treated as a capital lease because the present value of the minimum lease payments equals the fair value of the computer, or because the lease term > 75% of the economic life of the asset, or the title transfers to the lessee.

Breton Corporation (Lessee)
January 1, 1998

	Debit	Credit
January 1, 1998		
Cash	680,000.00	
Computer		580,000.00
Unearned Profit on Sale-Leaseback		100,000.00
Leased Computer Under Capital Leases	680,000.00	
Obligations Under Capital Leases		
($110,666.81 x 6.14457)		680,000.00
Throughout 1998		
Executory Expense	5,000.00	
Accounts Payable or Cash		5,000.00
December 31, 1998		
Unearned Profit on Sale-Leaseback	10,000.00	
Profit from Sale-Leaseback* ($100,000 ÷ 10)		10,000.00
Depreciation Expense	68,000.00	
Accumulated Depreciation ($680,000 ÷ 10)		68,000.00
Interest Expense ($680,000 x .10)	68,000.00	
Obligations Under Capital Lease	42,666.81	
Cash		110,666.81

*The credit could be to Depreciation Expense.

Note to instructor:

1. The present value of an ordinary annuity at 10% for 10 periods should be used to capitalize the asset. In this case, Conrad would use the implicit rate of the lessor because it is lower than its own incremental borrowing rate.
2. The unearned profit on the sale-leaseback should be amortized on the same basis as the asset is being depreciated.

The lease should be treated as a direct financing lease because (1) at least one of the criteria for a capital lease is met, (2) collectibility of the payments is reasonably assured, (3) no important uncertainties surround the costs yet to be incurred by the lessor, and (4) the lessor does not earn a dealer profit. The present value of the minimum lease payments equals the cost of the leased asset to the lessor.

Liquidity Finance Co. (Lessor)

January 1, 1998		
Computer	680,000.00	
Cash		680,000.00
Lease Payments Receivable ($110,666.81 x 10)	1,106,668.10	
Unearned Interest Revenue—Leases	426,668.10	
Computer	680,000.00	
December 31, 1998		
Cash	110,666.81	
Lease Payments Receivable		110,666.81
Unearned Interest Revenue—Leases ($680,000 x .10)	68,000.00	
Interest Revenue—Leases		68,000.00

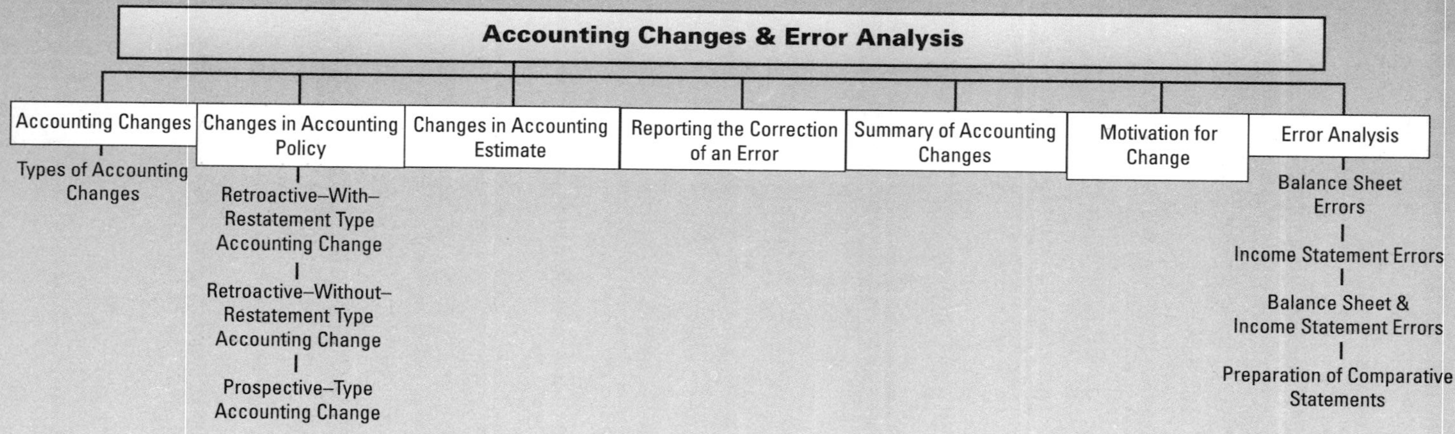

Accounting Changes & Error Analysis
Accounting Changes
Types of Accounting Changes
Changes in Accounting Policy
Retroactive–With–Restatement Type Accounting Change
Retroactive–Without–Restatement Type Accounting Change
Prospective–Type Accounting Change
Changes in Accounting Estimate
Reporting the Correction of an Error
Summary of Accounting Changes
Motivation for Change
Error Analysis
Balance Sheet Errors
Income Statement Errors
Balance Sheet & Income Statement Errors
Preparation of Comparative Statements

chapter 22

ACCOUNTING CHANGES & ERROR ANALYSIS

PERSPECTIVE

The chapter on changes summarizes the different types of changes in financial reporting and how they should be implemented and reflected in the financial statements. Keep in mind that a change in the way the financial statements are prepared may make them more confusing for users and may indeed cause users to question what was wrong in the first place that the statements had to be "corrected". Therefore, it is very important that changes only be made when there is good reason to do so.

INSIGHTS

This area is not complex and the material here gives an overview of the types of changes and how they affect the financial statements. The section on error analysis is not emphasized since it is fairly mechanical and therefore lends itself to self-study. There are multiple choice questions and a problem below, as well as, good exercises in the text that should be attempted for practice.

STUDY STEPS

1. Understanding the Nature of Changes

STUDY STEPS

Below is a summary of how changes should be accounted for:

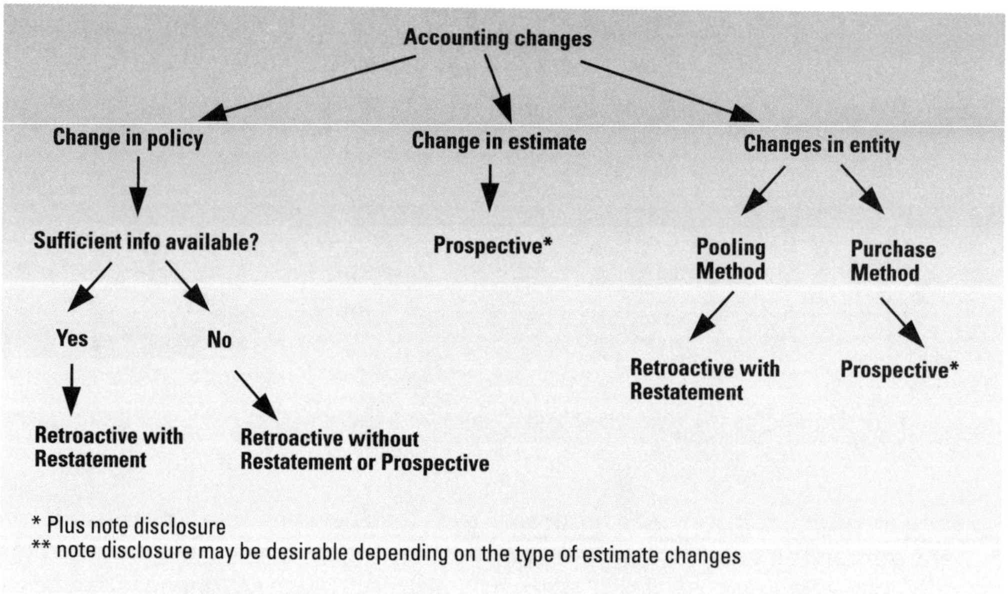

Changes in accounting policy

Generally, accounting policy choices are discretionary and, therefore, different people would select different methods in the same situation. Hopefully, a change will result in better accounting. Therefore, it makes sense to show the impact of the change on a retroactive basis.

Tip! **Retroactive application also results in consistency.**

Change in estimate

A change in accounting estimate usually results from **additional new information** or a **change in circumstances** (e.g., a change in the obsolescence provision for inventory might result from an inventory count, or a change in the estimated remaining useful life of an asset may result from real-life experience in that the asset physically lasts longer than originally expected). Therefore, it does not make sense to adjust retroactively since the situation was different in those earlier periods.

Tip! **If in doubt as to whether something is a change in policy or in estimate, treat it as a change in estimate.**

Correction of an error

A correction of an error is accounted for **retroactively with restatement** since once the error is found, the previous statements may be incorrect or misleading and should be adjusted.

Tip! **Be careful to differentiate between changes in estimates from corrections of errors due to the different accounting procedures.**

Tip!

Remember that estimates are made everyday in accounting. And, as long as the estimates are made with care and consider available information, they are acceptable for that time and would not be subsequently adjusted even though they proved to be incorrect in hindsight.

Any type of change or adjustment should be noted in the notes to the financial statements if they are material, except for changes in estimates since they are considered to be a normal part of financial reporting. Even changes in estimates may warrant some additional disclosure, however, depending on how significant the change is.

MULTIPLE CHOICE QUESTIONS

1) Assume that a company decides to change depreciation policy from straight line to sinking fund since it feels that the change will result in a better presentation. At the same time, the company decides that the remaining service life is longer than originally estimated. Assume that the impact of any change on earlier years may be determined. This should be treated:

   a) as retroactive incorporating the new life.

   b) as retroactive with old life. New life should be taken into account only prospectively.

   c) prospectively with new life and new method.

   d) retroactive with cumulative adjustment through opening retained earnings.

2) In the past, B Company leased cars annually for its sales representatives. At the end of each year, the cars were traded in for new ones under new leases. The accounting policy has been to account for these as operating leases.

   B Company has decided to change its policy such that the cars will be under five-year leases from now on, and these will be accounted for as capital leases. The company did not keep sufficient records to enable it to go back and restate each previous year if required. This should be treated as which of the following:

   a) a change in accounting policy with full retroactive application.

   b) a change in accounting policy with a cumulative adjustment through opening retained earnings.

   c) a change in accounting policy applied prospectively.

   d) a new accounting policy.

3) C Company has decided to increase its provision for obsolescence to 3% of ending inventory. In the past, the obsolescence provision has always approximated 2% of the ending inventory balance. The main reason for the change this year is to account for some old stock that has been on hand for two years. The stock would have normally been provided for last year under the old policy; however, the inventory count

records for the warehouse where the stock is located were lost just before the provision was calculated. The stock was therefore valued at full value last year. This should be accounted for as:

a) a change in estimate applied prospectively.

b) a change in accounting policy applied retroactively.

c) a correction of an error applied retroactively.

d) a change in accounting policy applied prospectively.

4) JMT used the cash basis to account for its operations. In 1998, JMT decided to get its financial statements audited for purposes of raising more capital. The auditors advised JMT to switch to accrual based financial statements. Adequate records exist to make any necessary adjustments. This change would be accounted for as:

a) a change in policy—retroactive.

b) a change in policy—cumulative restatement through opening retained earnings.

c) a correction of an error.

d) a change in policy—prospective application.

5) On January 1, 1992, A Ltd. purchased a vehicle for $20,000 cash. A Ltd's fiscal year-end is December 31. At the time of acquisition, the vehicle was expected to last five years and had an estimated salvage value of $1,400. A Ltd. uses the straight-line method to depreciate its vehicles. On January 1, 1993, A Ltd. changed its total estimated useful life of the vehicle from 5 years to 4 years and the estimated salvage value from $1,400 to $2,300. In 1993, A Ltd. Would record depreciation on the vehicle amounting to:

a) $3,495

b) $4,193

c) $4,425

d) $4,660

(CMA adapted—June 1994)

6) KLM Limited changes its accounting for inventory from the LIFO method to the FIFO method on the basis that the new method provides better matching of costs to revenues. Because prices have remained constant over the past several years, the impact on retained earnings and inventory is immaterial. The change should be accounted for as follows:

a) a change in accounting policy—retroactive.

b) a change in estimate—prospective.

c) a correction of an error—retroactive.

d) a change in accounting policy—prospective.

7) Under which of the following situations would a change in accounting policy not be acceptable under GAAP:

a) to conform with industry practice.

b) to avoid breaking a debt covenant.

c) to conform to new Handbook recommendation.

d) to conform to legislative requirements.

8) Noncounterbalancing errors are described as errors that:

a) will reverse in the following period.

b) will not reverse in the following period.

c) will never reverse.

d) need not be adjusted for.

9) YVT Incorporated discovered a balance sheet classification error in its prior year's financial statements. The error does not materially affect financial statement presentation. It is now in the process of preparing its current year financial statements. What if any adjustments should be made?

a) No adjustment is required since it does not affect net income of current or prior year.

b) Adjustment is required to the prior year. Reclassify comparative numbers and note that the numbers have been restated.

c) No adjustment is required since the error is not material.

d) Adjustment is required to the prior year. Reclassify comparative numbers, but do not note that the numbers have been restated, due to immateriality.

10) Goodwyn Company undervalued its inventory in its 1998 financial statements. It is now 1999 and the company is preparing its 1999 financial statements. Assuming that the 1998 error is counterbalancing, what action is required for the 1999 statements? Assume the books are closed.

a) No action is required since error counterbalancing and the books are correct on a cumulative basis.

b) Correct the books and adjust the financial statements.

c) Adjust the current year financial statements only.

d) Adjust the current and comparative financial statements.

SOLUTIONS TO MULTIPLE CHOICE QUESTIONS

1) b) Generally, this would be seen as a change in accounting policy with retroactive application since all numbers are determinable. The change in life, however, is based on new information and would only be adjusted on a going forward basis. Having stated this, however, the Handbook requires that accounting policies be reviewed annually as part of management's ongoing review of the estimates in the financial statements. It could be interpreted that this would put these types of accounting

changes (assuming that they are based on new information) in the realm of changes in estimates and therefore it would require prospective application.

2) d) This is not a change in accounting policy. Since B Company has never entered into capital leases before, this is merely a new type of transaction that must be accounted for in a manner that reflects its substance. The old leases are rental type arrangements that are correctly treated as operating leases and should not be adjusted. The accounting policy has not changed; rather, it has been augmented to take into account the new type of leases.

3) c) This is really a correction of an error. The inventory was obsolete last year and should have been written off then. The only reason that it was not is that of carelessness. Last year's records are incorrect due to an estimating technique that failed to consider all obsolete inventory when it should have.

4) c) This is technically a correction of an error since GAAP requires accrual based accounting.

5) d) 1992 depreciation = ($20,000—$1,400)/5 = $3,720

   1993 depreciation = ($20,000—$2,300—$3720)/3 = $4,660

6) d) This is an accounting policy change that would normally have retroactive application. However, since the change is immaterial, there would not be retroactive application.

7) b) It is not acceptable to change accounting policies in order to bias financial reporting.

8) b) These are errors that will not reverse in the following year but that will likely reverse in subsequent periods, except in unusual circumstances.

9) c) Anything that is not material should not be adjusted for since retroactive adjustments tend to confuse users and undermine the accounting process. Users will begin to lose confidence in the process, wondering if current financial statements are also misstated.

10) d) Since the books are already closed and the error is counterbalancing, there is no need to adjust the books. The financial statements, however, are misstated for both years. In 1998, inventory is undervalued and the cost of sales overvalued. In 1999, the opposite is true. This could tend to distort key ratios such as gross profit and should therefore be adjusted for.

SHORT PROBLEM

Purpose: To illustrate the difference in accounting for adjustments retroactively and prospectively.

Changes Limited (CL) has always costed out its manufactured inventory to include direct labour, materials, and variable overhead. In order to provide better information for pricing the inventory, CL has decided to included fixed overhead as well. Therefore, beginning January 1, 1998, fixed overhead has been included in inventory as part of the cost of the product. In prior years, fixed overhead was expensed as a period cost.

Other information is as follows:

	1997	1996
Opening inventory	100,000 units	98,000 units
Production	498,000	412,000
Units sold	412,000	410,000
Fixed overhead	$1,000,000	$1,000,000

There are no unfinished goods at year-end. All goods produced in 1996 were sold in 1997. The company uses the FIFO method of accounting for inventory costs. Fixed overhead per unit for 1995 was $2.00.

Required

(a) Prepare the journal entries to account for this change in accounting policy retroactively. Ignore income taxes.

(b) Prepare the journal entries to account for this change, assuming that, for some reason, the information for prior years was missing.

SOLUTIONS TO SHORT PROBLEM

(a) Each unit of inventory would increase by total fixed costs / number of units produced. Ending inventory would increase as follows:

1997	\$1,000,000 / 498,000 = \$2.008 x 186,000 units = \$373,494
1996	\$1,000,000 / 412,000 = \$2.427 x 100,000 units = \$242,718

Cost of goods sold (COGS) would increase in 1997 by the \$242,700 in opening inventory and \$626,496 relating to inventory produced and sold in 1997 (412,000 units sold—100,000 units from 1996 = 312,000 units produced in 1997; 312,000 x \$2.008 = \$626,496).

Cost of goods sold for 1996 would increase by the \$196,000 (98,000 x \$2.00) in opening inventory plus \$757,224 relating to inventory produced and sold in 1996 (410,000 units sold—98,000 units from 1996 units produced in 1996 = 312,000; 312,000 x \$2.427 = \$757,224).

Therefore, the adjusting journal entries would be as follows:

1996

dr. COGS	757,300 (rounded)	
dr. COGS	196,000	
dr. inventory	242,700	
cr. general expenses		1,000,000
cr. opening retained earnings		196,000

1997

dr. COGS	242,700	
dr. COGS	626,500 (rounded)	
dr. inventory	373,500	
cr. general expenses		1,000,000
cr. opening retained earnings		242,700

In 1997, we do not need to adjust for the \$196,000 again since, by 1997, it would have been debited through retained earnings both under the old way, as general expenses, and the new way, as COS.

(b) If the information for prior years was missing, the only entry that would be booked would be for the 1997 overhead:

dr. COGS	626,500	
dr. inventory	373,500	
cr. general expenses		1,000,000

Net income would be higher by the \$242,700 relating to fixed overhead that should have been included in the COGS under the new method had the amounts been known. This amount would have been charged to income in 1996. Also, 1997 and 1996 are not really comparable since, in 1996, the full fixed overhead has been expensed and, in 1997, some has been deferred.

Note: This one problem serves as an example of retroactive versus prospective application, and is not intended to serve as a comprehensive review of all the different types of changes. Additional questions/exercises from the text should be done for practice for the other types of changes. A good solid knowledge base is required for these types of questions about different depreciation methods, inventory costing methods, and revenue recognition methods, etc. Therefore, a review of that material is warranted.

CASES

1) Harvey's Hotels Limited

Harvey's Hotels Limited (HHL) uses the sinking fund method to depreciate its hotel buildings. It has used this method for the past 20 years on the advice of accountants who no longer audit the company. Originally, the company was perceived to be in the real estate business, with the operation of hotels as a sideline business. But gradually, HHL has changed the emphasis such that the main business is now in hotel operations.

Recently, HHL received a letter from the securities commission, which reviews financial statements of companies whose shares trade on the stock exchange. The letter pointed out that the use of the sinking fund method of depreciation for buildings was not really acceptable in Canada any more, except for the real estate industry. The securities commission requested that the matter be brought to the attention of the company's auditors and suggseted a response within three weeks.

HHL had also recently received a research report from a local university that corroborated the observation of the securities commission. There had not been any such study available previously in Canada. HHL had been considering switching from sinking fund to straight line, since they were now at the point where the depreciation charges under the sinking fund method were quite large and growing. The increasing depreciation charges under the sinking fund method were causing net income to decrease.

The CICA Handbook had recently come out with a new section stating that the amortization method and estimates of the remaining lives of assets should be reviewed on a regular basis as part of the ongoing annual assessment of the financial statements. In that respect, HHL had had their hotels appraised. The appraiser noted that the residual value at the end of the expected life of the hotels would likely be about five times higher than the original estimates in many cases due to a strong demand.

HHL would like to know whether the change to straight line would be accounted for prospectively or retroactively, and how to incorporate the information from the appraisal.

Required

Respond to the concerns of HHL, noting any relevant points ,as well as, any other issues.

2) Inco Limited—www.incoltd.com

In its 1996 financial statements, Inco reported the following note relating to a change in accounting policy:

> Effective January 1, 1995, the company adopted accrual accounting in respect to post-retirement benefits other than pensions. This change in accounting policy provides for the actuarially determined accrual of the cost of such benefits over the service life of the employees prior to their retirement. Previously, the costs of these benefits were accounted for on a pay-as-you-go basis after the employees retired.

The change has been applied retroactively and, accordingly, the consolidated financial statements for 1994 have been restated to reflect the company's obligation for accumulated post-retirement benefits other than pensions attributable to the services of retired and active employees prior to 1995..."

Post-retirement benefits other than pensions are generally benefits, such as dental and medical, which an employer extends to its employees even after retirement. The pay-as-you-go method allows employers to record the payouts only when a claim is made (which would be only after retirement, by definition). Therefore, it is recognized on a cash basis.

Required

Analyze the way that the change has been accounted for.

SOLUTIONS TO CASES

1) Harvey's

Overview

HHL has changed its business from real estate to hotel operations. It is concerned about the impact of the present depreciation policy on net income and has had a letter from the securities commission stating that the method being used is no longer acceptable.

HHL is interested in changing the method for these reasons, and would likely want to minimize the negative impact on the financial statements. **GAAP** appears to be a constraint since the shares are publicly traded. Any recommendation must be defensible since the securities commission will be reviewing it.

Analysis

The issue seems to be whether a change in method from sinking fund to straight line should be accounted for **retroactively** or **prospectively**.

The sinking fund method provides for minimal depreciation up-front and increasing amounts until the end. It is acceptable for the real estate industry due to the increasing values of real estate, and presumably, the increasing ability for real estate to generate increasing revenues from the property. The straight line method, however, would yield constant depreciation charges for the life of the asset.

Retroactive Treatment

- Traditionally, a change in method of amortization has been accounted for retroactively.
- This would require a large retroactive adjustment to accumulated depreciation and retained earnings since, in earlier years, straight line depreciation would be significantly higher than sinking fund depreciation.
- The current depreciation would be lower and have a less negative impact on net income, especially if the new estimated residual value were incorporated, which it should be.
- It might be argued that this is a correction of an error since the sinking fund method is not allowable for non-real estate companies. Therefore, retroactive treatment must be afforded. However, there are several arguments against this:
- The previous auditors had agreed to the acceptability of the use of the sinking fund method.
- There has been a change in operations from real estate to hotels.
- It was not clear prior to this point that use of the method was not acceptable.
- Retroactive application will make the statements more comparable from year to year.

Prospective

- Since the *CICA Handbook* requires a review of amortization methods on an ongoing basis, it might be argued that this is part of the ongoing annual review of accounts to incorporate new information. As such, prospective treatment might be more appropriate. This is supported by the fact that HHL's situation has changed. They are no longer in the real estate business, but rather in the hotel industry. Furthermore, since it was not earlier codified that the sinking fund method was not acceptable to non-real estate operations, it might be argued that this is also new information which will presumably affect their accounting.
- Prospective treatment might be preferable since retroactive adjustments, especially large debits to retained earnings, cause users to doubt the integrity of the decision and management, and undermine the credibility of financial statements in general. If they can change last year's statements, who is to say that the current statements will not be changed next year?

- Prospective treatment would take the present net book value from the old calculations under the sinking fund method and use that as a starting point to depreciate using straight line on a going forward basis. This might result in higher depreciation charges in the next few years than by using the sinking fund method.

Recommendation

It could be argued either way; however, HHL might opt for retroactive since it will have a more positive impact on their statements on a going forward basis.

2) Inco Limited

Inco has treated this as a change in accounting policy and, since the numbers are available for full restatement, this has been done. This change was likely precipitated by the changes in U.S. GAAP regarding post-retirement benefits other than pensions, since Inco's shares trade on the New York Stock Exchange.

The issue arises as to whether this is a **correction of an error** or a **change in policy**. Prior to an analysis, we must first define what an error is. An error would occur if Inco had been using a non-GAAP accounting policy and had switched to a GAAP policy. GAAP for post-retirement benefit plans other than pensions has traditionally been ill-defined, with many methods being used in **practice**, such as **pay-as-you-go**. In this regard, Inco would successfully argue that the previous method used was one of many acceptable methods.

On the other hand (and this applies to all companies, not just Inco), it might be argued that the pay-as-you-go method is based on the **cash basis** of accounting. Since GAAP is **accrual based**, wouldn't the pay-as-you-go method be considered inappropriate? It could also be argued that with a very base level of analysis, the post-retirement benefit represents a **liability** to the company that should be accrued while the employee is still working for the company (i.e. in order to **match** compensation costs with revenues). Indeed, this is what U.S. GAAP now requires and also what the new CICA Exposure Draft on retirement benefits proposes for the most part.

Although Inco is technically correct in the treatment as a change in accounting policy, it is interesting to note that, **in substance**, this change is more like a **correction of an error**. The only difference is that the error has been previously accepted as GAAP!

SELECTED SOLUTIONS FROM THE TEXTBOOK

EXERCISE 22-2

(a)

Accumulated Depreciation—Equipment ($408,000—$306,000)	102,000	
Retained Earnings—Cumulative Effect of Change in Accounting Policy—Depreciation		102,000

Computations:

Sum-of-the-years'-digits depreciation:		Straight-line depreciation:	
1995 (5/15 x $510,000)	$170,000	1995	$102,000
1996 (4/15 x $510,000)	136,000	1996	102,000
1997 (3/15 x $510,000)	102,000	1997	102,000
	$408,000		$306,000

(b) Comparative data:

	1998	1997
Income as originally computed	$375,000	$400,000
Effect of change in estimate*	8,250	
Income adjusted for change in principle and change in estimate	$383,250	$400,000
Basic earnings per share:		
Basic earnings per share	$3.83	$4.00

*Depreciation expense per books 1998 (693,000 ÷ 30)	$23,100
Depreciation expense after change in estimate [($693,000—($23,100 x 3)) ÷ (45 -3)] =	14,850
Increase in net income	$ 8,250

EXERCISE 22-9

(a) Inventory for 1998 should be reported at $499,510 under an average cost approach.

Beginning inventory under average cost	
3,000 @ $21.00 =	$ 63,000
5,000 @ $24.00 =	120,000
4,000 @ $30.00 =	120,000
6,000 @ $32.00 =	192,000
5,000 @ $34.00 =	170,000
5,000 @ $36.00 =	180,000
28,000	$ 845,000

Average cost = $845,000/28,000 = $30.18

Beginning inventory value = 8,000 @ $30.18 = $241,440

Ending inventory under average cost (11,000 units)

8,000 @ $30.18 =	$ 241,440
2,000 @ $45.00 =	90,000
5,000 @ $47.00 =	235,000
5,000 @ $50.00 =	250,000
7,000 @ $54.00 =	378,000
3,000 @ $56.00 =	168,000
30,000	$1,362,440

Average cost per unit is $1,362,440/30,000 = $45.41
Ending inventory value = 11,000 @ $45.41 = $499,510

Ending inventory under FIFO (11,000 units)

3,000 @ $56 =	$ 168,000
7,000 @ $54 =	378,000
1,000 @ $50 =	50,000
	$ 596,000

Note: 1997 ending inventory using FIFO would be 3,000 units at $34 each and 5,000 units at $36.

(b) When an enterprise changes to the average cost method of inventory valuation, the cumulative adjustment is difficult to determine unless average costs are available for each previous year-end inventory. Disclosure involves showing the effect of the change on the results of operations in the period of change and on opening retained earnings. The effect of the change is to decrease net income by $57,894 ([$596,000—$499,510] x 60%). The impact on 1997 net income would be [($282,000—$241,440) x 60%] $24,336. A description of the change would be included in the notes along with a disclosure that the 1997 financial statements had been restated.

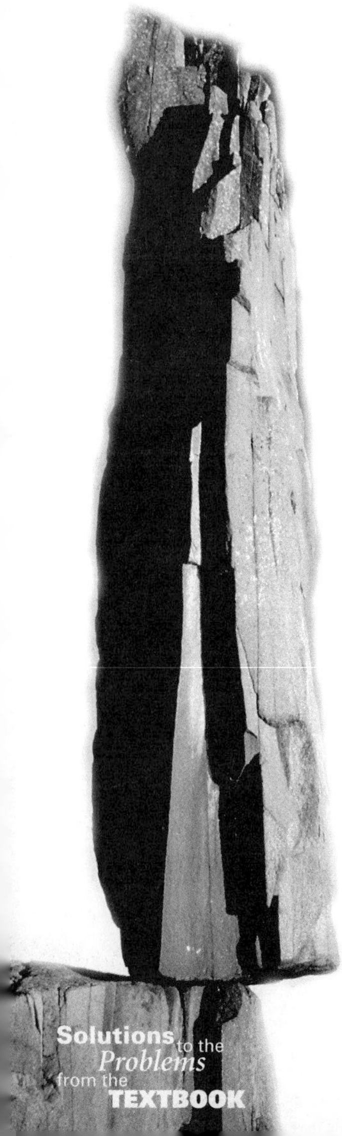

SOLUTION TO PROBLEM

PROBLEM 22-1

(a) 1. Depreciation Expense	36,000	
Accumulated Depreciation		36,000
Original cost		$880,000
Depreciation recorded in 1997 ($880,000 x 10/55)		160,000
Book value January 1, 1998		720,000
Depreciation rate (7/28)		x .25
Depreciation to be recorded		180,000
Depreciation recorded ($880,000 x 9/55)		144,000
Adjustment		$ 36,000

2.	Retained Earnings ($11,000 + $9,000)	20,000	
	Inventory	19,000	
	Income Summary ($20,000 + $15,000)		39,000

Income Overstated (Understated)

	1996	1997	1998
Beginning inventory	$(11,000)	$(20,000)	
Ending inventory	$11,000	20,000	(19,000)
	$11,000	$9,000	$(39,000)

3.	Retained Earnings	3,000	
	Wage Expense	600	
	Wages Payable		2,400

Income Overstated (Understated)

	1996	1997	1998
Beginning	(1,600)	$(3,000)	
Ending	1,600	3,000	2,400
	$1,600	$1,400	$(600)

4.	Furnace A	400,000	
	Depreciation Expense ($400,000 ÷ 5)	80,000	
	Accumulated Depreciation		160,000
	Retained Earnings		320,000
	Furnace B	450,000	
	Depreciation Expense ($480,000 ÷ 5)	90,000	
	Accumulated Depreciation		90,000
	Maintenance Expense		450,000

(b)

	1998	1997
Income—as reported	$900,000	640,000
Depreciation revision	(36,000)	
Inventory error correction	39,000	(9,000)
Wage accruals	600	(1,400)
Changes in policy:		
Maintenance expense	480,000	400,000
Current depreciation A	(80,000)	(80,000)
Current depreciation B	(96,000)	
Net income—revised balance	$1,207,600	$949,600

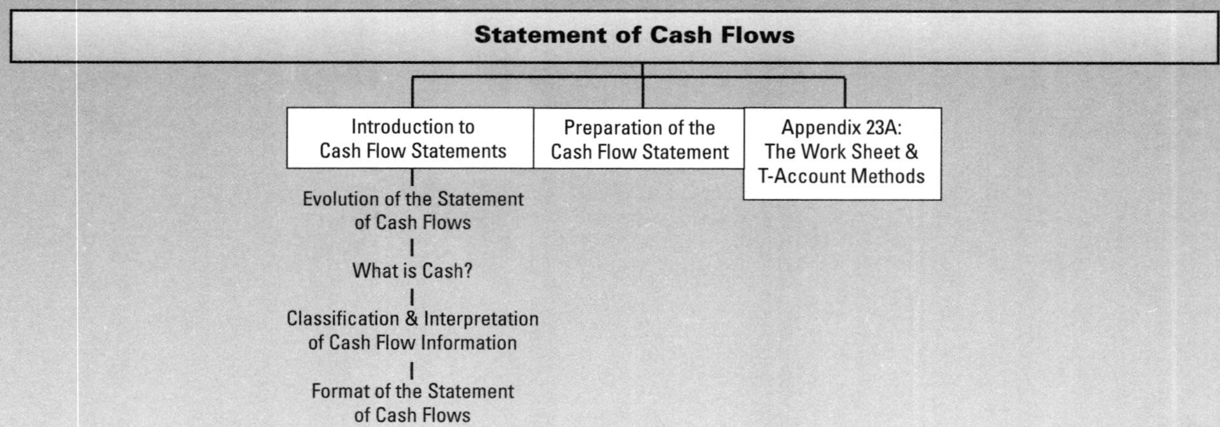
Statement of Cash Flows
Introduction to Cash Flow Statements
Preparation of the Cash Flow Statement
Appendix 23A: The Work Sheet & T-Account Methods
Evolution of the Statement of Cash Flows
What is Cash?
Classification & Interpretation of Cash Flow Information
Format of the Statement of Cash Flows

chapter 23

STATEMENT OF CASH FLOWS

PERSPECTIVE

The statement of changes in financial position gives information to users that is not provided by the other statements, such as the balance sheet and the income statement. Like the income statement, the focus is on transactions, rather than balances;, however, while the income statement primarily includes operating transactions on the accrual basis, the statement of changes in financial position includes operating, investing, and financing transactions on a cash basis.

The CICA has recently (at the time of writing this book), issued an Exposure Draft entitled Cash Flow Statements. The ED brings Canadian standards in line with international standards. This material assumes that the ED will become part of the Handbook with little modification since the changes are not controversial and since the CICA is concerned with international harmonization of standards.

INSIGHTS

- *Remember that the cash flow statement is a very critical statement and that many users begin an analytical review of the company with this statement.*
- *Like other statements, this statement has key numbers on it. The most important number is "cash from operations" since a company must generate cash from its primary operations if it plans to succeed in the long run.*
- *It is important to learn the mechanics of preparing the statement of cash flows. Therefore this chapter will focus on a method for doing this (the worksheet method).*
- *It is equally as important to be able to interpret the statement.*

STUDY STEPS

1. Understanding the Value of the Cash Flow Statement

STUDY STEPS

The primary value of the statement of changes is to show where a company gets its cash (e.g., from operations, by selling off assets, by borrowing, etc.) and how it spends its cash (e.g., on operations, paying off debt, buying assets, etc.). The focus is on liquidity and solvency. A company may be profitable according to the income statement but may be having cash flow problems. This is highlighted by the cash flow statement.

Tip! **Just because a company is profitable does not mean that it is generating cash from its operations.**

The key number on the statement is the line that shows cash provided by operations. Ideally, the greater the cash from operations, the stronger the company, since it can use these internally generated funds for expansion, dividends, and other. The point is that if the company is able to generate these funds internally, then it does not have to rely on external funding, such as borrowing or issuing shares. External funding often carries with it commitments for paying out a return to outside parties (e.g., interest) and for repayment of principal, which can put an undue strain on the cash flows of the company.

Tip! **Users put great value on this statement since it is felt to be more objective than the income statement (cash is cash). The measurement of net income is felt to be very subjective and dependent on the accounting principles and procedures selected by financial statement preparers.**

STUDY STEPS

2. Becoming Proficient in Related Calculations

This topic involves learning how to **prepare the statement** and learning how to **interpret** it. There are two different approaches that are often taught for the preparation of the statement:

- The work sheet approach.
- The T-account approach.

This chapter will focus on the former, although both are equally as effective and acceptable.

Preparation of the statement using the work sheet approach-the mechanics

The objective of the statement is to show changes in cash and cash equivalents over the period. Where the company gets its cash and where it spends it is important and, therefore, the statement is divided into three main areas as follows:

- Cash provided from/used in operations.
- Cash provided from/used in investing.
- Cash provided from/used in financing.

Definition of cash and cash equivalents:

Cash and cash equivalents are defined as cash on hand, demand deposits, and short-term, highly liquid investments that are readily convertible to known amounts of cash and which are subject to insignificant risk of changes in value (ED on Cash Flow Statements).

In preparing the statement, the objective is to first **identify all cash transactions** and then to **classify them between operating, investing, and financing activities**.

Identifying Transactions

Which transactions should be on the statement and how do we know that we have included all the ones that should be there? This is where the work sheet approach comes into play.

Theoretically, all transactions end up affecting the balance sheet because the general ledger consists of balance sheet accounts and income statement accounts. Since the income statement is closed out to retained earnings at year-end, and retained earnings is a balance sheet account, all transactions are eventually booked to the balance sheet.

Therefore, if we identify changes in the balance sheet from one period to the next, we will ensure that all transactions are identified. The problem is that looking at the net change in an account (e.g., land), does not give us detailed information about individual transactions that have happened. For instance, if land increased by $100,000 from one year-end to the next, this may be due to one transaction (e.g., a purchase of land costing $100,000) or multiple transactions (including off-setting purchases and disposals). Therefore, although changes in balance sheet accounts are a good starting point, information is required from other sources as well. This will be discussed later.

In order to ensure that all relevant transactions are captured, the work sheet is set up such that the change in each balance sheet account is calculated as a starting point. **Tip!**

For example, assume the following balance sheets for a company for the years ended December 31, 1997 and 1998. The change from 1997 to 1998 is also calculated.

Work Sheet

	12/31/98	12/31/97	change
		dr./(cr.)	
Cash	$50,000	70,000	(20,000)
Accounts receivable (AR)	75,000	75,000	-0-
Land	100,000	-0-	100,000
Accounts payable (AP)	(80,000)	(80,000)	-0-
Long-term debt (LTD)	(80,000)	(50,000)	(30,000)
Common stock (CS)	(15,000)	(15,000)	-0-
Retained earnings (RE)	(50,000)	-0-	(50,000)

The next step is to re-create the transactions and the related journal entries used to book them. As previously mentioned, the change is a "net" amount and could have arisen due to one transaction or to several. Therefore, we need more information than is provided by the balance sheet or the income statement.

Assume the following:

1. Land was purchased for $100,000 cash.
2. The company borrowed $30,000.
3. Net income for the year-ended 12/31/98 was $50,000.

The next step is to reconstruct the journal entries for the above as follows:

1.	dr. land	100,000	
	cr. cash		100,000
2.	dr. cash	30,000	
	cr. LTD		30,000
3.	various		

For the net income (i.e. #3), we abbreviate the numerous journal entries required to book sales and expense transactions and focus on net income and the journal entry required to close it out to retained earnings. Remember, the focus is on changes in the balance sheet, and net income eventually gets closed out to retained earnings. In this case, since we have income, there will be a credit to retained earnings. Where should the debit be booked? For this part of the entry, we must make an assumption that the net income is cash and, therefore, the journal entry is as follows:

3.	dr. cash	50,000	
	cr. retained earnings		50,000

Tip! **To facilitate the analysis, assume as a starting point, that all net income is cash.**

The problem with this entry is that we know that net income is not necessarily cash since net income is calculated using the accrual method of accounting. Therefore, at some point, we will have to adjust it for any non-cash items such as depreciation, credit sales, and accrued expenses.

Next, we post the journal entries (JE) to the work sheet. There are two parts to the work sheet: the first part, which we have already started above, and the second part, which forms the basic structure of the statement.

Work Sheet—Part 1
dr./(cr.)

	12/31/98	12/31/97	Change	JE
Cash	$50,000	$70,000	$(20,000)	see W/S Part 2
AR	75,000	75,000	-0-	
Land	100,000	-0-	100,000	100,000 (1)*
AP	(80,000)	(80,000)	-0-	
LTD	(80,000)	(50,000)	(30,000)	(30,000) (2)*
CS	(15,000)	(15,000)	-0-	
RE	(50,000)	-0-	(50,000)	(50,000) (3)*

* Reconciled

Every time a journal entry affects cash, we will post it in the second part of the work sheet. The second part of the work sheet is really the "cash" line from above; however, we have expanded it to make room for all the entries. For each entry, we will classify it into one of the three categories: operations, investing, or financing. Before we post the other side of entry 1, we must decide which category a purchase of land should be included in.

Classifying Transactions

An easy way to determine this is to break the balance sheet down into quadrants as follows:

I Current assets (excluding cash)	II Current liabilities
III Long-term assets	IV Long-term debt and equity

Any transactions that affect quadrant I or II are classified as operating activities. Those affecting quadrant II are investing activities, and those affecting quadrant IV are financing activities. There are some exceptions to this general rule. For instance, the current portion of long-term debt is included in quadrant II; however, it is really a financing activity since it relates to the financing of the company.

A purchase of land involves the purchase of long-term assets and, hence, is an investing activity. The borrowing of money on a long-term basis affects quadrant IV and is, therefore, a financing activity. The process of earning net income is an operating activity (intuitively and since sales and purchases affect accounts such as AR, AP, inventory, etc.).

Work Sheet—Part 2

	Cash inflows—dr.	Cash outflows—cr.
Operating activities		
Net income	$50,000 (3)	
Investing activities		
Cash required for land purchase		$100,000(1)
Financing activities		
Cash from loan proceeds	$30,000 (2)	
Net change in cash during the year outflow or credit		$20,000

The work sheet balances since the net change in cash is a $20,000 credit and, in Part 1 of the work sheet, cash declined from $70,000 to $50,000 over the year. In this case, assume that the net income was all cash and, therefore, there were no reconciling items.

TO RECAP: In the process of preparing the work sheet and Part 2, we have:

1. **Identified** the detailed transactions that account for the net change in each balance sheet account.
2. **Classified** the transactions as either operating, investing, or financing activities.

Tip! **Don't forget to balance the statement by adding up the debits and credits in Part 2 and comparing it to the change in cash in Part 1.**

Tip! **A balanced statement is not necessarily correct. There are three other things to consider:**

1. Have all transactions been **identified** (i.e., there may be some transactions that offset each other that have not been identified)?
2. Also, transactions may be incorrectly **classified** on the statement (e.g., classified as operating instead of investment activity).
3. The manner in which the statement is **presented** must also be considered and will often be a function of user needs (i.e., how much detail and which numbers are emphasized or de-emphasized).

Presentation

The **direct** and **indirect methods** are different ways of presenting the same information in the operating activities section. Either way is acceptable, although the ED encourages the use of the direct method. Many companies use the indirect approach. Under both methods, the objective is to reconcile net income, which is accrual based, to cash from operations.

Extraordinary items should be dealt with as separate line items and income from discontinued operations should also be segregated.

Recap of steps in preparing a statement of changes using the work sheet approach:

1. **List balance sheets for both year–ends** and **determine change** during year. Keep track of credits and debits. This is Part 1 of the work sheet.
2. **Prepare Part 2 of the work sheet** by putting in headings such as operating, investing, and financing activities.
3. **Obtain additional detail** about significant transactions that occurred during the year (both cash and non–cash). This information is usually given in a question but, in real life, it would have to be obtained from sources such as the general ledger, the controller, minutes of Board of Directors meetings, etc. **Re-create or obtain corresponding journal entries**. Note that the ED stipulates that non-cash activities be excluded from the statement.
4. **Post journal entries to work sheet**. Any journal entry that affects cash will affect both parts of the work sheet. Assume that net income is cash to begin with and adjust for non–cash or accrued items. An example will also follow in the problems.
5. **Summarize Part 2 of the work sheet** by totaling net cash change by activity. Balance to "change in cash" in Part 1. Ensure that all changes in each line of the balance sheet are accounted for. Part 2 is the statement. All that must be done is to recopy it in form and put a heading on it.

Interpretation of the statement

The best place to start when analyzing a company's financial position is with the statement of changes in financial position. The focus is on cash from continuing operations, since this indicates whether the operations are self-standing and able to pay dividends and interest and repay debt.

As previously discussed, the statement also offers insight into where a company received its cash during the year and where it spent its cash.

MULTIPLE CHOICE QUESTIONS

1) On June 30, 1998, D Ltd., a manufacturing company, sold a piece of land for its book value of $250,000. D Ltd. accepted $170,000 cash plus a mortgage in the amount of $80,000 in exchange for the land. How would D Ltd. report this on its December 31, 1998 annual cash flow statement?

   a) $250,000 inflow under investing activities
   b) $170,000 inflow under operating activities
   c) $250,000 inflow under investing activities and $80,000 outflow under financing activities
   d) $170,000 inflow under investing activities

(CMA adapted—June 1995)

2) During 1999, Cominco Limited declared dividends of $50,000-a material amount. How would the dividends be reported on the statement of cash flows?

   a) outflow under operating activity
   b) outflow under financing activity
   c) outflow under a fourth section-dividends
   d) dividends would not be shown on the statement

3) Which of the following would not be included as "cash and cash equivalents"?

   a) bank overdraft
   b) demand deposits
   c) common shares of publicly traded company
   d) six month term deposit due in three months

4) The ED on Cash Flows allows either the direct or the indirect method of presenting the statement to be used; however, the use of the direct method is preferred. Which of the following statements is most true under the direct method:

   a) cash flow from operations is greater.
   b) cash flow from operations is less.
   c) details under cash flow from investing and financing activities are different.
   d) the statement is the same except for details under operating activities.

The following information pertains to the next four questions:

Manny Limited is in the process of preparing its cash flow statement for the year-ended December 31, 2000 and notes the following transactions. Manny buys and sells shares for clients on commission. In some cases, he takes ownership of shares. However, the intent is to resell them to clients as soon as possible. This is the first year of operations.

• net income	$100,000
• loss on resale of marketable equity securities (cost $30,000 paid in cash)	3,000
• equity securities held at year-end by Manny Limited at cost	50,000
• long-term bank loan	50,000
• cash at year-end	100,000

5) What amount would Manny Limited show as cash from operating activities?
   a) $103,000 inflow
   b) $100,000 inflow
   c) $50,000 inflow
   d) $130,000 inflow

6) What amount would Manny show as investing activities?
   a) $0 outflow
   b) $50,000 outflow
   c) $80,000 outflow
   d) $53,000 outflow

For the next two questions, assume the same information as for 5) and 6) and assume further the following. The bank loan was used to buy the equity securities. The equity securities have a market value at year-end of $40,000. The loss has not been included in the net income figure reported above although the $3,000 loss on sale is included.

7) What amount would Manny show as cash from operating activities
   a) $100,000 inflow
   b) $113,000 inflow
   c) $90,000 inflow
   d) $103,000 inflow

8) What would Manny show as cash from investing and financing activities?

	Investing	Financing
a)	$80,000	$50,000
b)	$0	$0
c)	$3,000	$0
d)	$53,000	$50,000

9) The ED introduces a clarified presentation for comparative numbers and for a reconciliation between cash and cash equivalents on the balance sheet and the income statement. What are the required disclosures under the ED?

Reconciliation	Comparatives
a) required	required
b) required	not required
c) not required	required
d) not required	not required

10) Thane Company's accounts receivable increased during the year as did their accounts payables. How does this affect cash from operations?

AR	AP
a) increases CFO	increases CFO
b) increases CFO	decreases CFO
c) decreases CFO	decreases CFO
d) decreases CFO	increases CFO

SOLUTIONS TO MULTIPLE CHOICE QUESTIONS

1) d) The sale of the land would be an investing activity since this is a manufacturing company. Note that the land would have been recorded as a long-term asset (quadrant III) and, therefore, it would be classified as investing. The ED requires only cash transactions be disclosed on the statement and, therefore, only the cash portion would be shown.

2) d) The declared dividends would not be shown on the statement since they are non-cash. If they were cash dividends, they could be shown as either operating or financing per the ED. Note that this might change before the ED is finalized since it adds more choices than allowable under U.S. GAAP.

3) c) Equity shares are not included in the definition. Even though the shares have a ready market, they are less liquid than other forms of cash and cash equivalents, and they are also subject to the risk of change in value.

4) d) The only difference is the amount of detail shown in the operating activities section. The direct method gives more detail as to operating cash inflows and outflows and this is why it is the preferred method.

5) c) $100,000 + 3,000 + 27000 (proceeds on resale)—$80,000 (purchase of both lots of shares) = $50,000. Note that the marketable securities are not cash and cash equivalents since they are equity securities. They are, however, operating activities since Manny buys and sells shares as the main operating activity.

6) a) Since the buying and selling of shares is considered an operating activity, Manny does not have any investing activity.

7) a) Cash inflows from operations would be $100,000 or $90,000 after write-off + 3,000 +10,000 -30,000 (purchase) +27,000 sale.

8) b) Manny would show $0 as cash from investing and financing activities since all purchase and sale of securities is considered operating and since financing activities are non-cash.

9) a) Both are required under the ED although this may change when the standard is incorporated into the Handbook.

10) d) When AR increases, this means more credit sales and less cash. Likewise, when AP increases, this is more credit purchases and more cash.

SHORT PROBLEMS

1) Purpose: To illustrate the use of the indirect method and the calculation of cash flow from operations. This problem also deals with scenarios where other information about the transactions is not available.

The following information was taken from the financial statements of Cash Flow Limited (CL) for the year-ended December 31, 1997:

CL
Income statement
year-ended December 31, 1997

Sales	$450,000
Cost of sales	290,000
Gross margin	160,000
Selling, general, and administrative expenses	100,000
Depreciation	25,000
Net income before taxes	35,000
Income taxes	20,000
Net income	$15,000

CL
Balance sheet
December 31, 1997

	1997		1996
		(000s)	
Overnight deposits	$45		$-0-
Accounts receivable (AR)	50		75
Inventory (INV)	98		75
Fixed assets (FM)—net	209		220
Total assets	$402		$370
Bank overdraft (OD)	14		24
Accounts payable (AP)	49		70
Long-term debt (LTD)	150		150
Common stock (CS)	126		50
Retained earnings (RE)	63		76
Total liabilities and equity	$402		$370

Assume that all transactions are material, including non-cash transactions. Fixed assets were purchased with cash.

Required

Prepare a statement of changes in financial position for CL for the year-ended December 31, 1997. Use the indirect method and prepare a work sheet.

2) Purpose: To illustrate the use of the direct method of preparing the statement of changes.

Required

Assume the same data as in 1 and prepare the statement of changes in financial position for CL for the year-ended December 31, 1997. However, this time, use the direct method.

3) Purpose: To illustrate how discontinued operations are presented in a statement of changes.

CF Limited (CFL) decided to discontinue operations of their Moncton subsidiary. A formal plan of disposal was agreed upon on January 1, 1997 and the operations were closed down mid-year. The operations represented a separate business segment. Related fixed assets were sold at a loss for $2 million cash, and CFL accrued an additional $150,000 for employee severance. The two items resulted in a total loss of $300,000. The income statement for CFL for the year-ended December 31, 1997 is as follows:

CFL
Income statement
for the year-ended December 31, 1997
(000s)

Sales	$5,897
Expenses	3,989
Net income from continuing operations	$1,908
Discontinued operations:	
Loss from operations	$1,200
Loss on disposition	300
Net loss from discontinued operations	$1,500
Net income	$408

Other information:

- Non-cash current operating assets increased from the previous year-end by $900,234. There is nothing in the ending balance relating to the discontinued operations.
- Current operating liabilities also increased from the previous year-end by $786,090. This included the additional accrual of $150,000 for the severance pay.
- All other changes in the balance sheet pertain to investing and financing activities.

Required

Prepare the first part of the statement of changes in financial position that shows cash flows from operations. Use the indirect method.

SOLUTIONS TO SHORT PROBLEMS

1) In order to prepare this statement, since there is no additional information given regarding transactions during the year, certain assumptions must be made. Assume that all transactions are material.

Tip! **Use the 5-step work sheet approach noted above.**

Begin by listing the balance sheet accounts for both years and calculating the change. Be careful to keep debits and credits straight.

Tip! **Each column should add up to zero since debits are offset by credits.**

The second step is to set up Part 2 of the work sheet.

Tip! **Remember that this second part of the work sheet is the "cash" account. This is where we analyze all the changes in the cash account and segregate them by type of activity (i.e., operating, investing, and financing).**

Identify the change in cash that you are trying to explain. Normally, this would be the "cash" line on the balance sheet, but it also makes sense to include "cash equivalents", such as bank overdrafts, overnight deposits, liquid investments, etc., in order to get the full cash position. Here, we have overnight deposits and bank overdraft. Therefore, we will be attempting to explain why both accounts have changed (the net change). The statement should balance to the net difference between the two accounts (i.e., a dr. change of $55).

Next, obtain additional information and begin to re-create and post journal entries. The easiest place to start is with net income.

Tip! **Net income is an operating activity, but is calculated using the accrual basis and likely contains non-cash items. To simplify, assume that the net income is a cash item.**

The journal entry (JE) is dr. cash from operating activities and cr. retained earnings (JE #1). Next, attempt to adjust net income for non-cash items.
From the income statement, we can see that depreciation has been deducted. This is a non-cash item since the money was spent when the asset was purchased or when the associated loan was paid off. Depreciation is merely an accounting allocation. The journal entry to record depreciation was dr. depreciation expense, cr. accumulated depreciation (JE #2). This gets posted to the second part of the work sheet even though it is not

cash. The reason for this is because we are adjusting the net income number so that we end up with a "cash from operations" number.

Other non-cash items that can easily be identified are credit sales, accrued expenses, and non-cash purchases. Alternatively, any changes in the quadrant I or II balance sheet accounts generally pertain to operations and will help reconcile from accrual-based net income to cash from operations.

Credit sales can be identified by looking at accounts receivable (AR). In this case, AR is $50. This means that there are $50 of credit sales at year-end that have not yet been collected. However, we must also look at the opening AR balance. These are credit sales from last year that have been collected. We must adjust the net income by deducting the year-end credit sales (AR) and adding the previous year-end credit sales that have now been collected. (As an alternative, the two can be netted for an adjustment of $25 add back: dr. cash from operations, cr. AR (JE#3).

Non-cash expenses and purchases of operating assets can be identified by looking at the accounts payable (AP) and accrued liabilities accounts. At year-end, AP is $49. This means that there are expenses or purchases booked that have yet to be paid for. These should be added back to net income, assuming that they are for operating expenditures (rent, telephone, inventory, supplies). Usually, this is the case. We must also look at the previous year's balance. These items have since been paid off and, therefore, we must deduct them from net income as additional cash paid out in 1997 for operations. The two can also be netted: dr. AP, cr. cash from operations (JE#4).

Any other changes in current operating assets or liabilities should also be accounted for. In this case, the only other current operating asset or liability is inventory. Inventory should be treated the same way as other operating assets in quadrant I (i.e., AR) for purposes of the statement. That is, the year-end balance should be deducted and the opening balance added back: dr. inventory, cr. cash from operations (JE#5). All current operating assets (quadrant I) should be dealt with in the same manner, while current operating liabilities (quadrant II) should be dealt with in the same manner as AP.

Having dealt with all the operating items (quadrants I and II), we will next deal with investing activities (quadrant III). We have already partially explained the change in fixed assets (depreciation) and will assume that the difference of $14 must be due to a fixed asset purchase ($220—$25 = $195—$209 = $14). According to the question, this is a cash transaction: dr. fixed assets, cr. cash from investing activities (JE#6).

Last but not least are the financing activities (quadrant IV). Long-term debt has not changed but common stock has increased by $76. We will assume that this reflects an issue of shares: dr. cash from financing, cr. CS (JE#7). The change in retained earnings has not yet been fully explained and there is yet an unexplained difference of $28 dr. ($76 + $15 = $91—$63 = $28). Since there is no other information, the most likely reason for a decrease in retained earnings, other than a loss, is dividends. dr. retained earnings, cr. cash from operating activities. This may be shown under operating, financing, or a fourth category on the statement.

Tip! **As a check to ensure that we have identified and reconciled all balance sheet changes, put an "X" beside each line that has been explained on the balance sheet part of the work sheet.**

CL—SCFP—Work sheet—12/31/94

Quadrant		1994 dr./(cr.)	1993	Change	dr.	cr.	Reconciled
I	Deposits	$45	$ -0-	$45			X
I	AR	50	75	(25)	$25 (3)		X
I	Inv	98	75	23	$23 (5)		X
II	FA—net	209	220	(11)	14 (6)	25 (2)	X
III	Bank OD	(14)	(24)	10			X
III	AP	(49)	(70)	21	21 (4)		X
IV	LTD	(150)	(150)	-0-			X
IV	CS	(126)	(50)	(76)		76 (7)	X
IV	RE	(63)	(76)	13	28 (8)	15 (1)	X
Total		-0-	-0-		-0-		

	Cash inflows dr.	Cash outflows cr.	
Operating activities:			
Net income	$15 (1)		
Adjust for non-cash items:			
Depreciation	25 (2)		
Change in AR	25 (3)		
Change in AP		$21 (4)	
Change in inventory		23 (5)	
Cash from operating activities			$21
Dividends		28 (8)	(28)
		7	
Investing activities:			
Fixed asset purchase		14 (4)	
Cash outflow from investing activities			(14)
Financing activities:			
Issue of shares		76 (7)	
Cash inflow from financing activities			76
Net increase in cash during period			55
Opening balance in cash and cash equivalents			(24)*
Closing balance in cash and cash equivalents			$31**

* Deposit $0 plus overdraft 24 = $(24)

** Deposit $45 plus overdraft 14 = $31

We must balance the statement, which is the lower half of the work sheet, to the change in the cash and cash equivalents lines on the balance sheet. This is easily documented by doing the reconciliation on the statement as above. To prepare a statement in good form, all we need is a heading and an explanatory note explaining what has been included in "cash and cash equivalents".

There is a risk that we have not included all transactions, in that there might be some transactions that offset each other. Since we do not have any other information, however, this cannot be determined.

Finally, consideration should be given to presentation. In the above scenario, there are few changes. However, where there are many changes, consideration should be given to grouping "like" items.

Part 2 of the work sheet above forms the basis of the statement. It should be recopied, headed up properly, and the definition of cash and cash equivalents should be noted at the bottom.

2) The only part of the statement that changes when the direct method is used is the "cash from operating activities" section. The rest of the statement stays exactly the same. In fact, the cash from operating activities $ amount remains the same. The only thing that is different is the manner in which the information is presented. While the indirect method begins with net income and shows reconciling items to cash from operations, the direct method begins with each individual line on the income statement (or a grouping) and shows reconciling items which adjust each line.

The journal entries remain the same. Let us begin with the income statement. This statement is already fairly condensed and, therefore, we will use the same line items. The cash from operating activities of the work sheet will therefore begin with the entire income statement, rather than just net income, and will take a tabular form as shown below. (The statement itself would just show the far right hand column in the work sheet.)

Next, instead of posting the journal entries as deductions or add backs to net income, we must determine which lines in the income statement they affect. For instance, JE#2 regarding depreciation will affect the depreciation line and is therefore posted directly to that line.

JE#3 pertains to sales and will therefore be shown on the sales line. JE#4 could pertain to purchases of inventory, in which case it belongs on the cost of sales line. It could also pertain to accrual of tax, or selling, general, and administration expenses, in which case, it would belong on each of those lines respectively. Since we do not have a breakdown of the AP account showing whom the money is owed to, we will assume that the bulk of it is owed to suppliers (a reasonable assumption).

JE#5 shows the change in inventory and, therefore, relates to inventory movements and belongs on the cost of sales line. JE#8 pertaining to dividend, will also be grouped here.

CL—Statement of changes—Part 2

Cash from operating activities:

	Inflows/ (outflows)	Cash Inflows	Cash Outflows	Operating cashflows in/(out)
Sales	$450	$25 (3)		$475
Cost of sales	(290)		$21 (4)	
			23 (5)	(334)
Selling, general and administrative expenses	(100)			(100)
Depreciation	(25)	25 (2)		-0-
Income taxes	(20)			(20)
Net income	$15(1)			
Cash from operations				21
Dividends			28 (8)	(28)
				$(7)

Tip! **The far right-hand column shows cash movements for operating activities in greater detail than in the indirect method.**

We can tell from the statement that cash collected from customers in the period regarding sales was $475, cash payments to suppliers during the period was $334, etc. Therefore, some feel that this statement is more informative. However, since it is often only the far right-hand column that is shown, some users find it more difficult to follow than the indirect method, which begins with the net income number from the income statement. Note that the ED prefers the direct method, although the use of the indirect method is acceptable.

3) Since the full balance sheet is not given and the objective of the problem is merely to illustrate presentation, a work sheet will not be prepared. Instead the statement will be drafted straight away. Inflows or debits to cash will be shown unbracketed and outflows or credits to cash will be shown bracketed.

We will begin with the net income. However, since most users will be interested in CFL's continued ability to generate income, we should segregate income between continuing and discontinued operations.

Since the year-end current assets (quadrant I) contain no assets pertaining to the discontinued operations, the whole change will be attributed to continuing operations. Theoretically, we should look at the opening balances to determine if there are any pertaining to discontinued operations. If so, these would be adjusted for under discontinued operations in the statement. Since current assets have increased, this is shown as a reduction: dr. current assets, cr. cash from continuing operations.

Current liabilities (quadrant II) have also increased. We are told that the increase pertains partially to accrued severance pay. This must be adjusted for under discontinued operations, leaving $786—$150 = $636 to adjust under continuing operations. dr. cash from continuing operations, cr. current liabilities.

This leaves us with a cash inflow from continuing operations:

Next, we deal with discontinued operations, by showing the net loss per the income statement as an outflow. Then we adjust for quadrant I and II balance sheet items that pertain to discontinued operations. The only one that we know of is the accrual for severance pay: dr. cash from discontinued operations, cr. current liabilities.

The only other item is the loss on sale. This is a non-cash item and must be added back.: dr. cash from discontinued operations, dr. cash from investing activities, cr. fixed assets.

CFL
Statement of Changes in Financial Position
Year-ended December 31, 1997
(000s)

Cash from operations:	
Net income from continuing operations	$1,908
Adjust for non-cash items:	
Increase in non-cash current assets	(900)
Increase in non-cash current liabilities	636
Cash inflow from continuing operations	1,644
Net loss from discontinued operations	(1,500)
Adjust for non-cash items:	
Increase in accrued liabilities	150
Loss on disposition	150
Cash outflow from discontinued operations	(1,200)
Net cash inflow from operations	$444

Note how much better this makes the company look. If the operations were shown together, the cash from operations would only be $444. However, if we split out discontinued operations the cash amount from continuing operations increases to $1,644! Again, this latter number is the one that most users would use in order to predict future cash flows from operations.

CASES

CROWN LIFE—www.crownlife.com

Below is an excerpt from the published financial statements of Crown Life. Crown Life is in the life insurance industry.

Consolidated Statement of Changes in Financial Position
(thousands of dollars)

Years ended December 31	1996	1995
Cash Provided By (Used In) Operating Activities		
Net income	47,932	46,896
Decrease in policy liabilities	(397,592)	(642,001)
Sales and maturies of invested assets, net of purchases	394,403	517,938
Net change in other assets and liabilities	(8,902)	74,414
	35,841	(2,753)
Cash Provided By (Used In) Financing Activities		
Common shares issued	98	—
Convertible subordinated debentures issued	—	—
Preferred shareholders' dividends	(9,135)	(9,185)
Preferred shares purchased for cancellation	(429)	(98)
	(9,466)	140,717
Cash Provided By Investing Activities		
Subsidiary companies sold	—	41,100
	—	41,100
Increase in Cash Position	26,375	179,064
Cash Position, Beginning of Year	46,797	(132,267)
Cash Position, End of Year	73,172	46,797

Required

Which presentation method is the company using on its cash flow statement?
Explain the second and third items under the operating activities section. Discuss the appropriateness of classifying these items as operating activities?

2) PAPADOPOULOS LIMITED

Papadopoulos Limited (PL) sells retail merchandise in Canada. The company was incorporated last year and is now in its second year of operations. PL is owned and operated by the Papadopoulos family, and Iris Papadopoulos, the president of the company, has decided to expand the company into the American marketplace. In order to do this, bank financing will be necessary.

The books have always been kept by Tonya, Iris' daughter. Tonya is presently studying accounting in university. Financial statements had only been prepared for tax purposes in the past. For the year-ended December 31, 1997, Tonya prepared the following statement showing cash inflows and cash outflows:

Sources of cash:	
From shareholder loan	$150,000
From sales of merchandise	350,000
From truck financing	50,000
From term deposit cashed in	100,000
From interest income	10,000
Total sources of cash	$660,000
Uses of cash:	
For fixed asset purchases	$100,000
For inventory purchases	250,000
Operating expenses including depreciation of $70,000	160,000
For purchase of investment	55,000
For purchase of truck	50,000
For interest on debt	30,000
Total uses of cash	$645,000
Net increase in cash	$15,000

Tonya showed the statement to her mother, noting that the bank was sure to give them a loan, especially since they were profitable in their second year and since cash had increased over the year, indicating that it had been a good year. Iris is not convinced and decides to have the statement looked at by a "real" accountant.

Required

Adopt the role of the accountant and redraft the statement, if necessary, in good form for the bank. Discuss the issues.

SOLUTION TO CASES

1) Crown Life

a) The company is using the indirect method since they begin with net income and reconcile to cash from operations.

b) Policy liabilities are the company's estimate of future payouts required under the life insurance policies. These amounts must be accrued as a liability when the policy is sold and, each year, the amount is re-estimated. This would normally be a long-term liability; however, it is listed under operating activities because it is a normal ongoing cost of doing business.

   The invested assets are similar. As the company takes in premiums, they must invest and save some money to ensure that they will have sufficient funds to cover payouts under the policies. Are these amounts investment activities? On the one hand, they are included in the definition per the ED: "acquisition and disposal of long-term assets and other investments…". However, since these are the main source of funds that will be used to settle the policy liabilities, it would not make sense to split them up (i.e., if the policy liabilities are operating activities, then the investments should be as well).

   These two items are like accounts payable and accounts receivable in manufacturing companies. The main difference is that for life insurance companies, the operating cycle is significantly longer. As a point of interest, because of the long operating cycle, the company does not classify its balance sheet either.

2) Papadopoulos Limited

Overview

The bank is the main user of the financial statements and will use them to assist in determining whether a loan will be granted. They will likely want **GAAP**-based financial statements to enhance credibility and reliability. The financial statements prepared will be different from the statements prepared in the past (tax basis). Further, the statement prepared by Tonya does not conform to GAAP and must therefore be converted.

Analysis

Before any issues are dealt with, the statement must be redrafted as follows:

PL

Statement of Changes in Financial Position
for the year-ended December 31, 1997

Cash from operations:		
Sales	$350,000	
Purchases of inventory	(250,000)	
Operating expenses	(160,000)	
Add back depreciation	70,000	
Other income	10,000	
Interest on debt	(30,000)	
Cash used in operations		$(10,000)
Cash from investing:		
Term deposit cashed in	$100,000	
Fixed asset purchase	(100,000)	
Investment	(55,000)	
Truck purchase	(50,000)	
Cash used in investing		(105,000)
Cash from financing:		
Shareholder loan	$150,000	
Truck financing	50,000	
Cash from financing		200,000
Net cash inflows		$85,000

This statement shows that **operations** are not generating cash; rather, cash is required to maintain operations. This will be looked upon in a negative light by the bank, since internally generated cash from operations is what the company should be using to repay any loan granted. However, since it is only the second year of operations, the company is profitable, and the cash required to run operations is not that great, the bank may be somewhat flexible.

That the company is liquidating what appear to be non-essential assets (term deposit) and using the money to buy productive assets to be used to generate income will be seen in a positive light. That excess cash is being invested will also be seen in a positive light as good management (i.e. will maximize return on excess cash by investing).

The excess cash is only present, however, due to a shareholder loan. This is better than outside borrowings since the shareholders (all family) may be more flexible if the company can not make interest and principal repayments on time.

In conclusion, when the financial statements are redrafted, PL will be seen in an unfavourable light by the bank primarily because it is a new company and the cash flow from operations is negative. The only reason there is excess cash is due to a shareholder loan.

SELECTED SOLUTIONS FROM THE TEXTBOOK

EXERCISE 23-12

(a)

Yarmouth Company
Statement of Cash Flows
For the year Ended December 31, 1998

Operating Activities		
Net income		$1,050
Add back noncash expense - depreciation		50
Add (deduct) changes in noncash working capital		
– accounts receivable increase	$(450)	
– inventory decrease	300	
– accounts payable increase	300	
– accrued liability decrease	(100)	50
		1,150
Deduct dividends paid		(500)
Net cash inflow from operating activities		650
Investing activities		
Proceeds on sale of long-term investments	$100	
Purchase of plant assets	(200)	
Cash used by investing activities		(100)
Financing activities		
Proceeds on issuance of share capital	$200	
Retirement of bonds payable	(100)	
Cash flow from financing activities		100
Net increase in cash		650
Cash balance, January 1, 1998		1,150
Cash balance, December 31, 1998		$1,800

Additional disclosures required:

Interest and dividends received: information not provided
Interest paid: information not provided
Income taxes paid: information not provided

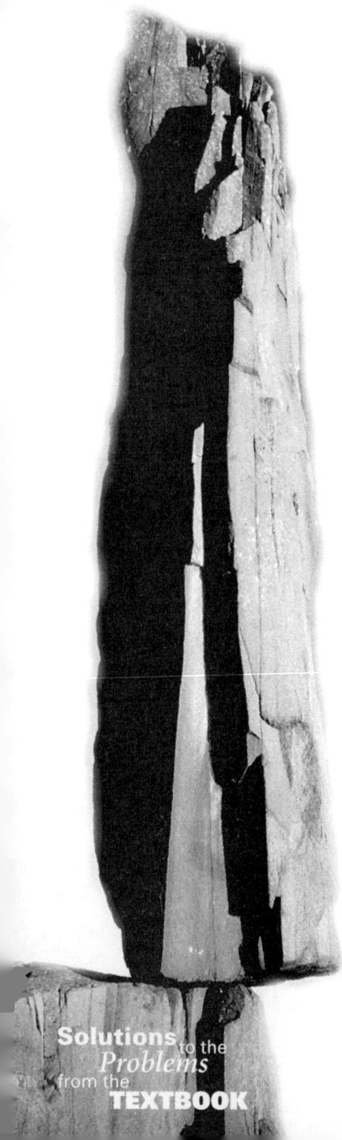

(b)

Yarmouth Company
Statement of Cash Flows
For the Year Ended December 31, 1998

Operating Activities		
Cash received from customers*		$6,450
Cash paid to suppliers for goods and services		(5,300)
Cash dividends paid to shareholders		(500)
Net cash inflow from operating activities		650
Investing Activities		
Proceeds on sale of long-term investment	$100	
Purchase of plant assets	(200)	
Cash used in investing activities		(100)
Financing Activities		
Proceeds on issue of shares	$200	
Retirement of bonds payable	(100)	
Cash from financing activities		100
Net increase in cash		650
Cash balance, January 1, 1998		1,150
Cash balance, December 31, 1998		$1,800

Additional disclosures required:
- Interest and dividends received: information not provided
- Interest paid: information not provided
- Income taxes paid: information not provided

* $6,900 - $450
** $4,700 + $450 + $650 - $300 + $100 (Assumes accounts payable applies to amounts owing on selling and administrative expenses as well as merchandise purchases.)

Rough draft of operating activities section:

Cash from customers	+6,900	-450	+6,450
Cash to suppliers of goods and services	-4,700	+300	
	-450	+300	
	-650	-100	
Depreciation expense	-50	+50	-0-
Dividends		-500	-500
	+1,050		+650

Problem 23-6

Seneca Limited
Statement of Cash Flows
For the Year Ended December 31, 1998

Operating Activities		$15,750
Net income (1)		
Add back (deduct) noncash expenses, gains and losses		
Gain on sale of long-term investments	$(2,500)	
Extraordinary gain—flood damage (2)	(9,250)	
Loss on disposal of equipment (3)	4,100	
Amortization expense	1,250	
Depreciation expense	1,900	(4,500)
Add (deduct) changes in noncash working capital		
Increase in net accounts receivable	$(3,750)	
Increase in inventory	(3,000)	
Increase in accounts payable	2,000	(4,750)
		6,500
Deduct dividends paid		(6,000)
Cash provided by operating activities		500
Investing Activities		
Proceeds on sale of investments	$5,500	
Proceeds on sale of equipment	2,500	
Purchase of equipment	(15,000)	
Proceeds from flood damage to building, extraordinary item	37,000	
Income tax paid on extraordinary gain, flood damage (4)	(4,000)	
Cash provided by investing activities		26,000
Financing Activities		
Repayment of short-term note payable	(1,000)	
Cash used in financing activities		(1,000)
Increase in cash		25,500
Cash balance, January 1, 1998		13,000
Cash balance, December 31, 1998		$38,500

Additional disclosures:
Dividends and interest received: (insufficient data provided)
Interest paid: $2,000 (given)
Income taxes paid: $5,000 (given)

Supporting Computations:

(1) $5,000 + net income - dividends declared = $20,750
$5,000 + net income - 0 = $20,750
net income = $15,750

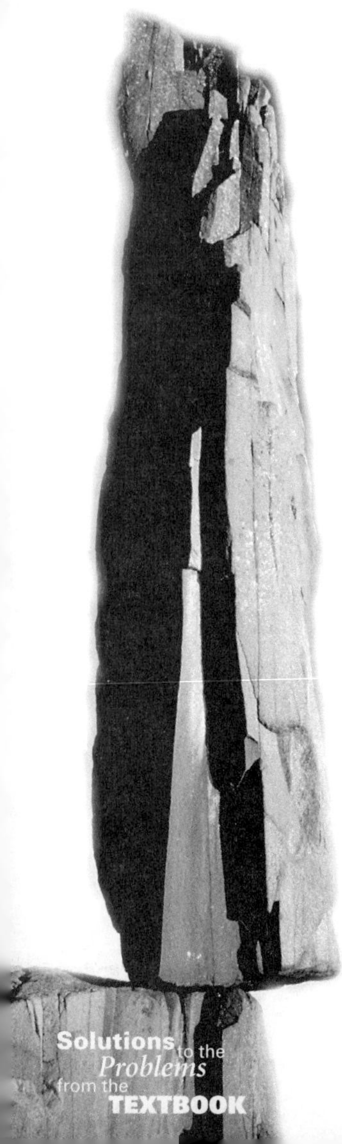

(2)	Insurance proceeds ($33,000 + $4,000)		$37,000
	Deduct carrying amount		
	Cost of building	$29,750	
	Accumulated depreciation	(6,000)	23,750
	Gain on flood damage		13,250
	Less income tax		(4,000)
	Extraordinary item reported		$9,250

(3)	Cost of equipment sold	$11,000
	Deduct accumulated depreciation (40%)	(4,400)
	Carrying amount	6,600
	Proceeds on sale	2,500
	Loss on sale of equipment	$4,100

(4) In this case, the income tax payment associated with the extraordinary item can be specifically identified with the investing activity. Because no income taxes remain unpaid at year end, it is known that the cash outflow was $4,000. It would also be correct to include the tax as part of the operating cash outflows instead.

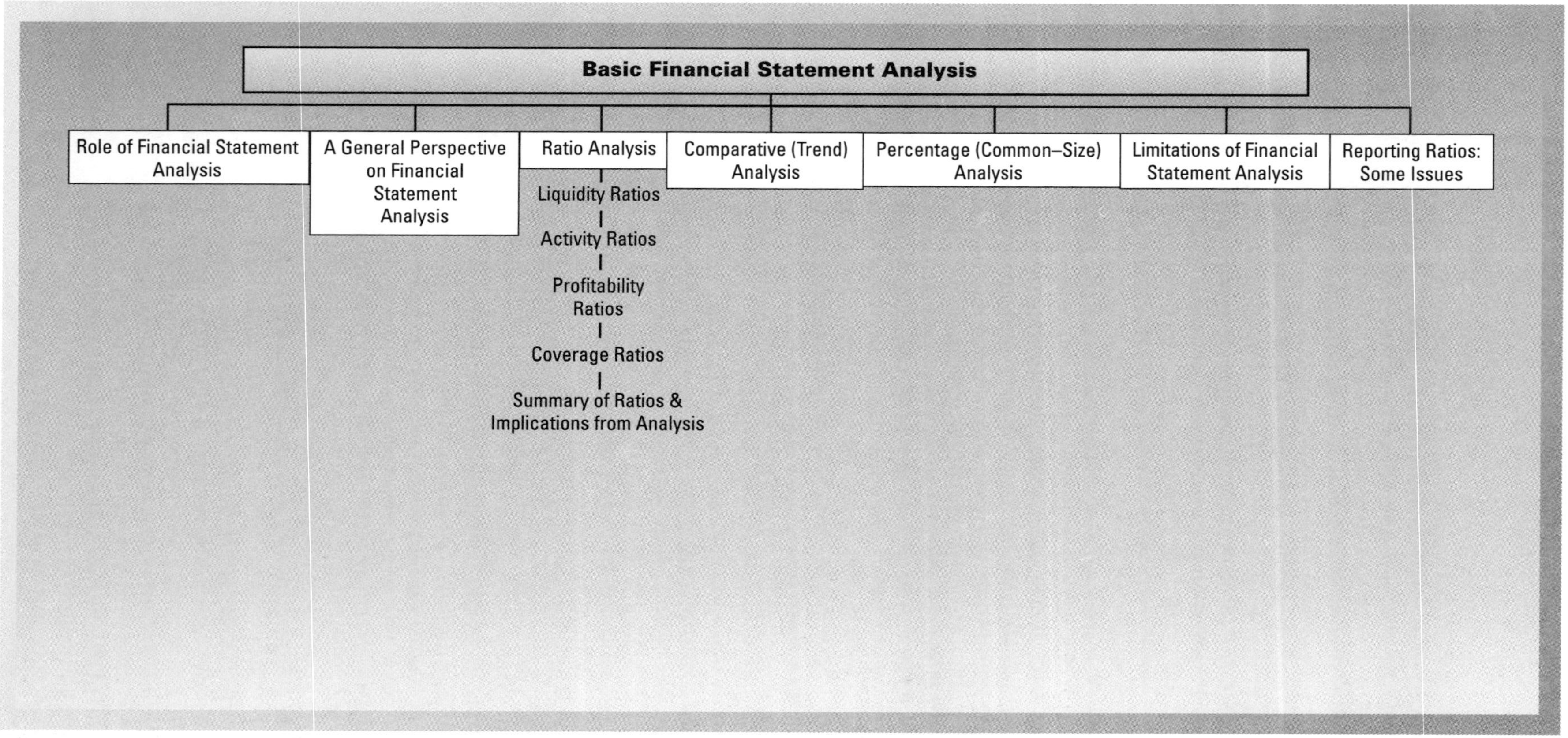

Basic Financial Statement Analysis
Role of Financial Statement Analysis
A General Perspective on Financial Statement Analysis
Ratio Analysis
Liquidity Ratios
Activity Ratios
Profitability Ratios
Coverage Ratios
Summary of Ratios & Implications from Analysis
Comparative (Trend) Analysis
Percentage (Common–Size) Analysis
Limitations of Financial Statement Analysis
Reporting Ratios: Some Issues

chapter 24

BASIC FINANCIAL STATEMENT ANALYSIS

Perspective

This is an area that is grossly misunderstood by students. Most students think of calculations when they think of financial statement analysis; however, this is only a very small part of the topic. Knowing when to use ratio analysis versus other types of analysis is important, as well as, knowing the limitations not only of the financial statement analysis but also of the financial statements that are used as a base for any calculations. It is also important to know what to do with any number, ratios, or trends that are identified. The calculations are not an end in themselves; rather, they are a means to an end.

Insights

- *The calculations will not be emphasized since they are mechanical in nature and are repetitive. This is not to say that they should be ignored by students; however, there are many excellent exercises in the text, along with problems and multiple choice questions below that may be attempted for self-study.*
- *Use the TOOLKIT summary of ratios to assist you when you practice.*
- *The emphasis of the material here will be on the other aspects of financial statement analysis and the use of judgement in deciding how analysis can augment what the statements tell us, if indeed it can.*

Study Steps

1. Understanding the Nature and Significance of Financial Analysis

STUDY STEPS

Financial statement analysis really consists of taking readily available financial information and manipulating it in such a way that it provides further information.

Since the analysis begins with the financial statements, it suffers from the same shortcomings as follows:

Financial statement shortcomings:

- Financial statements are an historic accounting of past transactions.
- They are based on historic costs, not current or market values.
- There are many soft numbers in the statements such as estimates of obsolete inventory and bad debts, etc.
- Different companies use different accounting policies and this makes it difficult to compare ratios between companies.
- There is much information that is not included in the balance sheet and income statements that therefore does not get included in numerical analysis, such as information about uncertainties (e.g., lawsuits).
- The quality of earnings as reported by different companies varies widely, making it difficult to cross-compare ratios (e.g., How much judgement has gone into calculating net income? Were the statements prepared aggressively? Does net income include nonrecurring income or exclude recurring losses?).

Tip! **It is necessary to take care in interpreting the information from the analysis. If the financial statements are deficient then the analysis will be too.**

STUDY STEPS

2. Becoming proficient in related calculations

There are three basic types of analysis:

Types of financial statement analysis

- Ratio analysis.
- Trend or horizontal analysis (i.e., year to year).
- Common-size or vertical analysis (i.e., expenses, etc., as a percentage of sales).

Whichever type of analysis (or combination) is selected, the **objective** of the exercise is to **highlight relationships, trends, or problems**. The calculations will not necessarily give any answers (e.g., assuming that gross margin has declined does not explain why it has declined, which is critical to the analysis). They are really just the **starting point**.

An approach to analysis:

1) **Select the tools** (i.e., which type of analysis and which ratios).

Tip! **Do not blindly perform all the calculations, as it is a waste of time and may obscure the more important/relevant analysis.**

Consider the industry (i.e., for some industries, some ratios are more important). Consider the environment (i.e., in a recessionary environment, a trend analysis will yield declining income and sales and, therefore, perhaps the more important analysis is a gross margin calculation to determine whether the company has been able to hold its margins).

2) **Know what you are looking for**. You should have some idea of the outcome before the analysis is done (i.e., what do you expect the trend analysis to show?). This is a matter of judgement. Factors such as the economy, prior years' performances, industry performance, new products, sales of part of the business, etc., all contribute to having a benchmark against which the outcome of the calculations might be judged or compared. Often, benchmarks in dollars or percentages are set (e.g., if sales decline by more than 5% this is cause for concern). Adequate research must be done prior to any numbers being calculated!

Designing the analysis is sometimes the most important step. **Tip!**

3) **Perform the calculations**.
4) **Identify items that need follow-up** (i.e., those that do not yield results consistent with your expectations).
5) **Follow-up**. Find out why the discrepancies/problems exist. This is usually done by discussions with management or further research.

As you can see, the calculations are really only a small part of the analysis.

Use the chart in the TOOLKIT that summarizes financial ratios and how to calculate them. **Tip!**

MULTIPLE CHOICE QUESTIONS

1) An unexpected decrease in which of the following ratios could indicate that fictitious inventory has been recorded:

   a) price-earnings

   b) total asset turnover

   c) current

   d) average collection period

(CMA adapted—June 1995)

2) For 1995, Pat-Claire Inc. had sales of $2.5 million, a gross profit of $1 million, and a net income of $125,000. Inventory was $250,000 at the beginning of 1995 and $300,000 at the end of the year. Which one of the following numbers represents the inventory turnover for 1995?

   a) 5 times

   b) 5.45 times

   c) 6 times

   d) 9.09 times

(CICA—September 1996)

3) Dentine Limited has the following current assets and current liabilities:

	1999	1998
Cash	$123,000	$100,000
Accounts receivable	45,000	56,000
Inventory	222,000	200,000
Accounts payable	500,000	400,000

Calculate the quick ratio for 1999

   a) .336 to 1

   b) .78 to 1

   c) .89 to 1

   d) .39 to 1

4) Classify the cash flow per share ratio.

   a) liquidity ratio

   b) activity ratio

   c) profitability ratio

   d) coverage ratio

The following applies to the next two questions:

The following transactions relate to KLM Limited.

- net income of $500,000
- non-cumulative preferred share dividends declared-$30,000
- cumulative preferred share dividends not declared-for current year $28,000, for last year $26,000
- weighted average # of common shares—1,000,000
- market price per share-$4.50

5) Calculate the EPS for KLM.

   a) .44
   b) .50
   c) .42
   d) .47

6) Calculate the price earnings ratio for the current year.

   a) 10.2 times
   b) 9 times
   c) 10.8 times
   d) 9.6 times

7) An increasing defensive interval ratio could be signalling:

   a) an increase in marketable securities and inventories.
   b) an increase in cash and net receivables.
   c) an increase in cost of goods sold.
   d) an increase in administrative costs.

8) Raymond Inc. sold inventory for cash equal to book value. What impact will the transaction have on the following ratios?

	Current ratio	Acid test ratio
a)	increase	increase
b)	decrease	increase
c)	increase	no change
d)	no change	increase

9)Assume the same information as 8 except that the inventory was sold at a loss. What will the impact be on the following ratios?

	Current ratio	acid test ratio
a)	increase	increase
b)	decrease	increase
c)	increase	no change
d)	no change	increase

10) The capital market's viewpoint on financial statement analysis argues the following:
   a) Financial statement analysis is not useful even for privately held companies since the share prices already incorporate all publicly available information including information in the financial statements.
   b) Financial statement analysis is useful since share prices do not incorporate all publicly available information.
   c) Financial statement analysis is useful for privately held companies and other companies where there isn't a well organized market since the information may not be incorporated into the share price.
   d) Financial statement analysis is always useful since it will yield insight into factors that would not otherwise be incorporated into the market price.

SOLUTIONS TO MULTIPLE CHOICE QUESTIONS

1) b) Asset turnover is net sales/average total sales. If inventory increased, then so would the denominator and, therefore, the ratio would decrease.

2) b) Cost of goods sold is the sales of $2.5 million less gross profit of $1 million. Average inventory turnover is $275,000, giving a turnover of 5.45 times.

3) a) The quick ratio excludes inventory = ($123,000 + 45,000)/500,000 = .336 to 1

4) c) It is a profitability ratio since it gives a good indicator of cash generated from operations, which over time, should be equal to profits from operations. It is not a liquidity ratio since liquidity ratios are looking at year-end ability to cover immediate cash outflow requirements. The cash flow per share is an historic number.

5) a) The EPS would consider declared dividends and undeclared dividends on the cumulative stock for the year only = ($500—30—28)/1,000 = .44

6) a) 10.2 times = $4.50/.44

7) b) The defensive interval is calculated as (cash + securities + net receivables) / operating costs. If operating costs increase, the ratio decreases. Inventory is not considered a defensive asset.

8) d) The current ratio would not change since inventory will decrease by the same amount that cash increases. The acid test ratio will increase since inventory is not included and, after the sale, cash will increase.

9) b) The current ratio will decrease since the inventory will decrease by more than the cash. The acid test ratio will increase for the same reason as 8 above.

10) c) Generally, this theory holds for publicly traded shares. The theory rests on the premise that the shares prices and markets will incorporate efficiently all publicly available information including information in the financial statements. For private companies with inefficient pricing mechanisms, there may be some value in analysis.

SHORT PROBLEM

1) Purpose: To demonstrate how to selectively approach financial analysis of the financial statements of a company.

The following are the condensed income statements and balance sheets of PepsiCo Inc. (PI) for 1991:

Consolidated Income Statement
years ended December 28
(in millions of dollars)

	1991	1990	1989
Net sales	$19,607.9	$17,802.7	$15,242.4
Cost of sales	9,395.5	8,549.4	7,421.7
Selling, General, and Administrative Expenses	7,880.8	7,008.6	5,887.4
Amortization	208.7	189.1	150.4
Gain on joint venture stock offering	–	(118.2)	–
Interest expense	615.9	688.5	609.6
Interest income	(163.3)	(182.1)	(177.2)
	17,937.6	16,135.3	13,891.9

Income from continuing operations before taxes	1,670.3	1,667.4	1,350.5
Provision for income taxes	590.1	576.8	449.1
Income from continuing operations	1,080.2	1,090.6	901.4
Discontinued operations (net of tax)	–	(13.7)	–
Net income	$1,080.2	$1,076.9	$901.4
Income per share:			
Continuing operations	$1.35	$1.37	$1.13
Discontinued operations	–	0.02)	–
Net income per share	$1.35	1.35	1.13
Average shares	802.5	798.7	796.0

Consolidated Balance Sheet
December 29
(in millions of dollars)

	1991	1990
Current assets:		
Cash and cash equivalents	$186.7	$170.8
Short-term investments at cost which approximates market	1,849.3	1,644.9
	2,036.0	1,815.7
Accounts and notes receivable less allowance: $97.5 in 1991 and $90.8 in 1990	1,481.7	1,414.7
Inventories	661.5	585.8
Prepaid expenses and other current assets	386.9	265.2
Total current assets	4,566.1	4,081.4
Investments in affiliates and other assets	1,681.9	1,505.9
Property, plant and equipment, net	6,594.7	5,710.9
Goodwill and other intangibles, net	5,932.4	5,845.2
Total assets	$18,775.1	$17,143.4
Current liabilities:		
Short-term borrowings	$228.2	$1,626.5
Accounts payable	1,196.6	1,116.3
Income taxes payable	492.4	443.7
Other current liabilities	1,804.9	1,584.0
Total current liabilities	3,722.1	4,770.5
Long-term debt	7,806.2	5,600.1
Non recourse obligation	–	299.5
Other liabilities and deferred credits	631.3	626.3
Deferred income taxes	1,070.1	942.8

Shareholders' equity:		
Capital stock, par value 10 cents per share authorized 1,800 shares, issued 863.1 shares	14.4	14.4
Capital in excess of par value	476.6	365.0
Retained earnings	5,470.0	4,753.0
Currency translation adjustment	330.3	383.2
	6,291.3	5,515.6
Less: Treasury stock, at cost: 74.0 shares in 1991, 74.7 shares in 1990	(745.9)	(611.4)
Total shareholders' equity	5,545.4	4,904.2
Total liabilities and shareholders' equity	$18,775.1	$17,143.4

During the financial statement period, North America was in a significant recession. PI operates in three different areas: snack foods (29% sales), restaurants (36%), and soft drinks (35%). The company is also committed to growth and follows an aggressive expansion policy. Assume that you are looking to buy shares of a company and have selected this one as a potential investment. You have decided to begin with the income statement.

For most manufacturing and food service companies, the key things to look for on the income statement in an overview analysis are sales and gross margins. Increasing sales are desirable and keeping manufacturing and food service costs in line are equally important. Watch for increased sales at the expense of uncollectible accounts receivable, although in the restaurant business, most revenues are from cash and bankable credit cards.

Required

Perform a limited analysis that will give you information on the above. What questions are raised by the analysis? Also, note what additional information you would need in order to perform a satisfactory analysis. Do not do a complete analysis.

The annual report includes a wealth of information that has not been reproduced here. The objective of this problem is really to focus on the analysis, see what questions are raised, and demonstrate how to approach an analysis. This is by no means meant to be a full and complete analysis of the company.

SOLUTION TO SHORT PROBLEM

Remember:

1. Select which type of analysis is appropriate for the situation.
2. Think about what you expect the analysis to yield given the environment, the industry, etc.
3. Perform the calculations.
4. Identify areas for follow-up.
5. Attempt to explain/identify additional areas.

Sales:

A trend analysis on the sales shows increases as follows:

1990 over 1989 = $17,802.7/$15,242 = 1.168 = 16.8%
1991 over 1990 = $19,607.9/$17,802.7 = 1.101 = 10.1%

Is the decline in sales growth a concern? Interestingly enough, with a recession going on, you would expect sales to decline or stay the same at best. Therefore, even though sales growth has declined, this is still very positive. You would want more information on how PI was able to maintain positive growth, especially since most people "eat out" less during a recession and perhaps have less disposable income to spend on non-essential items like snack food and pop.

According to the annual report, sales increases were due to additional restaurant units, acquisition of bottling operations, and increased international pricing. International sales volumes also accounted for some of the increase. Growth through acquisition is one way to increase sales. It also brings additional risk, however. These comments might warrant a closer look at how the expansion was financed. Has the company taken on more debt? If so, is their debt/equity ratio still acceptable? What about the ability to service interest payments? These concerns also need to be analyzed.

Since the company seems to be in several different businesses, it would be optimal to look at individual sales trends in each of the three operations. Furthermore, since PI is expanding rapidly on an international scale, sales by geographic markets would also be of interest to see where the growth is and how PI is faring in the recession. Although not reproduced here, this information is available in the annual report and would normally be reviewed as part of the analytical review.

Can the company sustain this growth? Is the risk level of the different segments acceptable to you? Is the aggressive expansion policy acceptable to you as an investor? These are questions that you would ask yourself based on the above.

Gross margin:

This vertical analysis would be calculated by year and then compared year to year to determine if PI is able to hold its gross margin.

\$7,821/\$15,242=	51%
\$9,253/\$17,803=	52%
\$10,212/\$19,608=	52%

As you can see, the gross margin is deteriorating marginally. This might be due to a shift in business from one area to another. Is this significant? What did we expect to see? Ideally, this margin should remain constant or improve. Remember that the restaurant segment will have different margins than the snack food (manufacturing) and soft drink segments. Therefore, if they have shifted emphasis from one operation to another, the margins would change justifiably.

The segmented information in the annual report shows that restaurant sales are growing at the expense of soft drink sales. It also shows that sales in the United States are declining as a percentage of total sales. PI may be able to obtain higher margins in the United States.

According to the Management Discussion and Analysis section (MD&A), higher pricing in soft drinks and lower domestic ingredient costs were offset by higher snack food manufacturing costs and snack food international pricing that could not keep pace.

Will gross margins continue to deteriorate, especially given the expansion into international markets where the pricing structure does not appear to be as optimal?
Other analysis stemming from the above review:

Have sales increased at the expense of more uncollectible accounts?

A vertical and ratio analysis comparing these from year to year might give us this information:

Allowance for doubtful accounts/accounts receivable

1990 = \$90.8/(\$1,414.7 + \$90.8) = 6.03%
1991 = \$97.5/(\$1,481.7 + \$97.5) = 6.17%

Number of days sales in receivables

1990 = \$1,414.7/(\$17,802.7/365) = 29 days
1991 = \$1,481.7/(\$19,607.9/365) = 27.58 days

These show that the allowance has increased, although this would be expected during a recession due to the number of companies going bankrupt. The increase is not significant. The number of days of sales in receivables has actually dropped, meaning that they are collecting receivables faster. Less than 30 days is good by any standard, especially in a recession. We would want to review the accounting policy notes and any other related notes for information that might be affecting our calculations.

Has the acquisition policy compromised the company's flexibility or threatened liquidity?

The debt-to-equity ratio will show the extent of any additional leverage:

1990 = ($1,626.5 + $5,600.1 + $299.5 + $626.3): $4,904.2 = 1.66
1991 = ($228.2 + $7,806.2 + $631.3): $5,545.4 = 1.56

There are many ways to calculate this ratio. Total debt (including current liabilities, long-term liabilities, and deferred taxes) divided by total debt and equity shows the following:

$$1991 = \frac{3722.1 + 7806.2 + 631.3 + 1070.1}{18775.1} = 70.5\%$$

$$1990 = \frac{4770.5 + 5600.1 + 299.5 + 626.3 + 942.8}{17143.4} = 71.4\%$$

Should current operating liabilities or deferred taxes be included? There are differing opinions. The most important thing to look at is the trend. Is it getting better or worse? How does it compare to industry statistics? Under the two above calculations, it appears to be getting better. How then are the acquisitions financed? The statement of changes is a good place to look for investing and financing activities and shows strong cash flow from operations. This was likely used to finance the acquisitions.

In any case, the company's ability to cover interest charges is good:
1990 = ($1,667.4 + $688.5—$182.1)/($688.5—$182.1) = 4.3 times
1991 = ($1,670.3 + $615.9—$163.3)/($615.9—$163.3) = 4.69 times

Therefore, the acquisitions do not appear to have jeopardized the flexibility of the company or its liquidity. It will be interesting to note in future, whether these operations contribute cash and acceptable profit levels to the organization.

Notice how we are looking for interrelationships between the numbers. This is critical to a successful analytical review.

Again, this is just a very limited analysis and is really only the tip of the iceberg, raising almost as many questions as it has answered. The objective was merely to show that selective, educated analysis is far better than across-the-board number crunching.

CASE

GRAPHICS AND RATIOS IN ANNUAL REPORTS

Most companies with publicly traded shares issue an annual report which includes the financial statements of the company. The report also includes information about the company, the industry, the environment within which the business operates, and lengthy discussions by management of the past, present, and future of the company.

Graphics and ratio analysis are being used more and more frequently as a vehicle to highlight financial information in the annual reports. Virtually all annual reports have some form of graphical analysis or ratios in them. It used to be that these analyses, as prepared by management, were clearly segregated from the audited financial statements. Now, however, much of the analysis either immediately precedes the statements, or follows it, making it hard to differentiate between the audited statements and management comments and analysis.

An interesting example is the 1991 annual report of PepsiCo Inc. The MD&A, which contains a fair bit of analysis and ratios, is interspersed with the statements. For instance, the income statement comes first, followed by the MD&A for operating results, which is on the next page facing the income statement. The balance sheet is next, followed by the MD&A for financial condition.

The auditors' report at the end has dealt with this presentation by making reference by page number to the financial statements upon which they are reporting. This is not usually done, however, since the MD&A has been mixed in with the statements, it is necessary for the auditors to emphasize what is part of the audited statements and what is not.

In 1993, the CICA published a research report entitled "Using Ratios and Graphics in Financial Reporting". The report was prepared after a survey was done on 200 Canadian public companies. The survey demonstrated the potential for misleading representation in the annual reports and the need for standardization. While the CICA found that graphs and charts can effectively highlight financial information, it also noted that they can just as easily distort trends and mislead users. The research report also evaluated ratios for capital markets, liquidity, solvency, profitability, asset activity, and productivity. It identified key ratios for assessing investment return, financial structure, and management performance.

Some feel that including graphs and ratios that mislead users undermines the whole reporting process and downgrades the credibility of the financial statements. Therefore, accountants should be involved in setting some standards to ensure certain minimum disclosures and to ensure that they are not misleading. Others feel that it is not the jurisdiction of the profession to monitor financial statement analysis.

Required

Comment on whether accountants should be involved in setting standards to regulate the presentation of graphics and ratios in annual reports.

SOLUTION TO CASE

This case is meant more to broaden thinking with respect to what the accountant's role is within society. There is no set answer but it is interesting to note that the CICA has to become involved by identifying the problem. Also interesting is the research report, which goes as far as to identify and evaluate key ratios.

Arguments for accountants becoming involved:

- As mentioned, the graphs and ratios are included in the annual report with the audited financial statements and, therefore, are often associated with the financial statements and the auditors. Auditing standards at present require that the annual report be reviewed for anything misleading and, therefore, the auditor is already involved with the information.
- At present, the auditor may have some legal exposure since it might be argued (as above) that they are already associated with the information. Therefore, it is in their best interest to protect themselves by becoming more involved. Especially in the PepsiCo case, the ratios and MD&A are interspersed with the financial statements and might give the impression that they are part of the audited financial statements.
- Setting some standards would help the auditor assess whether the information is misleading. At present, this is a very subjective call and an accountant is unlikely to wield much power in terms of convincing the client to change a presentation which, from the client's perspective, may not be misleading at all.
- If not professional accountants, then who should get involved? Is it not more cost effective for accountants and auditors to set standards and review these disclosures, since auditors are already looking at the annual reports as part of the annual audit anyway?
- Accountants are already involved in setting standards for calculating EPS. How is this justifiable if we can not justify accountants setting standards for other ratios? Besides, the emphasis on EPS might cause users to place more emphasis (perhaps unduly) on the EPS calculation.

In all likelihood, users probably think that auditors and professional accountants are involved with the preparation and presentation of the ratios anyway, since they are derived from the audited financial statements ("expectations gap").

Arguments against accountants becoming involved:

- Where does financial reporting end and financial analysis begin? Financial statement analysis is the responsibility of financial analysts who are specialists in their own right.
- If accountants get involved, it might cause users to rely blindly on the ratios (i.e., they may attach more credibility to them and be less wary of them if they know that professional accountants have mandated standards and are monitoring disclosures). At present, it is nice to think that users approach these ratios and graphs with a

healthy skepticism.

- Given that there is a multitude of ratios (including different ratios for different industries) and that different users need different ratios calculated for different purposes, how can there be any meaningful standard set that will apply to all situations and meet the needs of all users?
- Where would the responsibility of the auditor stop? At present, the auditor looks at the financial statements. If the auditor has to focus on graphs and ratios too, what will be next? Are accountants going to be arguing with the president of the company as to what should be included in the president's message to the shareholders?

SELECTED SOLUTIONS FROM THE TEXTBOOK

EXERCISE 24-1

Current ratio	1997	=	\$2,003,000/\$793,000	=	2.53
	1998	=	\$2,070,000/\$1,230,000	=	1.68
Acid-test ratio	1997	=	\$963,000/\$793,000	=	1.21
	1998	=	\$680,000/\$1,230,000	=	.55

Receivable turnover 1997 $= \frac{\$3,900,000}{\$198,000} = 19.70$

1998 $= \$4,400,000 \,/\, \frac{\$340,000 + \$198,000}{2} = 6.36$

Inventory turnover 1997 $= \$3,100,000 \,/\, \frac{\$980,000 + \$720,000}{2} = 3.65$

1998 $= \$3,250,000 \,/\, \frac{\$1,350,000 + \$980,000}{2} = 2.79$

Asset turnover 1997 $= \frac{\$3,900,000}{\$4,163,000} = .94$

1998 $= \$4,400,000 \,/\, \frac{\$4,650,000 + \$4,163,000}{2} = 1.00$

Profit margin on sales 1997 $= \frac{\$350,000}{\$3,900,000} = 8.97\%$

1998 $= \frac{\$630,000}{\$4,400,000} = 14.32\%$

Rate of return on assets 1997 $= \frac{\$350,000}{\$4,163,000} = 8.41\%$

1998 $= \$630{,}000 \,/\, \dfrac{\$4{,}650{,}000 + \$4{,}163{,}000}{2} = 14.30\%$

Rate of return on common equity

1997 $= \dfrac{\$350{,}000}{\$2{,}550{,}000} = 13.73\%$

1998 $= \$630{,}000 \,/\, \dfrac{\$2{,}720{,}000 + \$2{,}550{,}000}{2} = 23.91\%$

Debt to total assets

1997 $= \dfrac{\$1{,}613{,}000}{\$4{,}163{,}000} = 38.75\%$

1998 $= \dfrac{\$1{,}930{,}000}{\$4{,}650{,}000} = 41.51\%$

Exercise 24-8

(a) The cost of goods sold has remained about the same during each of the four years but the amount of inventory has increased. The inventory turnover for each of the last three years was:

1996 $= \$2{,}960{,}000 \,/\, \dfrac{\$456{,}000 + \$545{,}000}{2} = 5.9$ times

1997 $= \$3{,}000{,}000 \,/\, \dfrac{\$545{,}000 + \$601{,}000}{2} = 5.2$ times

1998 $= \$3{,}240{,}000 \,/\, \dfrac{\$601{,}000 + \$689{,}000}{2} = 5.0$ times

A larger amount of inventory is being carried with no corresponding increase in cost of goods sold; in other words, the inventory is being used less efficiently.

(b) The cause for the increase in inventory should be investigated. Perhaps new lines have been added, or larger quantities of the present lines are now carried, or obsolete or slow moving merchandise is being accumulated. Perpetual records should be examined to determine if larger than required quantities of some goods are being stocked, to determine if unwise purchasing policies are being followed, and to analyse the cause for the increase in inventories.

(c) If larger than required quantities are being stocked, then maximum and minimum quantities should be established for each kind of merchandise in order to prevent this in the future. If slow-moving goods are being accumulated, steps should be taken to see that requisitions and purchases are properly controlled and that the purchasing department is organized so that all orders are subject to appropriate approval before purchases are consummated.

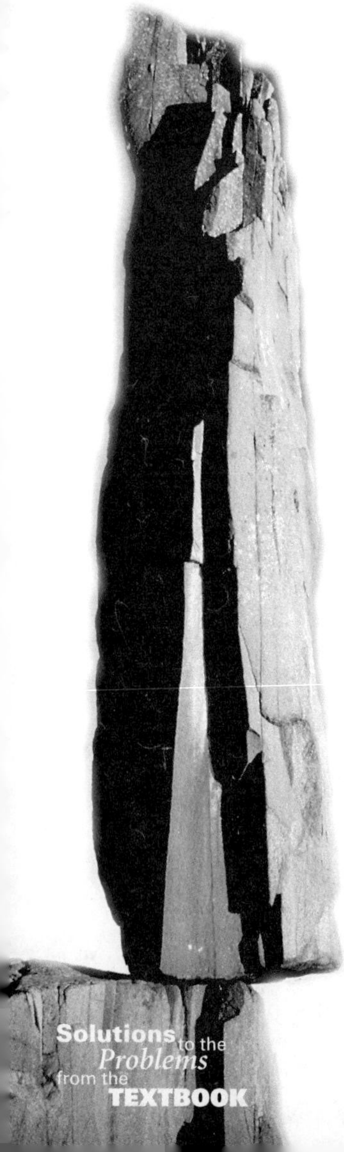

SOLUTION TO PROBLEM

PROBLEM 24-3

(a)	At Present	Plan 1	Plan 2	Plan 3
(1) Current Ratio[a]	$\frac{\$545{,}000}{\$238{,}000} = 2.29$	$\frac{\$845{,}000}{\$\ 238{,}000} = 3.55$	$\frac{\$845{,}000}{\$238{,}000} = 3.55$	$\frac{\$845{,}000}{\$428{,}000} = 1.97$
(2) Earnings per Share[b]	$\frac{\$85{,}000}{\$35{,}000} = 2.43$	$\frac{\$191{,}360}{\$\ 65{,}000} = 2.94$	$\frac{\$142{,}848}{\$\ 45{,}000} = 3.17$	$\frac{\$117{,}120}{\$\ 35{,}000} = 3.35$
(3) Rate of return on Shareholders' Equity[c]	$\frac{\$\ 85{,}000}{\$803{,}000} = 10.59\%$	$\frac{\$\ 191{,}360}{\$1{,}703{,}000} = 11.24\%$	$\frac{\$\ 142{,}848}{\$1{,}103{,}000}$ 12.95%	$\frac{\$117{,}120}{\$803{,}000} = 14.59\%$
(4) Ratio of Debt to Total Equity[d]	$\frac{\$\ 428{,}000}{\$1{,}231{,}000} = 34.77\%$	$\frac{\$\ 428{,}000}{\$2{,}131{,}000} = 20.08\%$	$\frac{\$1{,}028{,}000}{\$2{,}131{,}000} = 48.24\%$	$\frac{\$1{,}328{,}000}{\$2{,}131{,}000} = 62.32\%$

[a]Current Ratio

Under all three proposed plans, total assets will increase by $900,000. Of this increase, $600,000 will be used to increase fixed assets and $300,000 will be used to increase current assets, resulting in new current assets of $845,000. Under Plans 1 and 2, current liabilities will not change. Under Plan 3, current liabilities will increase by $190,000, which is the difference between the $1,090,000 needed to carry out the plan and pay off the long-term bank loan versus the $900,000 obtained by the sale of long-term bonds.

[b]Earnings Per Share

	Plan 1	Plan 2	Plan 3
Expected earnings before interest and taxes	$320,000	$320,000	$320,000
Less interest:			
On bonds: Plan 1—10% x $190,000	(19,000)		
Plan 2—12% x $790,000		(94,800)	
Plan 3—12% x $900,000			(108,000)
Other than bonds: total present interest of $21,000 less $19,000 interest on 10% bonds	(2,000)	(2,000)	(2,000)
On increase in short-term liabilities (Plan 3)			(27,000)
Expected earnings before taxes	$299,000	$223,200	$183,000
Less: Taxes at 36%	107,640	80,352	65,880
Expected net income	$191,360	$142,848	$117,120
Common Shares Outstanding:			
At present:	35,000	35,000	35,000
Additional: Plan 1—$900,000 / $30	30,000		
Plan 2—10,000 shares	10,000		
Plan 3—None			-0-
Total	65,000	45,000	35,000

[c]Rate of Return on Shareholders' Equity

	Plan 1	Plan 2	Plan 3
Present shareholders' equity	$803,000	$803,000	$803,000
Increase from sale of shares:			
Plan 1	900,000		
Plan 2—10,000 shares x $30	300,000		
Plan 3—None			0
Total	$1,703,000	$1,103,000	$803,000

[d]Ratio of Debt to Total Equity
Under all three proposed plans, total assets will increase by $900,000. Although $1,090,000 will be generated under Plans 2 and 3, $190,000 of the proceeds will be used to retire the existing long-term bank loan of $190,000. Total debt equals total assets less total shareholders' equity as determined above.

(b) Selection of the "best" alternative involves making judgements with which not all accountants and managers would agree. Plan 1 increases short-term liquidity (current ratio of 3.55) at the expense of earnings per share ($2.94) and return on shareholders' equity (11.24%). Plan 2 would result in the same current ratio as plan 1 and increased earnings per share ($3.17) and a higher return on shareholders' equity (12.95%). However, this is accomplished by assuming a higher degree of risk as indicated by the ratio of debt to total equity (48.24%). Plan 3 offers the greatest return ($3.35 per share and 14.59% on shareholders' equity) but reduces the current ratio (1.93) and raises the debt to total equity ratio (62.32%). Consequently, management must choose between a high return (plan 3) and acceptable levels of liquidity (current ratio) and financial flexibility

(debt to total equity). The latter two represent a degree of risk that is being assumed. A manager who wishes to avoid excessive risks would prefer plan 2, while those more prone to risk taking might prefer plan 3.

SOLUTION TO CASE

CASE 24-3

(a) In establishing a dividend policy, the following factors, among others, should be taken into consideration:

1. The expansion plans or goals of the organization and the need for monies to finance new activities.

2. The investment opportunities available to the enterprise versus the return available to shareholders on earnings distributed by way of a cash dividend.

3. The possible effect on the market value of the enterprise's shares of instituting a dividend, and the possible effect on financing alternatives.

4. The earnings ability and stability of the enterprise—past and future.

5. The ability of the organization to maintain a given dividend in future years. To offer a dividend this year that cannot be maintained may be harmful. It could also be harmful to establish a policy seeming to call for increasing dividends over the years in the event the increase could not be kept up.

6. The current position of the enterprise. Is cash available to pay the dividend? Will liquidity be decreased to a dangerous level?

7. The possibility of offering a stock dividend in addition to or rather than a cash dividend.

8. The dividend policies of other similar organizations.

9. The general condition of the economy in the area where the enterprise operates.

10. Availability of retained earnings.

11. Legal restrictions such as a restrictive covenant in a bond indenture.

12. Personal tax situations of shareholders if known—whether preference for dividends or capital gains.

13. Degree of dispersion of shareholdings and shareholders' needs or preference for dividends.

(b)	1998	1997	1996	1995	1994
Rate of return on assets	$2,900	$1,600	$800	$900	$250
	$22,000	$19,000	$11,500	$4,200	$3,000
	13.18%	8.42%	6.96%	21.43%	8.33%
Profit margin on sales	$ 2,900	$1,600	$800	$900	$250
	$20,000	$16,000	$14,000	$6,000	$4,000
	14.5%	10.0%	5.71%	15.0%	6.25%
Earnings per share	$2,900,000	$1,600,000	$ 800,000	$900,000	$250,000
	2,000,000	2,000,000	2,000,000	20,000	20,000
	$1.45	$0.80	$0.40	$45.00	$12.50
Price-earnings	$9	$6	$4		
	$1.45	$0.80	$0.40		
	6.2 times	7.5 times	10 times		
Current ratio	$8,000	$6,000	$3,000	$1,200	$1,000
	$4,400	$2,800	$1,800	$700	$600
	1.82 times	2.14 times	1.67 times	1.71 times	1.67 times

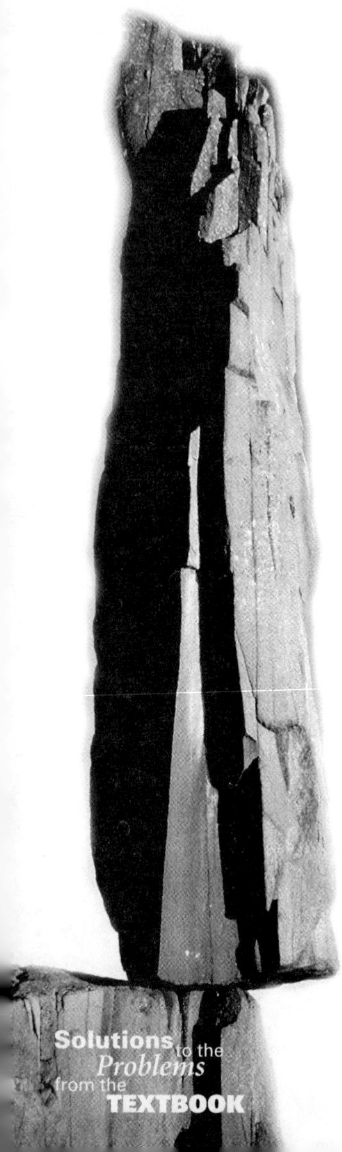

(c) While the return on assets, profit margin on sales, and earnings per share has been increasing, the market price of the shares has not given full recognition to these increases in that the price-earnings ratio is declining. This suggests that market factors (and perhaps industry factors) are having a depressing effect on the market price of the shares. While there has been increase in share price, it may be suggested that the relatively low market price of the shares relative to the growth in EPS may be due, in part, to the fact that dividends have not been paid in the past. It may be concluded that the enterprise is in an improving operating position, and appears to be able to pay a dividend, although the amount of cash is not given. It would, however, be wise to examine as many as possible of the other internal and external factors outlined in part (a) of this case.

A dividend in the range of 15c/ to 45c/, being 10% to 30% of earnings per share for 1998, would appear to be reasonable. Cash required would be $300,000 ($0.15 x 2,000,000) to $900,000 ($0.45 x 2,000,000). Payments considerably in excess of $900,000 could have a serious impact on the current ratio which, except for 1997 was not greater than 2:1. This would provide a dividend yield of between 1.7% and 5% on the average 1998 market value.

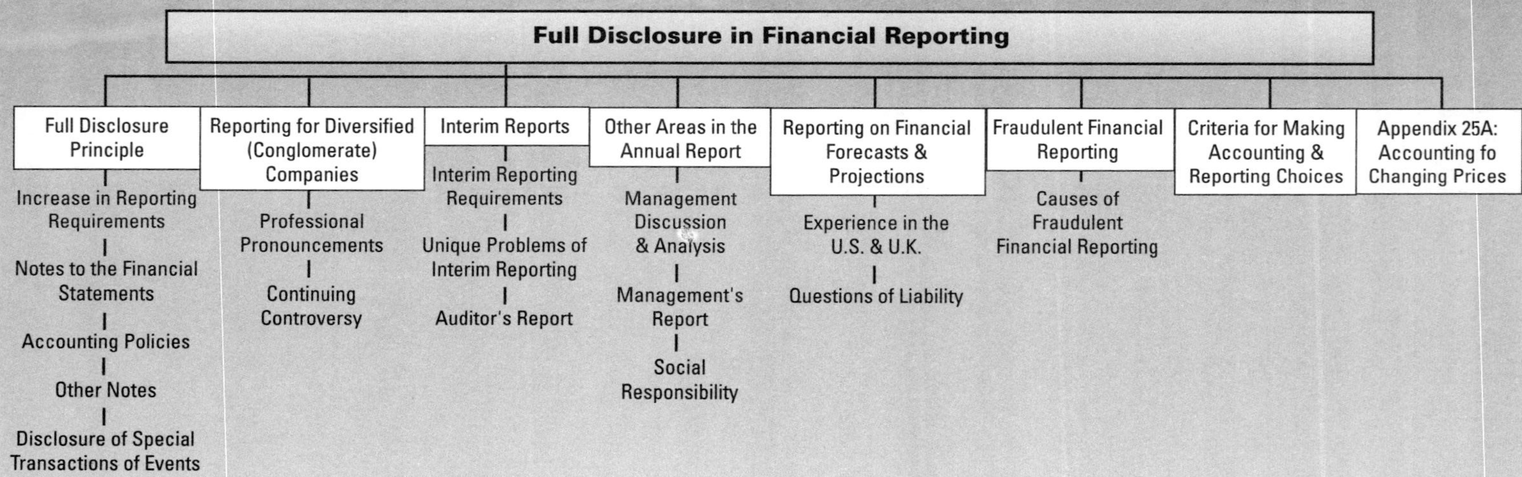

Full Disclosure in Financial Reporting
Full Disclosure Principle
Increase in Reporting Requirements
Notes to the Financial Statements
Accounting Policies
Other Notes
Disclosure of Special Transactions of Events
Reporting for Diversified (Conglomerate) Companies
Professional Pronouncements
Continuing Controversy
Interim Reports
Interim Reporting Requirements
Unique Problems of Interim Reporting
Auditor's Report
Other Areas in the Annual Report
Management Discussion & Analysis
Management's Report
Social Responsibility
Reporting on Financial Forecasts & Projections
Experience in the U.S. & U.K.
Questions of Liability
Fraudulent Financial Reporting
Causes of Fraudulent Financial Reporting
Criteria for Making Accounting & Reporting Choices
Appendix 25A: Accounting fo Changing Prices

chapter 25

FULL DISCLOSURE IN FINANCIAL REPORTING

PERSPECTIVE

A brief overview of the mandated disclosures not covered in other chapters will be given here. Accounting for changing prices will also be skimmed with an emphasis on finding a better accounting model that is more relevant to decision-making.

INSIGHTS

- *The calculations aspect of inflation accounting will not be emphasized since it is easy to get tangled up in the mechanics and not be able to then put the topic into perspective. Since no single model has gained acceptance, the emphasis will be on finding a solution, instead of memorizing models that are not accepted for various reasons.*

STUDY STEPS

1. Understanding the Importance of Disclosures

STUDY STEPS

The full disclosure principle

The full disclosure principle dictates what should be provided in financial reporting. It states that anything that will influence or change a user's decision should be disclosed in the financial statements. This is a very broad statement and is certainly open to interpretation.

As a general rule, if in doubt, disclose. Tip!

Tip! **Think about what users are expecting to see in the financial statements. If the preparer is presenting something unexpected, then more disclosure is generally better.**

Because financial statement preparers do not always follow the spirit of general principles like this one, especially if it is not in their own or the company's best interests, the CICA has begun to mandate increasing amounts of disclosures.

It is the general "catch-all" nature of the full disclosure principle that makes this area one of constant evolution and change. Users want more disclosures, preparers often want to give less. During the last few years, securities exchange commissions have also become involved and are changing the face of financial reporting by mandating their own disclosures that must be followed by any company whose shares are listed on a stock exchange.

Notes to financial statements

The notes to the financial statements are an integral part of the statements and often incorporate additional valuable information.

Tip! **Never analyze financial statements without reading the notes.**

A key note is the accounting policy note. It is usually note 1 and sometimes is presented before the statements to encourage users to read it first. All significant accounting policies should be disclosed here, especially ones where there is a choice.

Tip! **The accounting policy note gives important information about choices made by the financial statement preparers.**

Related party transactions

Disclosure of related party transactions is mandated by the CICA since, often, they do not reflect arm's-length terms. Since users expect that transactions are carried out at arm's length (reflecting market terms), it is wise to disclose those that are not.

Required disclosures under *CICA Handbook* Section 3840 are:

- A description of the nature and extent of the transaction.
- A description of the relationship.
- The recorded amount and measurement basis of the transaction.
- Amounts due to or from related parties and, if not otherwise apparent, the terms of settlement.
- Contractual obligations involving related parties.
- Contingencies involving related parties.

There is some judgement required in determining just who the related parties are. Note that the CICA has gone one step farther with these transactions, requiring that the transactions be revalued to carrying value in some cases.

As a general rule, if the transaction is in the normal course of business, is monetary and there is support for the price, the transaction is not revalued. If, however, these conditions are not present, the transaction gets revalued to book value and any gain/loss gets booked to equity. The following chart from the CICA HB 3840A summarizes the decision process.

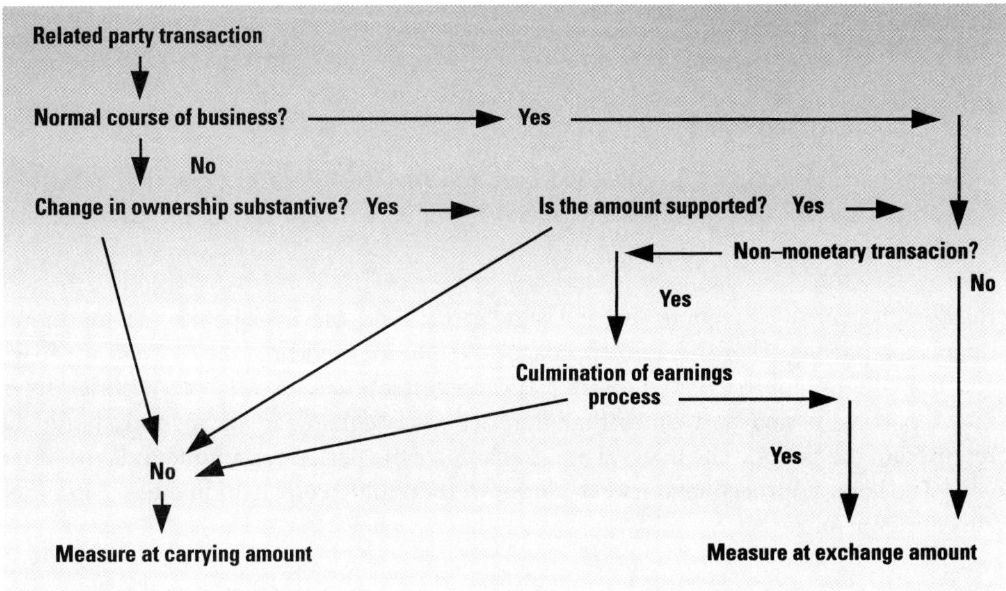

CICA HANDBOOK

Segmented information

Segmented information is also mandated by the CICA. Detailed information about sales, operating profits, and invested funds should be disclosed for different industry and geographic segments. This is encouraged because different industry and geographic segments carry different risks.

Users need information about risks in order to make decisions. **Tip!**

Only reportable segments should be disclosed. A segment would be considered reportable if it met one of the following criteria:

- Segment revenue is equal to or greater than 10% of total revenues.
- Absolute amount of profit or loss for the segment is equal to or greater in absolute amounts than the greater of the following:
    - Total of all operating profits.
    - Total of all operating losses.
    - Segment identifiable assets are equal to or greater than 10% of all identifiable assets for all segments.

Required disclosures include:

- Description of products or services.
- Segment revenues, profits, depreciation, and other disclosures

under *CICA Handbook* Section 1520.

- Identifiable assets of the segment.
- Accounting policies.

The table including the above information should add up to the totals on the financial statements where relevant.

Interim financial reporting

Interim financial reporting is governed by *CICA Handbook* Section 1750. It is important since, often, by the time the annual financial statements are issued, the information is no longer relevant.

Handbook Section 1750 requires that the same accounting principles be used as for annual financial reporting. There are two approaches to interim reporting: the discrete approach and the integral approach. The discrete approach treats each period as a distinct, separate reporting period and states that transactions occurring in the period should be reported in the period. The integral approach treats the periods as an integral part of the year. The latter approach favours calculating certain things on an annual basis and then allocating them.

The *Handbook* favours the discrete approach; however, there are some exceptions.

Required disclosures are listed in Section 1750 and include comparatives.

Financial projections and forecasts

Investors are increasingly calling out for more forward-looking information and the *CICA Handbook* has included Section 4250 on financial projections and forecasts governing disclosures. Areas of concern centre around what happens if the company does not meet the forecasted numbers and whether auditors should be involved.

Accounting for changing prices

At present, we use the historical cost to value transactions and balances, the nominal dollar to measure transactions, and the transactions approach to recognize income; that is, we do not recognize income until it is realized, usually through a transaction. Users of financial information continually question whether this model provides the most relevant information.

In most cases, historical costs bear no relationship to the real value of assets. If somebody wants to buy a business, they rarely rely on the net book value of the company to establish a price. Instead, an independent valuation must be made. Likewise, if a bank wants to lend money to a company, it will have the assets appraised for market value since this is the more relevant information.

In times of inflation, using the nominal dollar to measure transactions results in amounts that are not comparable from year to year. A dollar today is worth much less than a dollar

10 years ago, yet many trend analyses in annual reports show 10-year summaries of sales and net income for comparison.

Finally, we question whether revenues need to be realized before they can be recognized. For example, if an investment doubles in value by year-end but, is not sold until the following year, when is the income earned? Is it in the period of sale or in the year where the increase in value takes place? The former position is the presently accepted position.

To overcome these shortcomings in our present models, various alternatives have been proposed, with more activity in years of high inflation. Many industries, such as the brokerage business, have already incorporated changes such as valuing securities at market values versus historical cost. There is constant pressure to incorporate market values into the accounting model for other industries as well. The main criticisms of the alternative accounting models are subjectivity of the information and cost versus benefit.

2. Becoming proficient in related calculations.

The different models come and go; however, there are some concepts that underlie most of them. These concepts will be reviewed here.

Purchasing power gains and losses

This calculation measures the gain or loss to a company over time due to the change in the purchasing power of the dollar. It recognizes that a dollar today is worth less than a dollar from last year and attempts to measure just how the company is better off or worse off due to this.

If a company held $100 during the year and the price index was 100 at the beginning and 120 at year-end, the company is worse off since prices have gone up and it cannot buy as much with the $100. This is measured by restating the beginning-of-the-year balance to year-end dollars and comparing it to the year-end dollars.

Cash, opening balance restated to year-end dollars		
$100 x 120/100	=	120
Less: cash ending balance in year-end dollars	=	(100)
purchasing power loss		$20

If the company had spent that money at the beginning they could have purchased 20% more goods. This holds true for all monetary assets and liabilities. These are assets and liabilities whose face values are fixed in terms of dollar values (cash, AR, AP, long-term debt, etc.). Because these elements are fixed in face value (e.g., ignoring bad debts, $100 worth of accounts receivable will only bring in $100 cash when collected), the assets decline in real value during inflationary times. The longer the company waits to collect the $100, the lower the value will be, in terms of purchasing power,. Likewise, the liabilities increase in value. Since the amount of the debt is fixed, the longer you wait to pay it off, the better off you will be since you will be paying with dollars that are increasingly worth less and less.

Since the monetary assets and liabilities of a company change during the year, the calculation becomes more complicated. Basically, all transactions that affect monetary assets and liabilities must be restated into year-end dollars (YE$). (The restatement may also be done using average-for-the-year dollars). If the company noted above had spent $50 of the cash on inventory when the price index was 110, the purchasing power calculation would be as follows:

Cash, opening, restated to Y/E $ =$100 x 120/100	=	$120
Less: purchase of non-monetary asset(50) x 110/100	=	(55)
Equals equivalent value of Y/E $ $ 50		$65
Less: face value of cash at year-end		(50)
purchasing power loss		$15

The company is better off in this second scenario since it spent some of the cash when it had greater purchasing power. This concept is used when a different unit of measure is employed (e.g., a constant dollar versus the nominal dollar).

Holding gains/losses

Another important concept is a holding gain or loss. A holding gain or loss occurs because a company holds on to non-monetary assets or assets whose values generally increase in times of inflation because they can be sold for more. If a company has land worth $100 and at year-end the market value of the land has tripled, then the company has a holding gain:

Market value at year-end	=	$300
Historical cost	=	100
Holding gain		$200

This concept is relevant when a different basis of valuation (market value versus historical cost) is used.

Income recognition or capital maintenance

The last important concept relates to income recognition. If a company experiences holding gains, should they be recognized in income or not? Traditionally, we would argue no, not until the underlying asset is sold to an outside party and the gain is realized. Alternative models suggest that it may be appropriate to recognize these gains in the period in which they arise. Models that determine when revenue should be recognized are known as capital maintenance models.

Basically, capital maintenance theory states that income should only be recognized when the company is better off. This is measured by comparing the net worth of the company at the beginning of the year versus the end of the year. The trick is in measuring the net worth of the company. The net worth may be calculated using various bases of valuation (market values, historical costs, etc.) and various units of measure (nominal dollar, constant dollar).

Tip!

Physical capital maintenance theory suggests that the holding gains not be recognized in income, but rather be deferred on the balance sheet. Financial capital maintenance states that holding gains should be recognized on the income statement.

Below is a chart that summarizes various models:

	Present	Constant dollar	Current cost
Basis of valuation	HC	HC	CC
Unit of measure	ND	CD	ND
Capital maintenance	FCM	FCM	PCM

CD = constant dollar, CC = current cost, ND = nominal dollar, FCM = financial capital maintenance, PCM = physical capital maintenance.

Our present model uses historical costs to value assets, a nominal dollar to measure transactions, and recognizes any realized holding gains or losses in income for the most part (although there are some exceptions). In this model, holding gains are generally neither measured nor recognized in income until the assets are sold or used up.

The alternative models suggested above are not a comprehensive list and there are numerous variations to each model.

MULTIPLE CHOICE QUESTIONS

1) Which of the following would not be considered a related party to A company.
   a) A controls B Company
   b) A major shareholder of A (owns 55%)
   c) Management of A
   d) C company where A and C have a joint venture together but are otherwise unrelated

2) A Company is in the business of selling books. A sells a computer to C company, a related party for fair market value, which exceeds cost. In exchange, C gives A a used car of equal value. The change in ownership is not considered to be substantive but the transfer value is supportable. How should A record the sale?
   a) at exchange value since the value is supportable and there is a culmination of the earnings process (dissimilar assets)
   b) at exchange value since the value is supportable and the transaction is monetary
   c) at carrying amount since this transaction is not in the ordinary course of business and there is no substantive change in ownership
   d) at carrying value since the transaction is not in the ordinary course of business, the transaction is non-monetary and there is no culmination of the earnings process

3) D Company (a car dealership) sells a car to E company, a related party. E company pays D with computer repair services. How should D record this transaction?
   a) at exchange value since this is in the normal course of business, it is a non-monetary transaction and there is culmination of the earnings process—dissimilar assets

b) at exchange value since the transaction is monetary and is in the normal course of business

c) at carrying value since the transaction is monetary and there is no culmination of the earnings process

d) at carrying value since the transaction is non-monetary and there is no culmination of the earnings process

4) Which of the following statements would not describe a related party of a reporting enterprise under GAAP?

a) an individual having an ownership interest in a reporting enterprise that results in significant influence or joint control of the other party

b) the other party, when a management contract or other management authority exists and the reporting enterprise is either the managing or the managed party

c) the other party, when an investment is accounted for by the cost method and the reporting enterprise is either the investor or the investee

d) the other party, when an investment is accounted for by the equity or proportionate consolidation method and the reporting enterprise is either the investor or the investee

(CICA—September 1996)

5) The auditor of Westfair Limited has doubts that the company will be able to continue as a going concern. Which of the following statements represents what the auditor must do to fulfil his or her professional obligation?

a) ensure that the going concern problem is adequately disclosed in the financial statements

b) mention the going concern problem in the auditor's report

c) mention the going concern problem in the auditor's report and ensure that the problem is adequately disclosed in the financial statements

d) omit mention of the going concern problem because to do so may create a "self-fulfilling prophecy"

(CICA—September 1996)

6) According to GAAP, an industry segment must be disclosed separately if

a) the industry segment is completely unrelated to the major revenue producing activity of the organization.

b) the industry segment is operated in a foreign country.

c) the industry segment's revenue is equal to ten percent of the total segment revenue of the organization.

d) the industry segment's operating profit is identifiable.

(CMA—June 1994)

7) Gertrude Limited has three subsidiaries which operate in different geographic and

industrial segments. None of the subsidiaries meet the definition of reportable segment as far as revenues or identifiable assets are concerned. Gertrude has not yet reviewed the criteria as it relates to profits or losses. Sub A has a profit of $100, Sub B has a profit of $8 and Sub C has a loss of $30. Which of the subs would be reported as a separate segment?

	A	B	C
a)	yes	yes	yes
b)	yes	no	no
c)	yes	no	yes
d)	yes	no	no

8) Jutland Company is in the process of having its financial statements audited. The audit partner has called a meeting to discuss the fact that the company has not followed GAAP in accounting for advertising costs. The impact on net income is material but not so material that it renders the statements useless. This situation, if not fixed, could result in which type of audit opinion ?
   a) an unqualified opinion
   b) a qualified opinion
   c) an adverse opinion
   d) a denial of opinion

9) A financial forecast is defined as:
   a) prospective financial results reflecting management expectations and plans for future.
   b) prospective financial results reflecting one or more hypothetical assumptions and a course of action that is most likely.
   c) prospective financial results reflecting one or more hypothetical assumptions and a course of action that is not necessarily most likely.
   d) retrospective financial results of operations, financial position or changes in financial positions, reflecting management's expectations and plans for the period involved.

10) Assume that a company uses constant dollar accounting and revalues its assets to reflect holding gains. How would the holding gains and purchasing power gains be reflected in the financial statements under the financial capital maintenance concept?

	Holding gain	Purchasing power gain
a)	include in net income	include in net income
b)	include in net income	exclude from net income
c)	exclude from net income	exclude from net income
d)	exclude from net income	include in net income

SOLUTIONS TO MULTIPLE CHOICE QUESTIONS

1) d) Per Handbook 3840.05, as long as the venturers are not related then this would not be a related party transaction.

2) c) The only way to do these is with the chart.

3) a) The only way to do these is with the chart.

4) c) In the case of an investment accounted for by the cost method, there is no significant influence and therefore it is not a related party situation.

5) a)Note disclosure is all that is required. It is up to the company to disclose the situation. Otherwise users will assume that the company is a going concern. The auditor's role is to verify that the disclosures are adequate.

6) c) The test is a size test and is a function of revenues profits/losses or identifiable assets.

7) c) The test requires that the absolute profit or loss be compared with the greater of the total profits from all profit generating subs and the total losses from all loss generating subs. In this case the profits from profit generating subs are higher = $100 + $8 = $108 (versus $30). 10% of $108 = 10.8. This means A and C qualify.

8) b) A qualified opinion would be issued since this is an exception. The problem is not so material as to render the statements useless however. Hence, an adverse or denial would not be issued.

9) a) A forecast reflects management expectations for the future ,whereas a projection reflects one or more hypothetical assumptions and is not based on the most likely course of action.

10) a) Both would be included. Under both PCM and FCM purchasing power gains or losses are included in net income. Under PCM, holding gains would be excluded or at least segregated.

CASE

EXXON CORPORATION

Below is an excerpt from the 1989 financial statements of Exxon Corporation. The note deals with a large oil spill caused by one of the company's oil tankers.

Note 14 to the 1989 annual financial statements of Exxon Corporation.
On March 24, 1989, The Exxon Valdez, a tanker owned by Exxon Shipping Company, a subsidiary of Exxon Corporation, ran aground on Bligh Reef in Prince William Sound off the port of Valdez, Alaska, and released approximately 260,000 barrels of crude oil. More than one hundred and seventy lawsuits including class actions have been brought in various courts against Exxon Corporation and some of its consolidated subsidiaries. Most of these lawsuits seek unspecified compensatory and physical damages; several lawsuits seek damages in varying specified amounts. Some of the lawsuits seek injunctive relief.

The State of Alaska has filed a suit in Superior Court in Alaska against Exxon Shipping Company, Exxon Corporation and others seeking substantial civil penalties and unspecified damages arising from the oil spill. On February 27, 1990, an indictment was returned in the United States District Court in Anchorage Alaska, charging Exxon Shipping Company and Exxon Corporation with violation of the Refuse Act, the Migratory Bird Treaty Act, the Clean Water Act, the Ports and Waterways Safety Act and the Dangerous Cargo Act.
The potential total costs relating to the matters described above are difficult to predict and are not expected to be resolved for a number of years. It is believed that the ultimate outcome net of reserves already provided, will not have a materially adverse effect upon the corporation's operations or financial condition.

Required

(a) Why would the company want to disclose all the details given how it reflects negatively on the company?
(b) How much disclosure is necessary, and what level of detail is required?

SOLUTION TO CASE

(a) In order to understand the motivation behind this note disclosure, the reporting environment must be considered. At the time of the spill, there was public outrage. The unfortunate incident was splashed all over the headlines. There were also numerous editorials, commentaries, and documentaries that focused on the story. Even two and three years afterwards, there were still follow-up stories being written. This should give some idea of how much coverage the incident received.

The disclosure is very detailed and fairly lengthy compared to most disclosures relating to lawsuits. Perhaps this is because the incident was so highly publicized and this was their chance to tell their side of the story and perhaps set the record straight. This way, they come across as though they have nothing to hide and want to be totally open and honest with users.

The note is factual and straightforward, perhaps in an effort to calm the fears of investors and let them know that the incident will not threaten the existence of the company. Furthermore, it gives the impression that they acknowledge the disaster and have the situation well in hand.

(b) The full disclosure principle requires that any information that would affect the decisions of financial statement users should be disclosed. Due to the materiality of this event and the repercussions (lawsuits), it would be wise to disclose it. It would also be prudent since users might not have the correct information. The issue concerns how much detail to reveal. This is really a question of judgement.

CICA Handbook Section 3290 recommends the following where there is a contingent loss that has not been accrued:

- The nature of the contingency.
- An estimate of the amount of loss or a statement that no such estimate may be made.
- How the settlement of the contingency will be accounted for.

What we are discussing here is the contingent losses from the lawsuits and fines. The Handbook still leaves a fair bit of leeway in terms of how much detail to include.

In all likelihood, after meeting the above-noted requirements, management would likely want to emphasize that while it was a terrible tragedy, the company will be able to weather the consequences. However, management would want to be careful not to go out on a limb since there is the potential that it and the directors might be sued if they mislead users. Therefore, care has apparently been taken to make the note as informative and factual as possible, while still stating that the outcome will not materially, adversely affect the company.

SELECTED SOLUTIONS FROM THE TEXTBOOK

EXERCISE 25-1

Land ($140,000 x 150/100)	$210,000.00
Building ($200,000 x 150/100)	$300,000.00
Machinery ($80,000 x 150/100)	$120,000.00
($30,000 x 150/125)	36,000.00
	$156,000.00
Office Equipment ($25,000 x 150/120)	$31,250.00
($8,000 x 150/140)	8,571.43
	$39,821.43

EXERCISE 25-5

(a)

Current cost of goods sold	$215,000	
Historical cost of goods sold	196,000	$19,000
Current cost of inventory	107,000	
Historical cost of inventory	95,000	12,000
Current cost of land	190,000	
Historical cost of land	175,000	15,000
Total holding gain		$46,000

(b)

Albion Co.
Current Cost Income Statement
For the Year Ended December 31, 1998

Sales	$290,000
Cost of goods sold	215,000
Gross profit	75,000
Operating expenses	41,300
Current cost income from operations	33,700
Holding gain	46,000
Current cost net income	$79,700

Glossary

GLOSSARY OF TERMS

adverse opinion—required in any report in which the exceptions to fair presentation are so material that in the independent auditor's judgement a qualified opinion is not justified

antidilutive securities—securities that would create an increase in earnings per share (or a reduction in net loss per share) if common shares were issued by converting these securities or exercising options contained therein

bargain purchase option—a provision allowing the lessee to purchase the leased for a price that is lower than the property's expected fair value at the date the options becomes exerciseable

bargain renewal option—a provision allowing the lessee to renew the lease for a rental that is lower than the expected fair rental at the date the option becomes exerciseable

basic earnings per share—indicates income earned by each common share outstanding

capital lease—a lease whereby the risk and rewards of ownership are assumed to be transferred to the lessee

cash equivalents—short-term, highly liquid investments that are readily convertible to known amounts of cash and which are subject to an insignificant risk of changes in value

common shares—the residual corporate interest that bears the ultimate risk of loss and receives the benefits of success

contingency—an existing condition or situation involving uncertainty as to possible gain (gain contingency) or loss (loss contingency) to an enterprise that will ultimately be resolved when one or more future events occur or fail to occur

contributed capital—comprised of the share capital and contributed surplus

contributed surplus—includes items such as donations from owners and other sources, gain on forfeited shares, credits arising when the company's own shares are reacquired and canceled at a cost less than issue price, and amounts received in excess of par value when such shares are issued

covenants—restrictions placed on long-term debt for the protection of the lender

convertible bonds—bonds that are exchangeable into other securities of the corporation, such as preferred or common shares

coupon rate—the interest rate written in the terms of the bond indenture and ordinarily appearing on the bond certificate

denial of an opinion—is appropriate when the auditor has gathered so little information on the financial statements that no opinion can be expressed

derivative financial instruments—named because their value is derived from the value of some underlying instrument, such as stocks, bonds, or commodities, or is tied to a basic indicator such as interest rates, foreign exchange rates or Toronto Stock Exchange averages

dilutive securities—convertible bonds, convertible preferred share, share purchase warrants and contingent shares are called dilutive securities because a reduction (dilution) in earnings per share often results when these securities become common shares

direct financing lease—a lease that transfers the risk and rewards of ownership from the lessor where cost and fair value of the asset transferred are equal

discrete view—a view that states that each interim period should be treated as a separate accounting period; deferrals and accruals would therefore follow the principles employed for annual reports

dividends in kind—dividends payable in assets of the corporation other than cash

earned capital—retained earnings represents the earned capital of an enterprise and consists of all undistributed income that remains invested in the enterprise

effective rate—the interest rate used to compute the present value of these cash flows is the rate that provides an acceptable return on the investment commensurate with the issuer's risk characteristics

equity instrument—any contract that evidences a residual interest in the assets of an entity after deducting all of its liabilities

executory contract—a contract requiring both parties to perform under the contract at some point in the future

financial asset—any asset that is cash, a contractual right to receive cash or another financial asset from another party, a contractual right to exchange financial instruments with another party under conditions that are potentially favorable or an equity instrument

financial liability—any liability that is a contractual obligation to deliver cash or another financial assets to another party; or to exchange financial instruments with another party under conditions that are potentially unfavorable

financial reorganization—a procedure that enables a company that has gone through financial difficulty to proceed with its plans without the encumbrance of having to recover from a deficit

financing activities—activities that result in changes in the size and composition of the equity capital and borrowing of the enterprise

fully diluted earnings per share—indicates the dilution of earnings per share that has occurred if all contingent issuances of common shares that would have reduced earnings per share had taken place

guaranteed residual value—(1) the amount at which the lessor has the right to require the lessee to purchase the asset at the end of the lease, or, (2) the amount the lessee of the third-party guarantees the lessor will realize

implicit rate—the lessor's internal rate of return implied by the lease variables

incremental borrowing rate—defined as the interest rate that, at the inception of the lease, the lessee would have incurred to borrow, over a similar term and with similar security for the borrowing, the funds necessary to purchase the leased asset

integral view—a view that states that the interim report is an integral part of the annual report and that deferrals and accruals should take into consideration what will happen for the entire year

investing activities—cover the acquisition and disposal of long-term assets and other investments not included in cash equivalents

liquidating dividends—dividends based on other than retained earnings, thus implying that they are a return of the shareholder's investment rather than of assets generated from profits

loss carryback—when a corporation elects to carry the tax loss back against taxable income of the immediately preceding three years

loss carryforward—when a corporation elects to carry the tax loss forward to the seven years that immediately follow the loss

nonreciprocal transfer—a transfer of assets or services in one direction, either from an enterprise to its owners or another entity or from owners or another entity to the enterprise, without consideration

off-balance-sheet financing—an attempt to borrow monies in such a way that the obligations are not recorded or reported in the balance sheet

operating activities—the principal revenue-producing activities of the enterprise and other activities that are not investing or financing activities

operating lease—a lease that does not transfer the risk and rewards of ownership to the lessee

past service costs—represent the present value of the additional future benefits granted to employees for past services rendered by the employers

pre-emptive right—means that existing shareholders of a class of shares have a right to acquire additional shares of any new issue of that class in proportion to their existing holdings before the new issue of shares can be offered to others

property dividends—dividends payable in assets of the corporation other than cash

qualified opinion—states that, except for the effects of the matter that the qualification relates, the financial statements present fairly, in all materials respects, the financial position, results of operations, and changes in financial position in conformity with generally accepted accounting principles

related party transactions—arise when a business engages in transactions in which either of the transacting parties has the ability to influence the policies of the other

residual value—the estimated fair value of the leased property at the end of the lease term

sale-leaseback—describes a transaction in which the owner of property (the seller-lessee) sells the property to another party (the purchaser-lessor) and simultaneously leases it back from the owner

sales-type lease—a lease that transfers the risk and rewards of ownership from the lessor and where there is a profit or loss on the transaction

stock appreciation rights—represent the right to receive share appreciation, which is defined as the excess of the market price of the shares at the date of exercise over a pre-established price; stock appreciation rights are normally granted to executives

stock dividends—dividends paid in the form of company's own shares (of the same or different class)

stock option—an option to purchase common shares at a given price over an extended period of time

treasury shares—a company's own shares that have been purchased but have not been canceled; they are usually being held for reissue

unguaranteed residual value—that portion of the residual value that is not guaranteed or is guaranteed solely by a party related to the lessor and is not included in the definition of minimum lease payments

unqualified or clean opinion—when the auditor expresses the opinion that the financial statements present fairly, in all material respects, the financial position, results of operations, and its changes in financial position in conformity with generally accepted accounting principles

vesting—occurs when the rights to receive future benefits is conferred on an employee, whether or not the employee remains in the service of the entity

warrants—certificates that entitle the holder to acquire shares at a specified price within a stated period

WE WANT TO HEAR FROM YOU

By sharing your opinions about this Study Guide to Accompany Intermediate Accounting 5/E, you will help us ensure that you are getting the most value for your textbook dollars. After you have used the book for a while, please fill out this form. Either fold, tape, and mail, or fax us toll free @ 1-800-565-6802!

Course name: ______________________ School name: ______________________

Your name: ______________________

I am using: ❑ Volume 1 ❑ Volume 2

1) Did you purchase this Study Guide (check all that apply):

❑ From your campus bookstore

❑ From a bookstore off-campus

❑ New ❑ Used ❑ For yourself

❑ For yourself and at least one other student

2) Was this Study Guide available at the bookstore when you needed it?

❑ Yes ❑ No

3) Did you purchase it:

❑ Alone?

❑ Packaged with the vol. 2 Study Guide?

❑ Packaged with the book?

4) Did you find it a useful studying aid?

❑ Yes ❑ No

Comments: ______________________

____

____

5) How far along are you in this course? (put an X where you are now)

❑——————❑——————❑
Beginning Midway Completed

6) How much have you used this Study Guide? (put an X where you are now)

❑——————❑——————❑
None Half All

7) Have you read the introductory material?

❑ Yes ❑ No ❑ Parts of it

8) Even if you have only skimmed this Study Guide, please rate the following features:

Features:	Very valuable/effective	Somewhat valuable/effective	Not valuable/effective
Value as a reference			
Readability			
Design			
Study Steps			
Problems & cases			
Selected Solutions from Text			
TOOLKIT			
Overall perception			

9) What do you like most about this Study Guide?

____

____

____

____

____

10) How do you think we can improve future editions?

____

____

____

____

____

11) At the end of the semester, what do you intend to do with this Study Guide?

❑ Keep it ❑ Sell it ❑ Unsure

13) May we quote you? ❑ Yes ❑ No

If you would like to receive information on other Wiley business books, please fill in the following information:

Name: ______________________________

Mailing address: ______________________________

(Street) ______________________________ (Apt. #) ______________________________

(City) ______________________________ (Prov.) ______________________________

(Postal Code) ______________________________

Thank you for your time and feedback!

WILEY
Publishers Since 1807

You can contact us via e-mail at: cwells@wiley.com

(fold here)

MAIL POSTE
Canada Post Corporation / Société canadienne des postes

Postage paid
if mailed in Canada

Port payé
si posté au Canada

Business Reply

Réponse d'affaires

0108529899 01

0108529899-M9W1L1-BR01

COLLEGE DIVISION
JOHN WILEY & SONS CANADA LTD
22 WORCESTER RD
PO BOX 56213 STN BRM B
TORONTO ON M7Y 9C1